Modern Literary Theory and Ancient Texts

D1484469

Modern Literary Theory and Ancient Texts
An Introduction

Thomas A. Schmitz

Blackwell
Publishing

BLACKWELL PUBLISHING
350 Main Street, Malden, MA 02148-5020, USA
9600 Garsington Road, Oxford OX4 2DQ, UK
550 Swanston Street, Carlton, Victoria 3053, Australia

The right of Thomas A. Schmitz to be identified as the Author of this Work has been asserted in accordance with the UK Copyright, Designs, and Patents Act 1988.

The publisher and the author make no representations or warranties with respect to the accuracy or completeness of the contents of this work and specifically disclaim all warranties, including without limitation warranties of fitness for a particular purpose. No warranty may be created or extended by sales or promotional materials. The advice and strategies contained herein may not be suitable for every situation. This work is sold with the understanding that the publisher is not engaged in rendering legal, accounting, or other professional services. If professional assistance is required, the services of a competent professional person should be sought. Neither the publisher nor the author shall be liable for damages arising herefrom. The fact that an organization or website is referred to in this work as a citation and/or a potential source of further information does not mean that the author or the publisher endorses the information the organization or website may provide or recommendations it may make. Further, readers should be aware that Internet websites listed in this work may have changed or disappeared between when this work was written and when it is read.

First published 2007 by Blackwell Publishing Ltd

1   2007

Library of Congress Cataloging-in-Publication Data

Schmitz, Thomas A., 1963–
   [Moderne Literaturtheorie und antike Texte. English]
     Modern literary theory and ancient texts : an introduction / Thomas A. Schmitz.
       p. cm.
   Includes bibliographical references and index.
     ISBN 978-1-4051-5374-4 (pbk. : alk. paper) – ISBN 978-1-4051-5375-1 (hardcover : alk. paper) 1. Criticism–History–20th century. 2. Classical literature–History and criticism. 3. Classical literature–Criticism, Textual. I. Title.

       PN94.S2313 2007
       801'.95–dc22

                          2007018629

A catalogue record for this title is available from the British Library.

Set in 11/14pt Adobe Garamond Premier Pro
by the author
Printed and bound in Singapore
by Markono Print Media Pte Ltd

The publisher's policy is to use permanent paper from mills that operate a sustainable forestry policy, and which has been manufactured from pulp processed using acid-free and elementary chlorine-free practices. Furthermore, the publisher ensures that the text paper and cover board used have met acceptable environmental accreditation standards.

For further information on
Blackwell Publishing, visit our website:
www.blackwellpublishing.com

Contents

Contents

Contents

Contents

Acknowledgments

This book grew out of classes on modern theory that I taught at Kiel University in 1997 and Frankfurt University in 1999/2000. The idea of transforming this material into an introductory book was triggered by a (slightly tongue-in-cheek) remark by Heinz-Günter Nesselrath. Concentrated and continuous work was made possible by a scholarship of the German Research Foundation (DFG) which enabled me to spend the academic year 1997/8 at Harvard University, in a stimulating environment ideal for scholarly research, free from administrative or teaching obligations. A number of colleagues were generous with their time and provided intellectual stimuli; my thanks are due to Susan Suleiman, Albert Henrichs, and Richard F. Thomas.

Conversations and discussions with many other colleagues gave encouragement and inspiration; I am happy to acknowledge the help of Toni Bierl, Heinrich Detering, Stephen Harrison, Stephen Hinds, Glenn Most, and Jürgen Paul Schwindt. Susanne Eiben was a wonderful research assistant in Kiel; her help with bibliographical difficulties was most valuable. The late Gudrun Langer gave a number of most helpful suggestions for chapters 1 and 4.

When the manuscript was already in an advanced state, I accepted a new position at Frankfurt University, and my new obligations left hardly any time for continuous scholarly work. I am grateful to Martina Erdmann from Wissenschaftliche Buchgesellschaft for her friendly and sustained prodding which helped me finish the manuscript, and to the entire staff at Wissenschaftliche Buchgesellschaft for perfect collaboration.

As always, my greatest debt is to my wife, untiring interlocutor, keen reader, model of scholarly zeal, and mother of our two sons; one was born just as I was finishing this manuscript. This book is dedicated to Thomas and Benjamin.

T. A. S.
Frankfurt, March 2002

Acknowledgments for
the English Translation

This is a translation of the German edition of 2002; I have made only minor changes to the original text in order to update references. I was able to do most of the bibliographical work at Butler Library during a stay in February 2006 and want to thank Columbia University for their hospitality. Working with the staff of Blackwell has been a pleasure throughout; my special thanks go out to Juanita Bullough, who has been an exemplary copy-editor. I would also like to thank Hans Hagen and Taco Hoekwater, the developers of ConTEXt, for their wonderful typesetting program and for their patient help with technical questions.

After five marvelous years, I want to renew the dedication of the original edition with even greater enthusiasm: this book is dedicated to Thomas and Benjamin.

T. A. S.
Bonn, March 2007

Introduction

There is no shortage of introductory books on literary theory and literary criticism on the market. Publishing yet another one needs justification: what is its purpose, which the audience is it attempting to address, what is its methodology and strategy? I will try to answer these questions before introducing the subject itself.

What Is, and To What End Do We Study, Literary Theory?

First encounters with literary theory tend to be frustrating and discouraging. This book proposes to counteract the impression that literary theory is a closed room, hermetically sealed and accessible only to initiates. It wants to help the reader avoid mental reservations and unnecessary fears; it aims to provide an Ariadne's thread through the maze of confusing and contradictory theoretical approaches. It is primarily targeted at students of the classics. I have taken most examples from ancient, especially Latin, literature, and I have favored well-known ancient texts wherever possible. I hope that in addition to students, colleagues teaching ancient languages and literatures at high-school, college, or university level will also profit from reading this book. Finally, this book is written for everybody with an interest in literature, regardless of period or culture, everybody who cares about texts and the fundamental problems their understanding raises, everybody who is open to new questions and answers about familiar books. This book does not presuppose any prior knowledge or skills; it can be read by the famous Greekless and Latinless reader; all quotations from the classical languages are translated.

The aim of this book is to provide a first encounter with the most important ideas and concepts of the main theoretical approaches, thus enabling readers to pursue their forays into this territory independently. To facilitate this, every chapter has a Further Reading section containing a number of publications that will enable readers to deepen and broaden their understanding of the position explained in the chapter. I have made a conscious decision to keep these lists brief: I want to encourage readers to pursue their own way, not to browbeat them. I have only included works that I have read myself and found particularly helpful. If you want to do more serious work on a specific theoretical position, you will easily find further bibliographical hints in these works.

My optimistic assumption that it is possible to a give short and comprehensible account of a field as difficult as literary theory is based on the realization that most positions explained in this book, while they may be quite complex and intricate in their details, deal with a finite number of fundamental problems and questions. These fundamental problems may not allow for definitive and positive answers, but their core is most often easy to grasp. Some of the most important of these problems are:

- What *is* literature, and how can we distinguish it from non-literature?
- How does a literary text convey its meaning? Why is it that literary texts provoke a great number of different, often irreconcilable interpretations? How, then, can we guarantee that a text does not mean just anything or nothing at all?
- Who has the authority to interpret a text, and how do they obtain the right to claim validity for their interpretations?
- What is literature's relation to the world by which it is surrounded; how does it take its historical, social, political, or personal environment into account?

By their very nature, all these questions are infinite. But we must be aware that it is impossible *not* to give a preliminary answer to them: whether we like it or not, when we are reading literature (and especially when reading, interpreting, and teaching literature is our profession), we are bound to have more or less fixed ideas of why reading literature will enrich our life and what the right approach to literary texts should be, and during our reading, we cannot help interpreting the text. In fact, this might be the greatest advantage of studying literary theory: by forcing us to face these fundamental, seemingly trivial questions (as if anybody were unaware of what literature is!), it allows, even compels us to put our cards on the table and reflect upon our presuppositions. After studying literary theory for a while, you may still hold the same beliefs as before and make no changes about your attitude to and interpretation of literary texts – but your stance will be more self-conscious than it used to be, and this is a decisive advantage.

I am convinced that it is possible to explain most aspects of literary theory in plain, ordinary language. Nevertheless, I do not wish to prevent readers from encountering ideas and hypotheses that may at first appear confusing, bewildering, or simply absurd. Many recent pedagogical theories emphasize that we need to adjust the subject matter to the mental horizon of our students so they can more easily grasp what is at stake. I find this principle unhelpful. Meeting strange concepts that may at first strike us as incomprehensible, not the eternal return of familiar concepts, is what helps us learn new things and educate ourselves.

Some of the theoretical positions explained in this book are more than likely to evoke strong reactions (ranging from mild irritation to utmost anger) with readers who have not had much experience with this kind of thinking. They go against what common sense and our everyday knowledge seem to tell us. Therefore, I would recommend an ounce of patience to those who are making their first encounter with literary theory: when hypotheses and formulations strike us as absurd or perverse, this should not be taken as a personal insult, but instead, as a welcome invitation to reflect upon everything we thought we knew. Sometimes, you will have the impression that some theorists are systematically trying to conceal their thoughts behind a thick wall of opaque and impenetrable language. This should neither make you doubt your own intellectual capacities nor provoke you into throwing their books (let alone this book) into the trash can out of sheer desperation. Instead, you should remember the wonderful aphorism that the German philosopher Georg Christoph Lichtenberg (1742–99) wrote two centuries ago: "When a book and a head collide and there is a hollow sound, is it always from the book?"

Quite a few of the ideas that at first seem completely inaccessible will soon appear clear enough when you have understood the basic questions and assumptions upon which they rest. However, our patience should not be boundless, either: when I have read a book of literary theory carefully and with great attention, when I have made every effort to understand the issues and nevertheless am as unable to comprehend its basic ideas after reading as before, I have a moral right (maybe even a moral duty) to remember that life is just too short for such unfruitful endeavors – sometimes, the hollow sound comes from the book after all.

This introductory book wants to plead for a more composed attitude toward literary theory; it invites its readers to rid themselves of any inferiority complex they might feel toward literary theory and its adherents. This excludes a way of using theory that is unfortunately found all too often: in many academic debates, you will see scholars who consider literary theory as part of a rhetorical strategy that enables you to one-up your interlocutors (be they students, colleagues, or teachers). Lavish name-dropping, superficial allusions to the buzzwords and concepts of theories that happen to be in vogue at the moment ("What's the flavor of the day?"), a theatrical display of disappointment that your interlocutor has not read this theorist, is unaware what this term means, these are the telltale symptoms of this attitude. A corollary of this tactical use of theory is an all too earnest zeal about certain theoretical positions. Adherents tend to insist that only this or that theory offers a true approach to all literary texts, that it is not merely one model in a great number, but so revolutionary that it will forever change the way we look at literature ("Thou shalt have no other gods before me"). Theory is not a stick to beat people up (even if a minimum of knowledge about theory is an excellent tool to defend yourself in this kind of situation), and literature is not an area that any theory could monopolize for itself. Much rather, this book wants to invite its readers to pursue an attitude that the German critic Heinrich Detering has called "cheerful pluralism" [82.12]. We should be ready to play with different approaches, to test how far they can take us, to short-circuit texts and theories, and we should accept that this may either produce illuminating sparks or blow all the fuses. If I had to choose between daring novel readings at the risk of proposing wrong interpretations on the one hand and forever repeating the same old truths on the other, I would not hesitate to pick the former.

Literary Theory and Classics

There is no denying that this introduction is somewhat belated. During the 1970s and 1980s, literary theory was a field with a feverish pace, especially in the USA: hardly a week went by without some new contribution appearing, and every month brought a new fashion that ousted the previous month's favorite. Today, this fever has gone down; theory is no longer the most fashionable game in town. University bookstores still carry a "literary criticism" section, but it tends to be much smaller than it used to be, and most of the books date back to a period roughly from 1970 to 1990. Many of those who, in the 1980s or early 1990s, were climbing higher and higher into the unknown realms of theory, have now safely returned to the firm ground of the literary texts. The titles of some books and articles can serve to illustrate this change: as early as 1982, Paul de Man wrote an essay about "The Resistance to Theory" and another one about "The Return to Philology" (both reprinted in [74]). In the same year, Steven Knapp and Walter Benn Michaels published the essay "Against Theory" which led to a lengthy and intense debate in the scholarly journal *Critical Inquiry*. In one of the contributions, Stanley Fish flatly stated: "theory's day is dying; the hour is late; and the only thing left for a theorist to do is to say so" [108.341]. Since then, there has been a steady stream of books or articles with titles such as *The End of Literary Theory* [281] or "Beyond Theory" [103.200–23], and scholars wonder *What's Left of Theory?* [51]. Is theory dead (or a demon, as the French title of Antoine Compagnon's 1998 book *Le Démon de la Théorie* [58] has it)? Like Mark Twain, it might respond that all reports of its death are greatly exaggerated. And it continues to haunt departments of literature throughout the academic world.

Classics as a field has been rather slow to come to grips with modern literary theory (and this is especially true in Germany, where this book was written). This should not be too surprising; after all, our discipline has the longest tradition of scholarship in the entire field of humanities, and in the course of many centuries, it has developed its own methodology. It could be argued that this belatedness is an advantage rather than a drawback: while the turmoil of the last century has subsided and given way to a more dispassionate view, the fundamental questions that literary theory has raised remain with us. This is a turn of events that can be observed quite often in the humanities: basic problems appear to go away not because the ultimate solution has been found and everybody is happy with it, but because more interesting and novel debates seem to be taking place in other areas. But often, the same fundamental questions will crop up again after a short while (albeit in a slightly different outward appearance).

This situation should be considered an opportunity to take a calmer look at all these questions and problems, at a safe distance from the sound and the fury of earlier times. We may not be able to remain completely neutral and *sine ira et studio*, but we can now examine the contributions of the theoretical positions and the individual theorists with a less polemical eye – you no longer have to surf the latest theoretical wave to be considered hip. The historical distance has a liberating force, and we can now see the (sometimes exaggerated) pretensions that some theorists formulated for what they really were: there is so much noise and ballyhoo in the academic marketplace that some literary theorists thought it necessary to crank up their advertising to the highest volume in order to be heard at all. Every new approach could be nothing less than "revolutionary" and "groundbreaking," not only an innovative way of reading literature, but a new philosophy that changed our way of seeing the world.

In the last few years, a number of classicists have become aware of the chances and opportunities that literary theory offers and have developed fascinating new vistas on our ancient texts. But the acknowledgment that a basic understanding of the main streams of literary theory should be an integral part of the classics syllabus at our universities has been slow to gain acceptance. We have to catch up with most other disciplines in the humanities. The scathing words of a journalist in the leading German newspaper were not undeserved [31]: "If for classicists, literary theory ends with Emil Staiger ..., they should not be surprised that their field, which used to be the model of philology in general, is just the laughing stock of the other disciplines." In other words: a minimum of knowledge about the development, problems, and results of modern literary theory is necessary for classicists if they want to be able to communicate with members of the other disciplines, if they want to have a common language with the rest of the humanities. It is the only way we can argue successfully for our claims that without knowledge of the classical tradition, large areas of vernacular literatures and Western civilization in general cannot be appreciated and understood. It is the only way that interdisciplinary work in which each partner takes the other side seriously can function.

Objections Raised against Literary Theory

The study of literary theory has intensified in literature departments since the 1960s, and for the same period of time, arguments against studying theory have been around. Let us have a look at some of these arguments that are most frequently proposed.

Theory for theory's sake

A criticism that has been raised very often is the statement that some scholars have lost all contact with the literary texts themselves and are doing theory for theory's sake (see Karl Galinsky in [128.31]; a particularly silly formulation by Joachim Latacz can be found in [232.85]). In general, such an accusation is little more than a bogeyman to frighten the inexperienced: the percentage of studies that really do theory for its own sake is probably very low. And in a discipline like classics where theory has been neglected for such a long time, where numerous books on literary texts have been written without any knowledge of and regard for the theoretical foundations of interpretation, it would not be too disastrous if we were to err on the other extreme for a while.

Modern theories are inappropriate to ancient texts

Another frequent objection against literary theory is the criticism that these modern ideas are fundamentally incommensurable with texts from which they are separated by two millennia. For instance, Gregor Maurach, in his book on the "Methodology of Latin Studies," expresses as an iron rule that the interpreter of classical texts has to avoid "any form of modernity (e.g., contemporary sociology)" [249.7]. Even if we disregard the fact that this sentence demands something which is patently impossible (how can you avoid "any form of modernity" when you're using a computer to write your interpretation?), it is not even tenable as an ideal to aspire to. This would amount to the same thing as if we ordered archeologists to eschew the methods developed by modern engineering for analyzing ancient material. Literary theory claims to speak for literature in general, for all periods and cultures. It behooves the specialists of every literature to examine whether this claim holds water. Undoubtedly, the dicussion about literary theory has been dominated to an unhealthy degree by students of modern Western literatures who have had a tendency to draw untenable generalizations from the restricted corpus of texts they know. Hence, we classicists may and will come to the conclusion that some of these generalizations of modern theory rest upon special qualities of modern literature and cannot be applied to ancient literature – but this is an important realization that only classicists will be able to make. To put it bluntly: those who are skeptical about the (too) sweeping generalizations of modern theory will have to be particularly knowledgeable about it. A broad refusal to deal with it will be unfruitful and pointless, for it would isolate classics. And this is true not only for the status of classical scholars within the other humanities; it would also have negative effects for the subject itself: if it were true (as I firmly believe it is not) that classical texts cannot be understood in modern terms, if modern eyes and modern methodologies had no business looking into these texts, they would be dead for our time, and their existence would have to be considered a mere museum of leftovers from a long defunct culture. In that case, how could we possibly justify that students should still read these classical texts?

New wine in old wineskins

Another criticism takes the opposite direction, and yet, in a paradoxical manner, it is often raised by the same opponents of modern theory as the one just mentioned. It claims that all modern theories are, at a closer look, just repetitions of ideas that can be found in the scholars of the nineteenth century (or even in antiquity, in Aristotle and the ancient rhetoricians): "that's something we have always known and done!" Again, there's no denying that there is a certain amount of truth in this objection: some ideas that are promoted as being completely novel and unheard of are indeed just a slick version of old concepts, and we have already seen that literary theory is really about fundamental and primeval questions. It is also true that some concepts and problems in modern literary theory have antecedents in ancient rhetoric and philosophy (as George A. Kennedy pointed out in an article published in 1989 [214]). But if this criticism is generalized, it is certainly unjustified: concepts such as those developed by structuralism (Chapter 2) are really unprecedented. And every period of human history cannot but reformulate the old questions and search its own answers to them.

Literary theory is too fashionable

A variation on the objections just mentioned is the criticism that using modern theory in your scholarly research is just a fad, something that scholars will do just to embrace the *Zeitgeist* and have an edge in the ever intensifying race for academic positions and reputation; "traditional" scholars, on the other hand, are said to care about nothing but the beauty of the texts they treat and the truth of their interpretations. This may be right in some cases: some scholarly papers propose rather banal interpretations, bolstered by a plethora of quotations from modern theories and references to fashionable theorists, and one often cannot resist the impression that the same result could have been achieved by much simpler means. It cannot be denied that such quotations may be merely ornamental and be used to give a rather ostentatious display of scholarly credentials. On the other hand, a refusal to take literary theory into account can be just as ostentatious; pretending that you stay aloof from all this theoretical nonsense and the corruptions of modernity can also be just a strategy that is meant to reap benefits in certain academic quarters. Above all, we need to remember that the interpretive methodologies employed by traditional scholarship have not existed without a change forever; instead, they have a history, and, at one point in time, they were in turn the most recent methodology that was debated and bitterly fought over. And it is certainly open to question whether following the fashions of yesteryear is by definition morally superior to wearing the fashion of today.

Texts must be approached unprejudiced

Another criticism that is quite similar to the two objections just mentioned is the reproach that studying literary theory prevents us from being unprejudiced when we approach the literary texts about which we really care in our studies. Proponents of this position state that following the latest fad in literary theory will inevitably turn our head and seduce us into regarding these texts as mere playgrounds on which to build our theoretical sandcastles. However, I am absolutely convinced that there is no such thing as an unprejudiced approach to literary texts – in Terry Eagleton's wonderfully sarcastic words [90.x]: "Hostility to theory usually means an opposition to other people's theories and an oblivion of one's own." As we have already seen (above, p. 2), when we read a text, we do not have the choice whether to hold certain opinions and presuppositions or not – whether we like it or not, we have already answered certain questions and thus accepted certain prejudices before we read the first word on the page. The choice we do have is whether we want to be aware of these prejudices, whether we want to be able to consciously examine the arguments for and against a certain position. This will enable us to read our texts in the full knowledge that our position will always be provisional since we cannot expect to give final answers to the fundamental questions raised by literature. Indeed, the opinion (implied in the objection that theory will make us prejudiced and held by many traditional critics) that the only end of any form of literary criticism must be the interpretation of individual texts is such an unconscious and ill-considered prejudice. As early as 1964, the American critic Susan Sontag (1933–2004) wrote against it a poignant and well-known essay "Against Criticism" (reprinted in [334.3–14]). Sontag explains that every interpretation aims to translate a work of art and tell us what it "really" means. For her, this amounts to "a dissatisfaction (conscious or unconscious) with the work, a wish to replace it by something else" [334.10]. But even if we do not accept her position and hold that interpretation is indeed a legitimate aim of the study of literature, there can be no doubt that it is equally legitimate to attempt to grasp general principles of and in literature, such as the rules of epic narrative or even the rules of poetic style. Such studies do not have to be justified by the argument that they will help us interpret individual texts; they are important and fruitful in themselves.

Literary theory uses incomprehensible jargon

This is another objection which is not entirely unfounded. From everyday life, we all know that secret languages are a frequent phenomenon. They are an ideal means of establishing the togetherness of a group and giving it a sense of identity by excluding outsiders. A similar mechanism can sometimes be seen at work in literary criticism. An unnecessarily complex style, packed with neologisms and unusual words, can often be seen to serve no other purpose than to make all outsiders feel how stupid and ignorant they are. If you probe the real meaning of this pretentious jargon, you'll often find that the ideas behind it could very well have been expressed in a much easier way (a phenomenon that is by no means unique to literary criticism; intellectual mediocrity has always and in all fields had a tendency to hide behind walls made of impenetrable words). But this is only one side of the coin: every trade has its own specialized language which allows it to express (sometimes complex) ideas in a precise and succinct manner. Classics is no exeption to this rule, and most scholars have no qualms using terms such as "hyparchetype" or "anaclasis" to describe precise details in their field. We should thus not pretend that equally precise terms such as "heterodiegetic" or "signifier" are against human nature. Moreover, we should be ready to admit that some thoughts indeed *are* unusual and unorthodox and cannot be couched in a style that is immediately accessible. They may even strike "common sense" as being completely absurd. However, this does not mean that they are necessarily wrong – such apparent absurdities should be no more surprising or revolting in modern philosophy or literary theory than they are in modern physics. If you refuse to consider anything that is expressed in perplexing and difficult language as being empty jargon, without actually exploring and examining it, you would be forced to condemn classical texts such as Aristotle's *Metaphysics* or most of what the Neo-Platonist Plotinus has written.

All the objections raised against modern theory, then, contain a grain of truth, but they are by no means a sufficient reason for flatly condemning the study of theory. Above all, they often seem to spring from some sort of defense mechanism that has its origin in a lack of self-confidence: we, who have the privilege of a regular and easy access to the rich and enriching cultural heritage of antiquity, should view opinions that differ from our own not as a threat, but as a supplementation and a challenge, in the spirit of cheerful pluralism quoted above. My wish is that all those who teach and study classics adopt at least some of the attitude that Michel Foucault described, shortly before his death, in these words [117.8]: "There are times in life when the question of knowing if one can think differently than one thinks, and perceive differently than one sees, is absolutely necessary if one is to go on looking and reflecting at all."

How to Use This Book

When I first thought about planning and structuring this book, several options seemed feasible. It would have been possible to organize the material according to the main key concepts and have one chapter on the author, one chapter on the reader, one on interpretation, etc. The result would have been a useful work of reference, but not a readable book. Furthermore, the systematical arrangement would have been deceptive because it suggests that the system is a necessary or "natural" one while in fact, dividing the object "literature" in this way means accepting certain theoretical positions and rejecting others. On the other hand, a purely historical arrangement is difficult to maintain because there is no clear historical development in the course of literary theory: it would be misleading to pretend that all theoretical positions can be seen in a framework of argument and counter-argument; instead, several theoretical approaches are usually being elaborated at the same time, and it would be extremely artificial to construe a historical development or an image of progress out of this messy material.

There is one possible arrangement of such an introductory book which rests on a misunderstanding, and I want to be particularly clear about why I chose not to adopt it. When I was teaching classes on literary theory, students would time and again suggest that I should take one individual, well-known text and demonstrate the working of all main methods of literary interpretation: first, give a "structuralist analysis," then "deconstruct" it, and finally, give a "feminist" and "New Historicist" interpretation. What is at the core of such a suggestion is the view that literary theory is a toolbox which will always be ready to supply the right instrument for the job in hand. Moreover, it implies that all theoretical positions can somehow be harmonized and that the sum of all applied theories and methods will in some way supply a higher form of truth. In fact, many positions rest on completely divergent and mutually incompatible foundations, and they are interested in totally different aspects of literary texts; hence, such a procedure would be utterly impossible. Not every text lends itself to every theoretical approach; not every approach will aim to interpret texts at all.

It is thus obvious that there is no entirely satisfactory method of presentation. Hence, I have adopted an eclectic manner. In general, this book will provide a chronological account of the development of literary theory from the beginning of the twentieth century. However, I have taken the liberty of deviating from this course when objective or didactical reasons suggested close connections between positions whose historical place was wide apart. Classical literature is often referred to, both as a paradigm and for shorter examples to make points clearer. Moreover, there is a section in (almost) every chapter that presents a case where approaches shaped by modern theory have furthered our understanding of ancient literature or can be expected to do so.

Almost every chapter of this book could begin with the sentence that the theoretical position which will be described on the following pages is so important and vast that it can be regarded a field of its own and that the bibliography of relevant contributions could fill an entire book. This explains why most books which have aspirations similar to this one are edited volumes written by a group of specialists in the various fields. Nevertheless, after due consideration, my conviction was strong that the advantages of having a book like this, written by one person and thus having a uniform and consistent conception, outweigh the disadvantages of having to write about subjects that I am not entirely familiar with. My decision to write about all these divergent positions myself is most certainly foolhardy, yet it is also meant as an encouragement to colleagues. Undoubtedly, nobody can claim to be, in every field presented here, on a par with experts who have sometimes been working on the subject for years. Yet it is possible to gain a sufficient point of departure so that one can recognize what is interesting and important in the various positions and methodologies and can then go on to delve deeper into the subject in question.

The succinctness of the account in this book has most likely necessitated some crude simplifications and inacceptable shortcuts. Moreover, personal preferences may explain why I have decided to pay more attention to some positions than to others. Nevertheless, I am convinced that it is better to have an albeit superficial knowledge of a theoretical approach than to have no knowledge at all. Therefore, I have attempted to keep the discussion as comprehensible and straightforward as possible. I have not balked at using significant anecdotes and stories if they help us gain a better view of the concepts and problems that we are dealing with.

I am deeply aware of my own prejudices and limitations (and I became more and more aware of these as I was writing this book). I consider it an act of honesty toward my readers to be frank about these limitations instead of trying to hide them behind a specious display of impartiality. Hence, I have decided to put my cards on the table and make clear where my interest and preferences are so readers can see themselves what to expect from this book. Because of my academic education, I am more familiar with theoretical approaches coming from a French and American background than with German scholarship. If a colleague were more interested in this German tradition, he would certainly have had different priorities in his account. Furthermore, I am more sympathetic to positions that are "text-centered." This does not mean that I regard approaches which place particular emphasis on a text's wider context, perhaps with special regard to its social, cultural, or religious setting or to the foundations of literary activity in the human psyche, as unjustified or uninteresting; I can only say that my own preferences lie elsewhere. I have nonetheless attempted to be as clear and precise in presenting these positions as I could, but I prefer to be honest about my likes and dislikes and give reasons for them so readers can judge themselves whether they find these reasons convincing.

Let me briefly explain some of the conventions and practices used in this book: references to works quoted are given directly in the text itself. Numbers within square brackets such as [99] refer to the numbered bibliography on pp. 215–232. Readers who want to delve deeper into one of the theoretical approaches presented here will find suggested reading material at the end of each chapter. Moreover, I have given a few supplementary notes and further references to some questions raised in the text on pp. 209–214. It is a conscious decision not to have a symbol or footnote mark in the text itself flag these notes: I wanted to emphasize that this is additional material aimed to provide more in-depth information for those who are particularly interested in a topic, not "required reading." Whenever possible, quotations are taken from published English translations; where this was not possible, translations are my own.

Introductions to Literary Theory

The book market offers a wealth of reading matter for those who are curious to learn more about literary theory. The mass of introductions, handbooks, edited collections, encyclopedias, and historical accounts is difficult to survey, and an attempt to list them all would be fruitless and confusing. On the following pages, I will give a shortlist of some of the most well-known and useful titles, adding short commentaries as I go so readers can at least guess what they can expect from each book. After that, I add an unannotated list of a few further titles that I consulted while I was preparing this book. Since every reader has her or his own expectations, opinions, previous knowledge, and questions, I recommend that she or he browse as many of these books as (s)he can to find out which one will be most profitable for her or for him.

For those who, after reading this book, still feel the need to have some of the fundamental questions and concepts explained in a clear manner and in plain English, I recommend Peter Barry's 1995 book *Beginning Theory* [22]. In 11 chapters, Barry provides a patient and lucid explanation of the most important positions of modern literary theory. What makes his book special is his (typically British) no-nonsense approach and his willingness to be critical toward the ideas and theorists he describes.

Eagleton's *Literary Theory* [90], of which a second edition appeared in 1996, is rightly regarded as the classic introduction to the subject. It is for more advanced students. Eagleton is brilliant in giving a vivid, comprehensible explanation of complex problems, and he keeps a critical distance from his subject. However, readers (especially those who do not have much experience) must know that Eagleton himself holds a political (Marxist) view of literary criticism and that he judges other theoretical positions accordingly. Another problem is that the second edition is just a reprint of the first edition, printed in 1983, with an "Afterword" added at the end of the volume, so the account itself reflects the status of literary theory at the beginning of the 1980s. The bibliography (which had never been especially helpful in the first place) has not been updated. Another concise and clear account can be found in *A Reader's Guide to Contemporary Literary Theory* by Raman Selden, Peter Widdowson, and Peter Brooker [327]. Unlike Eagleton's books, the authors do not put much emphasis on the political and intellectual background of theory; their aim is not to explain why literary criticism developed in the directions we observe today. Yet they take the more recent developoments into account; every chapter contains a helpful bibliography which is subdivided into "basic texts" and "further reading."

These two books aim to give a continuous history of modern literary theory. The plan of *The Cambridge History of Literary Criticism*, especially volume 8 *From Formalism to Poststructuralism* (1995), edited by Raman Selden [326], is slightly different: here, a series of independent articles written by specialists in their respective field presents the various positions and theories. This volume is accordingly less homogeneous than the ones previously described, however, if read in succession, the articles give a history of twentieth-century literary theory. The volume is more thorough and comprehensive than the one mentioned before, and its bibliography aims to be fairly exhaustive and is hence immensely useful; on the other hand, it is meant more as a work of reference than as a readable account, and it might be a bit overwhelming for the beginner.

Another work of reference is the *Encyclopedia of Contemporary Literary Theory*, edited by Irena R. Makaryk in 1993 [246]. It does not aim at giving a historical account. Instead, it is a work of reference that offers short descriptive articles on different aspects of literary theory. There are three different parts: "Approaches" presents important developments and fields of theory; "Scholars" provides bibliographical and intellectual information about the most important critics (emphasis is put on scholars from the English-speaking countries); and "Terms" explains key concepts (such as "parody," "postmodernism," or "authority") in a succinct and clear manner. If you are not absolutely committed to having a continuous historical account of the development of literary theory, this may very well be the most useful book around. It was the one that I found myself consulting constantly while I was writing these pages, and I would recommend it to anyone interested in the subject. *The Johns Hopkins Guide to Literary Theory & Criticism*, edited by Michael Groden, Martin Kreiswirth, and Imre Szeman, follows a similar plan; the second edition appeared in 2005 [157]. In this book, however, the articles cover more general topics (such as "French Theory and Criticism") and provide broader surveys. Since this volume treats the development of literary theory from antiquity to the present day, Makaryk's book [246] tends to be more detailed about topics concerning the twentieth century.

For those willing to read books in languages other than English, there are a number of works that can be mentioned. *Methoden und Modelle der Literaturwissenschaft*, edited by Rainer Baasner and Maria Zens in 1996 [14], can be recommended to beginners. It successfully aims at being clear and didactic; the emphasis is on theory and criticism in German-speaking countries. *Grundzüge der Literaturwissenschaft*, edited in 1996 by Heinz Ludwig Arnold and Heinrich Detering [6], is more comprehensive; its extensive bibliography and its glossary of terms are immensely useful; however, the quality of the contributed articles varies. Another helpful book is the *Lexikon literaturtheoretischer Werke*, edited by Rolf Günter Renner and Engelbert Habekost in 1995 [301]: it offers short summaries of important books of literary theory from antiquity to the present day. If you read French, you will find a readable and comprehensive account of French literary theory in Jean-Yves Tadié's 1987 book *La Critique littéraire au XXe siècle* [345]. Tzvetan Todorov's *Literature and Its Theorists. A Personal View of Twentieth-Century Criticism* (published in 1984; English translation in 1987) [356] is a highly personal and thus deeply impressive story of the development of literary criticism. Antoine Compagnon's 1998 book *Literature, Theory, and Common Sense* (English translation 2004) [58] is very readable and well-informed, and it is structured in a systematic way. Last but not least, I can only name a few more books that I also found useful such as *Modern Literary Theory. A Comparative Introduction*, edited by Ann Jefferson and David Robey in 1986 [204]; *Contemporary Literary Theory*, edited by G. Douglas Atkins and Laura Morrow in 1989 [9]; *Redrawing the Boundaries. The Transformation of English and American Literary Studies*, edited by Stephen J. Greenblatt and Giles Gunn in 1992 [151]; there is the French volume *Méthodes du texte. Introduction aux études littéraires*, edited by Maurice Delcroix and Fernand Hallyn in 1987 [71]; and the German collections *Neue Literaturtheorien. Eine Einführung*, edited by Klaus-Michael Bogdal in 1990 [37]; *Literaturwissenschaftliche Theorien, Modelle und Methoden. Eine Einführung*, edited by Ansgar Nünning, Sabine Buchholz, and Manfred Jahn in 1995 [280]; and finally *Literaturwissenschaft. Ein Grundkurs*, edited by Helmut Brackert and Jörn Stückrath in 2000 [46].

When we come to our specific topic, the application of modern literary theory to classical texts, a word of warning is due: Thomas G. Rosenmeyer's 1988 book *Deina ta polla. A Classicist's Checklist of Twenty Literary-Critical Positions* [310] looks like the perfect reference to keep handy, yet the book is a big disappointment and not too useful. A number of collective volumes have been published during the last decades. Some cannot be recommended because their contributions either do not really engage with modern critical approaches or are marred by a shocking ignorance of the classical world and the ancient languages. In my view, this is the case for the volume *Contemporary Literary Hermeneutics and Interpretation of Classical Texts*, edited by Stephen Kresic in 1981 [218] and for *Post-Structuralist Classics*, edited by Andrew Benjamin in 1988 [34]. The contributions in the following volumes are generally of higher quality: some concrete examples for encounters between classics and modern literary theory (with varying degrees of success) can be found in *Innovations of Antiquity*, edited by Ralph Hexter and Daniel Selden in 1992 [179]. *Modern Critical Theory and Classical Literature*, edited by Irene J. F. de Jong and John Patrick Sullivan in 1994 [210] contains a number of interesting articles and is valuable because of its extensive bibliographies and good introduction. *The Interpretation of Roman Poetry: Empiricism or Hermeneutics?*, edited by Karl Galinsky in 1992 [127], is less systematic, but it offers fascinating insights into a still ongoing debate between adherents and opponents of the introduction of modern critical methodologies into classical studies. *Texts, Ideas, and the Classics. Scholarship, Theory, and Classical Literature*, edited by Stephen J. Harrison in 2001 [172], is an excellent, if somewhat heterogeneous collection; the introductions to the different sections are especially helpful. Last but not least, I refer readers to the article "Literary Theory and Classical Studies" [122] by Don P. and Peta G. Fowler in the third edition of the *Oxford Classical Dictionary* [190], which is a model of the presentation of a wealth of information in very little space.

Chapter 1
Russian Formalism

Like all intellectual activity, reflecting upon literature and its intepretation is a continuous process. It is almost as old as literature itself, and this probably means as old as humanity. Even revolutionary ideas usually have predecessors, sometimes in the form of small footnotes or forgotten ideas. Most approaches do not start at some zero point – even if some adherents of new ideas want to convince us that their methodology will take us where no man has gone before. Hence, there is no "starting point" for modern literary theory. However, since this introduction cannot cover the entire development of literary theory from antiquity to the twenty-first century, it cannot avoid setting such a point of departure. Starting with Russian Formalism is not entirely arbitrary. Not only were the Formalists the first clearly demarcated school of literary criticism in the twentieth century; they can also be called the founding fathers of modern literary theory in many other regards. Their movement put questions and problems on the agenda that were to play an important role in later discussions, and it is safe to say that today, Russian Formalism is not studied because of the concrete results and contributions of its chief thinkers but because of the important incentives it provided. Specialists will still value the Formalists (students of Slavic literatures emphasize, e.g., that their studies of Russian versification still merit reading), but in this introduction, they will be considered because of their influence on the later development of literary theory. The following pages, then, will concentrate on aspects and questions raised by the Formalists that can be said to have contributed to the development of literary criticism; I will not dwell on the more technical and specialized work performed by the Formalists.

Let us begin by making a few remarks on the nature and the history of Formalism. Unlike many of the approaches we will study in the course of this book, Formalism really was a close-knit school of literary studies. Most of its adherents knew each other, they discussed their work with each other and, despite occasional (and sometimes even fundamental) disagreements, they had a feeling of being a community of scholars. This feeling was certainly fostered by the fact that most Formalists were rather young scholars; they were keenly aware of being outsiders who had to fight against a well-established academic mainstream, and they were very fond of conducting this fight by means of provocations, bluffs, and polemics. These members of the Formalist movement would occasionally use words like "formal method" or similar words; however, the label "Formalistic" was by and large a polemical sobriquet applied by their adversaries. In the Soviet Union, "Formalistic" was used as a catch-all term to tar a number of cultural manifestations (in literature, music, film, or art) which the regime found suspect. Hence, the word degenerated into a polemical buzzword with little or no concrete meaning.

Nevertheless, it is important to remember that initially, the Formalists had not been opponents of the Communist Party. Their movement began in the cities of St. Petersburg and Moscow, shortly before the October Revolution of 1917, and many Formalists were convinced that their work was as revolutionary in the field of lingustics and literary criticism as the Bolsheviks' work was in the field of politics. During the turmoils of the revolution and the ensuing civil war, Formalism made a rapid and brilliant advance to prominence. But it was not long before some of the leading communist activists began to voice criticism against the Formalists, and this criticism grew ever more vociferous after Vladimir Ilich Lenin died (in 1924) and Joseph Stalin (1879–1953) took power. At first, the Formalists had underestimated just how determined and influential their opponents were; now they tried to make their ideology acceptable to the communist powers by retouching and rephrasing their work. But in vain: at the beginning of the 1930s, Formalism had more or less ceased to exist; its adherents had either gone into exile or had been forced to do their scholarly work in fields that were less political and thus less visible and less exposed to government scrutiny.

During its heyday, the Formalist movement comprised numerous scholars who followed similar approaches to the interpretation of literary texts and discussed the methodology and practice of the formal method. Two of the most important ones were Victor Shklovsky and Roman Jakobson (whom we will meet again in another chapter of this book).

ᢀ Victor Shklovsky (1893–1984) was in many regards the most brilliant representative of the Formalist movement. He provided a clear exposition of the fundamental tenets of the Formalists early in the development of Formalism. His contributions often show a plethora of original insights and ideas, but he also had a tendency to let himself get carried away by his penchant for provocative and polemical formulations.

ﻉ Roman Jakobson (1896–1982) can be called the most influential thinker of the Formalist school. He left the Soviet Union for Prague as early as 1920; in 1941, he settled in the USA where he became an established and famous academic teacher. The different stages of Jakobson's career in the Soviet Union, Czechoslovakia, and the USA are one factor that was responsible for the spread and development of Formalist ideas in literary scholarship. Jakobson was a linguist by training, yet his published work covers an impressively wide area of topics; he was especially interested in the connections between linguistics and literary criticism.

The Question of Literariness

What was new about Formalism? How did the Formalists influence the course of literary theory? Formalists were deeply unsatisfied with the state of literary scholarship at the beginning of the twentieth century. In particular, they had the impression that literary criticism had not yet developed a sufficient definition of its subject proper. At this time, literary critics in Russia were more interested in the philosophical and religious dogmas that could be extracted from literary texts than in the texts themselves; or they gave more attention to the authors of literature than to their works (even questions as important as "Was Pushkin a smoker?" would elicit articles). The Formalists, many of whom had linguistic training, endeavored to provide a new definition of the field: if we want to study literature, we must first find out what distinguishes literature from non-literature. "What makes a verbal message a literary work of art?" was thus the most important question that the Formalists asked, or, to put it more technically: what produces the "literariness" (*literaturnost'*) of texts?

Two logical consequences ensued from this postulate. (1) If a concept as abstract and as general as "literariness" is the subject of scholarly research, the interpretation of specific texts must necessarily be considered of secondary importance. It is true that a number of papers by the Formalists still attempt to interpret specific literary texts. But in general, it is safe to say that Formalism was most influential because of contributions that explore the qualities of a body of texts such as folktales or parodies. (2) Modern literary criticism had clearly shown that literariness cannot be defined by the objects depicted in the texts – a poem about a piece of machinery can be as "literary" as a poem about a rose; a novel set among the working class can be no less artistic than a novel about life at a royal court. Hence, literariness must be constituted not by the subject matter, but by a specific usage of the linguistic material. This basic observation is the single most important idea that Formalism developed; it exerted an immeasurable influence on the development of literary theory in the twentieth century. Literary criticism deals with a special usage of language; hence it has to develop its methodology and formulate its questions and problems by deriving its inspiration from linguistics: this was a lesson that was to be important for the course of literary scholarship during all of the twentieth century.

The question, then, was: how can we proceed to analyze this linguistic literariness? Our first reaction would be to distinguish literary from non-literary language such as everyday speech. In fact, this had been a method of looking at literature that had been used since antiquity; it is called "poetics of deviance" or "deviation" because in this view, poetic language is defined by deviating from the "ordinary" use of language. But it soon became clear that this method was riddled with problems: such a definition of literariness presupposes that one of the factors involved be stable and unchanging in order for deviations from the ordinary to be perceptible and measurable. Was this the case in the opposition "poetic vs. ordinary language"?

ᴈ❧ Ordinary, prosaic speech is no homogeneous phenomenon, but much rather an amalgam of different elements – most languages have several dialects (geographical differentiation), different social groups and strata use different forms of a given language (sociolects), and linguistic facts are defined by the genre of the text – an editorial in a newspaper will not use the same variant as the manual for a computer. How can we hope to define ordinary language in this bewildering plethora of linguistic forms?

ᴈ❧ However, defining literary language is not easier than defining ordinary language. Features that may strike us as being utterly poetic may have been quite ordinary in Shakespeare's times. And many literary works do not use any linguistic material that could be considered out of the ordinary, e.g., realist novels or many forms of modern lyrics. After all, we know that using extraordinary, "poetic" vocabulary does not constitute literature. Poetic language, then, cannot be defined as "ordinary language + x."

Hence, it is not the linguistic material itself that distinguishes literary language. This observation made the Formalists attempt new ways of defining literariness. Literary language, they claimed, plays a communicative role that is different from that of ordinary language; the difference lies in its function, not in its raw material. Ordinary language always serves specific, precise needs: e.g., it wants to convey information. Poetic language, on the other hand, has its aim in itself; it is autotelic or autonomous.

Roman Jakobson's Model of Linguistic Communication

This definition may appear somewhat cryptic at first sight. It will become clearer if we take a look at a model of linguistic communication that Roman Jakobson proposed in a now famous paper delivered at a conference in 1960 (reprinted in [197.62–94]). Jakobson here summarizes and develops ideas that the Formalists had brought up several decades earlier. He distinguishes between several sets (*Einstellung*) toward the linguistic message. In most acts of communication, we will find a mixture of these sets; having one of them exclusively is an exception, not the rule. This is how Jakobson schematizes these sets and the corresponding aspects of communication [197.66–71]:

	context	
addresser	message	addressee
	contact	
	code	

	referential	
emotive	poetic	conative
	phatic	
	metalingual	

The first part of this schema contains the various parts that a linguistic communication contains. In the center, we see the message proper. It is conveyed by an addresser to an addressee. This takes place in a specific communicative context, which can be a personal conversation, a public discourse, or the reading of a book. The context comprises all factors that are shared by addresser and addressee: a shared knowledge about certain details of the message, a common situation in which both communicate, and so on. The message exists in a certain code – in our case, this could be the English language, which is in turn divided into numerous subcodes: when engineers talk about their work, we might not be able to understand them even though they use the English language. Addresser and addressee must share this code, or communication will be impossible. Finally, we need a medium of contact. In the technical sense, the medium of contact in a conversation is the air that transmits the vibrations of the addresser's vocal cords to the addressee's tympanic membrane, or it could be the electric impulse of a telephone wire. However, in a looser sense, we call contact everything that stimulates the addressee's attention and makes her or him receptive to the message.

The second part of Jakobson's model contains the functions that correspond to these elements of verbal communication. If a message centers on the addresser, it has an emotive function – a good example could be an interjection or exclamation. If the message concentrates on the addressee, we have a conative function: the message tries (Latin *conari*) to influence the addressee. An order does not attempt to convey information or express the speaker's emotions; instead, it wants the addressee to do what (s)he is told. If the message revolves around its context, the function is referential; a good example of this would be a radio transmission of a football match: its aim is to depict the facts as accurately as possible, to give information about the situation. Communication is called metalingual when it is primarily concerned with its own code: this is the case in a scholarly paper about the English language, but it also occurs in everyday situations, when we have to come to an understanding of what certain terms may or may not mean. The phatic function of verbal communication comes to the forefront when the medium of contact is concerned, e.g., when we have a bad telephone line and constantly have to ask "do you hear me?" or when we try to ascertain if our interlocutor has understood what we are saying. Certain forms of communication could be said to be predominantly phatic – when I greet somebody by saying "good morning," this is neither a magical or religious incantation nor an order, but it is merely a means of establishing contact and beginning a communication.

Let us now turn to the poetic function of language. This will be easiest if we keep in mind what we just learnt about all the other functions and look at a literary work of art such as Virgil's *Georgics*. This text is not *referential*; its aim is not to convey information about agriculture and stock-farming. Nor is it *conative*: it does not urge its readers immediately to go and obey the rules and recipes it contains. Instead, the main point of this verbal message is to display its own aesthetic quality. Agriculture is merely the raw material that makes such an act of communication possible. Virgil's words do not serve any purpose outside of themselves; rather, they have their end in themselves. As readers, we are not invited to use these words as a transparent medium which will allow us to forget its existence and see the subject matter; instead, these words, the act of communication itself, is at the center of our attention. This is what is meant when we say that poetic language is autonomous. This concentration of the addressee's attention upon the message itself is produced by a number of linguistic means, the most obvious of which is undoubtedly the rhythm of Latin hexameter verse. It immediately draws the reader's attention to the message itself and emphasizes that this verbal message, not the context, nor the writer's emotions, are paramount in the act of communication.

Poetic Language as Defamiliarization

What is achieved by this poetic function; how does our perception of such an autotelic message differ from ordinary communication? The Formalists observed that everyday language follows a need for economy; it tries to facilitate communication as much as possible. Accordingly, our ordinary language tends to abridge and leave out things that are self-evident (in the linguists' professional language, this aspect is called "elliptical"). When we happen to overhear a conversation whose context is unknown to us (because we have no knowledge of the subject matter the speakers are talking about or because we can hear only part of the conversation), it is often impossible to supplement such an elliptical act of communication.

We could also say that everyday language tries to make itself as unobtrusive and transparent as possible. In ordinary communication, we care about the things we talk about, not about the linguistic means utilized to describe them; words are merely tools we have to use. In such a form of communication, we are not aware of the sound of our language; they just stand in for the things they refer to. This state was called "automatization" by the Formalists: if you happen to be a teacher and speak or hear the word "chalk" dozens of times every day in your classroom, you will no longer be attentive to its sound, you will not ponder upon the numerous connotations, nuances, and senses that this word can convey, but whenever you hear it, you will instantaneously, automatically see this all too familiar object. As will be clear from what we just learnt, poetical language acts against this automatization. It attempts to make us aware of the value and quality of the linguistic material that appears to be so familiar and ordinary, and it does this not by making communication easy, but more difficult.

With this effect, art offers us a fresh perception of everything that we normally just take for granted; it makes us "see" objects to which we have become accustomed and prevents us from merely "recognizing" them without paying attention. In the words of Victor Shklovsky [234.3–24], written in 1919, art makes "the stone stony" [234.12]. This quality of literary language is called deautomatization or defamiliarization. We can compare it to a strategy that has been used in literature for a long time: we tend to see our familiar world in a new light when this world is described by an outsider – this could be a foreigner for whom our own habits and customs are utterly novel (as in Montesquieu's *Persian Letters*), an animal that finds human behavior confusing (as in E. T. A. Hoffmann's *Tomcat Murr*), or an extraterrestrian (as in a number of movies and television shows). This unfamiliar perspective makes us reflect on attitudes and judgments that our habitual, everyday perception has made automatic.

But it is not only our everyday perception that has a tendency to become automatic and insipid; the same can happen to artistic devices. Think of linear perspective: when this technique was first developed by artists at the beginning of the early modern period, it must have been an unfamiliar and shocking experience for those who first viewed it; it must have unsettled their expectations of what a painting should be like. But after some period of time, people began to get used to this new form of presentation. Hence, artists began to experiment with increasingly more daring designs; they began to paint their objects from increasingly novel and unusual perspectives to demonstrate their skills and the possibilities of the device. But automatization could not be stopped, and artists set out to discover fresh and original forms of depicting (such as impressionism and cubism) that were not dominated by linear perspective; these new forms again defamiliarized their objects, made perception more difficult, and "deautomatized" our ways of looking at the world.

Similar developments, the Formalists claimed, can be observed in the course of literary history. Literature employs certain techniques to achieve defamiliarization. For a certain time, these techniques are so unusual that they succeed in arousing the readers' attention; the audience is aware of the fact that it is looking at literature, not at the ordinary communication of everyday facts. After some time, however, these techniques and devices tend to be become "automatized" themselves, and instead of making perception slower and more difficult, they become ossified as mere conventions that readers often do not perceive. When this happens, new tendencies appear that will attempt to defamiliarize these now conventional techniques, thus producing a new effect of defamiliarization. One of the devices that is particularly successful in achieving this effect is parody. For the Formalists, parody meant not only a comical distortion of a text or a literary form, but every method that tries to lay bare a device and to make it perceptible to the audience, thus exposing its conventionality and allowing for defamiliarization. In a brilliant paper published in 1921 [234.25–60],

Shklovsky demonstrates this by analyzing Laurence Sterne's (1713–68) novel *Tristram Shandy*, first printed in 1760–7. In it, Sterne parodies the conventional ways of narrating a novel – his hero Tristram Shandy sets out to tell the story of his life, but time and again, he loses the thread of his narrative and gets involved in a maze of digressions, excursuses, commentaries, and clarifications; the narrative thus departs more and more from its own goal, ending the day before the hero's birth. Sterne's novel thus renders the usual ways of storytelling impossible; by doing so, it exposes the conventionality of these norms (which had become familiar and automatic), thus reminding its readers that these are not natural, but artificial devices. But every literary current will in turn succumb to this tendency of becoming conventionalized and automatized, thus calling for a new countercurrent that will in turn lay bare its devices by parody and replace them with new techniques.

The Formalists saw this regular movement of device – automatization – parody – automatization as a decisive force in the course of literary history; they claimed that this history is determined by the fact that automatized forms die and are replaced by novel techniques. But these seemingly dead forms can also return (in a slightly modified manner) and become novel in turn, replacing what had once been new and exciting. In a paper published in 1927, Jurij Tynyianov (1894–1943) used this simple schema to develop a systematic and complex model of literary evolution [248.66–78].

Further Reading

Victor Erlich's book on the Formalists (first published 1954) [97] is still the standard account of the history and doctrine of Russian Formalism; the preceding chapter is largely based on this work, which provides a thorough introduction into all aspects of the movement. Several anthologies of important contributions by the Formalists have been published; in the English-speaking world, *Russian Formalist Criticism*, edited by Lee T. Lemon and Marion J. Reis [234] is the most well-known collection, but it contains just four (albeit important) essays. The bilingual (Russian–German) anthology edited by Jurij Striedter [342] has more essays; the excellent introduction by the editor has been translated into English in [340] and [341] and is an ideal point of departure for everyone interested in Formalist theory. A few of the most important essays by Roman Jakobson have been collected in the volume *Language in Literature* [197]; he has an exemplary way of giving a clear and helpful exposition of fundamental problems and concepts.

Chapter 2
Structuralism

As we saw in chapter 1, the "linguistic turn" can be called the most important heritage left by the Formalists; this was to be a decisive influence on most later developments in literary theory. The clearest case in point is structuralism. This is where the intellectual adventure of modern literary theory really starts – and this is where the immense rift in the study of literature began. Structuralism proposed a number of positions and hypotheses that more traditionally trained literary critics found unacceptable and that they attacked, often passionately. At times, the debate was emotional and irrational, and the structuralists were not least responsible for this. Quite a few of the scholars who, in the intellectual climate of France during the 1950s and early 1960s, called themselves structuralists, were young, and they were out for provocation. If the methodology and, above all, style of their contributions shocked the established professors in the field, so much the better! When we read some of the fiercely polemical essays and books today, now the frenzy has subsided, we cannot help thinking that in those days, being a structuralist meant not so much holding certain beliefs and using a certain methodology as being on the cutting edge, being progressive and innovative, and fighting against everything and everybody that was considered old hat. This debate was no less about power in the academe than about questions of theory and method, and it should not come as a surprise that the wearers of the old hats (and detainers of academic power) were not willing to give up their position without putting up a fight. Accordingly, structuralism gained a strong position in French universities after the turmoils of 1968, although some of its leading proponents had no sympathies at all for the rebellious students. Nevertheless, structuralism itself appeared to embody everything that was forward-thinking and capable of breaking up the ossified system.

It is thus less easy to speak about something like a unified structuralism than about Formalism because in the heyday of the movement, a number of quite heterogeneous elements were eager to adorn themselves with this fashionable label. Nevertheless, it is possible to detect, among the numerous byways and sidetracks, something we could call "standard structuralism," which has had an important influence on many areas of the humanities. It achieved this wide influence because many of the important problems and questions it raised were answered in a manner that was sometimes simplified to a rather violent degree. It is this standard structuralism that we will now try to understand.

The Founder of Structuralism: Ferdinand de Saussure

Three influences were decisive for the emergence of structuralism:

1   It inherits ideas from the Formalists. Roman Jakobson, whom we have just met in chapter 1, plays an important role: during his stay in Prague, he was one of the members of the "Prague Linguistic Circle" where he formulated a number of ideas that were forerunners of structuralism.
2   In 1942, the French anthropologist Claude Lévi-Strauss (b. 1908) attended lectures delivered by Jakobson in New York. He was fascinated by Jakobson's ideas and attempted to apply them to the study of foreign cultures, especially their religion and myths. This is how structural anthropology developed, and it has in turn exerted an influence on structuralism in linguistics and literary criticism.
3   By far the most important contribution, however, came from the field of linguistics. The Swiss scholar Ferdinand de Saussure (1857–1913) is rightly considered the founding father of structuralism, and it is his work that we will examine first.

In 1915, two years after Saussure's death, some of his students published notes from lecture courses he had given in the years from 1906 to 1911 in Geneva under the title *Cours de linguistique générale* ("Course in general linguistics," [315]). Like the Russian Formalists, Saussure believed that it was necessary to give a more precise definition of the field he was exploring. He distinguished two aspects of language [315.77]: on the one hand, the single utterance (*parole*), and on the other hand, the system of rules that underlies these utterances (*langue*). This system is not in the possession of one single user of a language; instead, it is the collective property of all its speakers. Our first reaction would be to assume that *langue* is just the sum of all *paroles* of a language or that it is an abstraction that has been made *a posteriori*. Yet Saussure emphasized that *langue* is not an artificial construct, but is as real as any single utterance [315.15]. Think of the way we see our own language: when we say that someone "speaks English," we do not mean that (s)he has knowledge of the abstract rules of English (native speakers usually do not know much about the grammar of their language), nor would we say this about someone who can merely reproduce sentences and expressions (s)he has heard, but is incapable of forming sentences herself or himself. Much rather, when we learn a language, we acquire a model which lets us form an infinite number of grammatically correct *paroles*; the American linguist Noam Chomsky (b. 1928) has called this skill "competence" [53.3–10] (in contrast to the "performance," the actual utterance). This model may be less obvious than a concrete speech act, yet it is clear that it exists in its own right. It is this system, then, that is the object of linguistic investigation, not the single *parole*.

Saussure's original analysis was only concerned with this system of human language, yet he himself pointed out that every system of signs can be analyzed according to the same criteria: e.g., traffic signs, or a deck of cards [315.16]. Later, we will see some examples of such extralinguistic systems. It was precisely this possibility of applying Saussure's methodology to other systems that was one of the reasons for the enormous influence of structuralist thought on such diverse fields as anthropology or literary criticism. This science of systems of signs in general is often called "semiotics," a term coined by the American philosopher Charles Sanders Peirce (1839–1914). In the following pages, I will occasionally take my examples from sign systems other than the human language to illustrate aspects of structuralism; this will also demonstrate the universal applicability of structuralist concepts.

Studying language as a system entailed one important consequence that brought Saussure in sharp contrast to the tendencies of scholarship in his time: he shifted the focus of linguistics away from historical problems. At the turn of the twentieth century, linguistic research was almost exclusively concerned with historical changes in sounds and words, syntactical structures, or semantical values. Saussure, on the other hand, saw language as a uniform system that is complete and functional at every period of its existence; he claimed that the aim of linguistics was to analyze the ways in which this system works. In Saussure's terms, his approach was about the synchronic structure of language, not about studying historical, diachronical developments [315.83–7].

The difference between both approaches is so fundamental that we should spend some time examining it. In classics, a diachronic model of studying language has always been preponderant, and it is still going strong today. If you look at a Latin dictionary or grammar, you will find that they usually distinguish between classical, preclassical, and postclassical usage of words and forms. But doesn't that mean that long periods of the Latin language are treated as being either "not yet" or "no more"? Saussure emphasized that the linguistic system does not manifest such preliminary or decadent stages; at every period of its existence, Latin was a tool perfectly suitable for communication. Studying the systematical functioning of Latin in late antiquity is as legitimate as examining how this late Latin differed from, say, Cicero's language.

On the other hand, as will shortly become clear, Saussure's methodology is indeed particularly suited for synchronic examination. Hence, critics have often reproached structuralism for being ahistorical. (This was sometimes connected with the criticism that it was politically suspect: if you have so little regard for historical developments, you are probably uninterested in influencing them and, hence, will refrain from any active participation in politics.) This lack of interest in history cannot be denied: it is difficult or even impossible to analyze the synchronic functioning of a system at the same time as you observe how it changes in history. What we have here is typical: a blind spot in a particular methodology. But every theoretical position has such a blind spot, and it seems rather unfair to censure structuralism for not explaining what it never wanted to explain. We should be aware of this omission in structuralist thought, but we should not therefore condemn structuralism.

Saussure's Definition of the Linguistic Sign

What, then, is Saussure's method of a synchronic study of language? For him, the linguistic system is made up of a multitude of signs. Every sign consists of two elements that are one inseparable unity: on the one hand, the sound-image (which Saussure called "*signifiant*," English "signifier"), on the other, the mental concept that is connected with this sound-image (the "*signifié*," or "signified"). This is best understood if we consider first the example of a concrete object like a tree (see the famous diagrams in Saussure's *Course* [315.66–7]), but, of course, it applies to abstract notions as well: in English, the sound-image "yes" is connected with the abstract mental concept "affirmation."

It is important to remember that the linguistic sign is always just a connection between such a sound-image and a mental concept. In Jonathan Swift's (1667–1745) novel *Gulliver's Travels*, the hero reaches the island of Balnibarbi and visits the academy in the capital Lagado. He is fascinated by the academy's project to make language more efficient: people will no longer speak words, but instead carry with them the objects about which they want to converse. Gulliver approves of the project but remarks that it "hath only this inconvenience attending it, that if a man's business be very great, and of various kinds, he must be obliged to carry a greater bundle of *things* upon his back, unless he can afford one or two strong servants to attend him." Swift's satirical description can help us understand one aspect of structuralism that can paradoxically be described both as a strength and as a weakness: the real objects behind the linguistic signs (or "referents" in expert terminology) are not part of the language; hence, they fall outside of the field that a (structuralist) linguist studies; the same is true for the connection between the linguistic sign and its referent. This limitation allowed structuralism a more focused and clearer examination of the relations between signs *inside* of the linguistic system. On the other hand, it resulted in another blind spot of structuralism: at times, structuralists seemed almost oblivious to the fact that linguistic utterances do have content, that they do relate to the outside world. This refusal to pay attention to the meaning of language is a predecessor of developments that should later result in deconstruction (see chapter 8) and led many people to regard structuralism with great suspicion.

Saussure explained that the connection between signifier and signified is arbitrary, yet necessary [315.67]. This sentence sounds somewhat paradoxical. What does it mean? There is no natural connection between the sound-image "key" and the concept of "a device to open locks"; the same sound image will, for a French speaker, evoke a different concept ("qui," which is the equivalent of "who"). Hence, the connection between sound-image and concept is arbitrary. However, within the linguistic system of the English language, the sound-image "key" can only signify a device for opening locks, and the connection between mental concept and sound-image cannot be broken – that is why this connection is considered necessary.

The Meaning of Differences

The next question we will ask, then, must be: in which way do signs produce meaning for the users of a given linguistic system? Saussure's answer to this question is the foundation of one of the most important tenets of structuralism, so we will be very careful when thinking about its implications and consequences. According to Saussure, linguistic systems assign meaning to the single elements in them because of differences, or even: the differences define the single elements and thus create them [315.117–22]. Let us look at an example concerning a single sound: the English words "coal" and "goal" (or, to be more precise, the sound-images "coal" and "goal" within the linguistic system of the English language) denote two different concepts. They differ by just one element: the first sound is either the "hard" velar plosive [k] or the "soft" velar [g]. The difference between these two variants is thus functional in the English language; they can define different signs and constitute what is called "phonemes." However, English does not differentiate between aspirated and non-aspirated plosives: for a speaker of ancient Greek, the words θείνω (*theinō*) and τείνω (*teinō*) were clearly distinct: the first meant "I strike," the second "I stretch." The only difference in their sound is that the first has an aspirated dental plosive (the "t"-sound is followed by audible breath) while the dental is not aspirated in the second. In English, the amount of breath heard after a "t" will depend on the speaker, the dialect or accent, or the emotional state, but it will not produce different concepts.

For Saussure, then, these differences are decisive in constituting the elements of a linguistic system. We can all observe that the human voice produces a continuum of sounds with almost imperceptible transitions: consider the vowel in words such as "hard," "hot," "hat," "hate," "pet," or "pit." There are no clearly distinct, discrete units in this continuum. We can only define what a certain vowel sounds like by contrasting it with related sounds: the vowel in "hat" is *not* like the one in "hard" or in "hate." Hence, every sound can only be defined negatively: it is what all the other elements are *not*. Saussure formulated this quality in the paradoxical sentence that "in language, there are only differences *without positive terms*," "dans la langue il n'y a que des différences sans termes positifs" [315.120]. Or, to put it more technically: linguistic elements have only a relational, not a substantial value.

A similar argument could be made for the concepts we express in language: they can be defined only in contrast to each other. If we want to define a word such as "shout," we can only do so by contrasting it with other words, in a negative manner: "shouting" is definitely louder than "whispering" or "speaking," but not as loud as "hollering." If we had enough time on our hands, we could go on and demonstrate that all elements of a linguistic system define each other in such negative terms.

But we must be aware of the fact that not all differences in a language function like this. If we recorded a number of English speakers of either sex and different ages, coming from different regional and social backgrounds, pronouncing the word "hot," the vowel in this word would, according to scientific criteria (which we could apply by using a spectrograph), cover an extremely wide range. But most of these differences in pitch, stress, and color of the sound are not functional – as long as we can hear that the vowel differs from the vowels in "hard" and "hat." We will see what this means if we take an example outside of language: imagine a number of people observing the stream of cars going along a busy thoroughfare. The environmentalist will classify the cars according to their emission of carbon monoxide; the marketing expert will consider the different marques; the agent from the local city council will view them according to their weight; a child will be interested in how many cars of a certain color will pass by; and for the police officer, only one criterion is of interest: there are cars going faster than the speed limit allows and cars staying within the limit. We can see that these cars are marked by an unlimited number of details. Which of these details is functional and marks an important difference, is defined by the rules of the system that we apply when we observe them. If I look at them without knowing this system, the differences will be so numerous as to make classification impossible.

The example also demonstrates that most differences have a number of categories – we can differentiate between dozens of colors and marques. Structuralists, however, have in general reduced these categories to so-called binary oppositions: either a car is speeding, or it is not. We have already seen a few of these binary oppositions such as synchronic vs. diachronic or signifier vs. signified, and some more will be found on the following pages. It is an open question (even among structuralists) whether favoring such binary oppositions is due to some factor in the nature of the world (whether indeed our world somehow rests on such "on or off" oppositions) or whether this is just a tool to facilitate scientific analysis because it makes complex systems easier to describe. In any case, we should remember that these binary oppositions are an important aspect of structuralist thought.

A language, then, produces meaningful content by combining several signs. Again, structuralism analyzes these combinations in terms of a binary opposition, on a syntagmatic and paradigmatic axis. Although these terms are indeed specialized linguistic vocabulary, we will understand them best if we look at an example outside of language. Every morning, we go to our closet and choose our clothing on such a syntagmatic and paradigmatic axis. We can choose between several shirts, pants, and socks, between black, blue, or brown shoes, etc. Every group just named can be described as a class of paradigmatic elements: I wear only one shirt as a representative of its group; all the other members of the group are absent. All the pieces of clothing I am wearing at any given time can be seen as standing in a syntagmatic relation: their combination follows certain clear rules: I have to wear my socks in my shoes (usually), not the other way round. This example is enough to demonstrate that the opposition "syntagmatic vs. paradigmatic" can be applied to a huge number of fields besides language.

It also has an application in literary criticism which is so fundamental that I will mention it at least briefly: the terms metaphor and metonymy can be explained in a clear manner if we look at this opposition (see the essential article by Jakobson in [197.95–114]). Metaphor can be described as using paradigmatic relations: a word "represents" and replaces another word because both belong to the same paradigmatic group and can be compared to each other (love is like fire). Metonymy, on the other hand, depends on a syntagmatic relation because it brings elements into a combinational contact: a ship has sails; hence, "four sails" can mean "four ships." The notions of metaphor and metonymy can then in turn be applied to other phenomena outside of language: magical actions can be performed either metaphorically or metonymically. In the former case, I will use an object that "stands for" something or someone; e.g., I pierce a puppet representing an opponent. In the latter case, I use something that has a syntagmatic relation; e.g., I burn a piece of clothing that belongs to my opponent.

Structuralism and Subject

Before we continue these reflections on the application of linguistic categories to other fields, we should consider one important aspect that has, more than anything else. made structuralism the *bête noire* of traditional scholars. As we have already seen, structuralism is interested in the linguistic system (*langue*), not in single utterances (*paroles*). Now this system cannot be owned and controlled by any individual speaker. Most people, most of the time, are not conscious of following rules that they are not free to control or change. We are born into a linguistic community, and if we want to be understood, we have to accept and adapt to its laws. Hence, our personal liberty is limited. The structuralists were keenly aware of this fact and have, time and again, emphasized that individual subjects do not possess any godlike power to have an unmediated perception of the outside world and express this perception at their discretion; instead, both perception and expression are governed by our language. This is a manifest blow against René Descartes's (1596–1650) famous sentence "cogito, ergo sum" ("I think, therefore I am") which placed the individual subject at the center of the world and made it the firm basis of all thinking and all knowledge. Instead, for the structuralists, the individual's mind is controlled by rules that she or he cannot change and possibly not even perceive.

This does not mean, as has sometimes been claimed, that structuralism flatly denies the existence of the subject – we are, after all, free to formulate any number of utterances *within* the linguistic system. But the subject does lose its position of supreme power; it is no longer the unquestionable center of all human activities and interest: it is "decentered." This decentering is at first difficult to accept for most of us because it contradicts the way we perceive ourselves and the world, and it raises a number of problems (such as: What, if the subject is no longer in control, becomes of the notion of personal responsibility?). It also assimilates structuralism to other intellectual currents of the twentieth century that were involved in dethroning the free subject, such as Marxism or psychoanalysis. It is thus justified to describe structuralism as anti-humanistic if we give this attribute the right meaning. As Eagleton writes [90.98]: "[this] means not that its devotees rob children of their sweets but that they reject the myth that meaning begins and ends in the individual's 'experience.'" This anti-humanistic tendency may be uncomfortable, but this is not enough to prove that the structuralist decentering of the subject is wrong.

Structural Anthropology

As has already been mentioned, Lévi-Strauss's anthropological studies constitute a second area besides Saussure's linguistics where structuralist methodology has been paramount. In an article first published in 1945 [238.31–55], Lévi-Strauss himself emphasized that his research uses Saussure's work as a model which will help us gain a better understanding of anthropological phenomena. In this contribution, Lévi-Strauss analyzes kinship relationships in different societies, especially with regard to the ways in which a young man's relationship to his father on the one hand and to his (maternal) uncle on the other hand is defined. Lévi-Strauss uses phonological analyses as they had been proposed by structuralist linguists as a model for his own work. He sees a number of fundamental rules in these linguistic studies that can be transferred to other areas of knowledge such as anthropology [238.33–4]: structuralism is not concerned with surface phenomena that are conscious to the agents within a certain system; instead, it is interested in unconscious structures below the surface that produce these phenomena. Structuralism does not consider the terms of such structures as independent items that can and should be studied in their own right, but rather as correlations that are defined by their function within the system governing them. And structuralism's aim is to study the general rules which control such systems.

It is not difficult to see elements in these programmatic statements that we have already observed in Saussure's approach to linguistics. Yet it is important to remember that the way in which Lévi-Strauss generalizes these tendencies is more important than might appear at first sight. By reducing his definition of what structuralism is about to a few core elements, Lévi-Strauss takes a decisive step that allows (or at least facilitates) the application of structuralist methodology to areas which are quite remote from linguistics. At the same time, this layer of generalization and abstraction carries a certain danger: the notion of "structuralism" could be reduced to such vague terms that almost anything might be called "structuralist."

We will not go into the details of Lévi-Strauss's analysis of family relationships; suffice it to say that he sees the relation to uncle and father as elements within a system and that these elements define each other via their function in the system. Accordingly, it would be impossible to study either of those elements without looking at the other. We will have a closer look at another contribution by Lévi-Strauss both because it constitutes one of his most well-known studies and because it will provide an exemplary demonstration of the possibilities and problems which arise when we try to apply structuralist methodologies to other areas such as literary criticism. In this article, which was first published in 1955, Lévi-Strauss undertakes "The Structural Study of Myth" [238.206–31]. Again, he refers to linguistics as an analogy, and he emphasizes that elements of myths cannot be studied in isolation, but must be seen in their relation to each other. Myths are made out of language, yet the elements that are decisive in their system are not single phonemes, words, or even sentences; much rather, they are the the single steps in the story. That is why, according to Lévi-Strauss, myths can be translated from one language into another without any problems: as long as the sequence of actions within the narration remains unchanged, the myth retains its original meaning even in translation. Hence, these steps constitute the smallest signifying units in a myth; in analogy to the phonemes, Lévi-Strauss calls them "mythemes." These mythemes can be represented in the form of simple sentences such as "Orestes kills his mother Clytemnestra."

Before we turn to studying these mythemes and their relation to each other, let us take note that this approach to myth is another important step in structuralist methodology. Typically, we encounter myths in the form of verbal communication, as narratives. In Lévi-Strauss's analysis, they are seen as a linguistic system at a secondary degree. Usually, when we undertake the scientific analysis of a language, the complete sentence is the most complex unit we analyze. A sentence produces meaning by arranging its linguistic signs in a certain order. In Lévi-Strauss's model, sentences are the smallest elements; sense is being produced by arranging sentences in a certain order. We could say, then, that on this level, the linguistic sign, consisting of signifier and signified, serves as a signifier in its turn. This is a model of analyzing semiotic systems which we will find again later in this book.

A scholar, when confronted with a myth, has to recognize the mythemes, the decisive actions, in it, and has to reduce the myth to these core elements by stripping it of all secondary material such as poetic or rhetorical ornamentation and concentrating on these significant aspects. Lévi-Strauss uses the myth of Oedipus as an example for his methodology. As you can see in table 1, Lévi-Strauss arranges its significant elements into four columns [238.214].

An ordinary narration of this myth would read this "score" like any text, starting at the top left corner and then proceeding line by line. Lévi-Strauss, on the other hand, arranges the mythemes by columns: the elements of each column are united by a correspondence which must be analyzed. As a working hypothesis, he suggests titling the correspondences in the columns of this table like this: 1. overrating of blood relations; 2. underrating of blood relations; 3. monsters being slain; 4. difficulties in walking straight and standing upright. He then

Cadmos seeks his sister Europa, ravished by Zeus.			
		Cadmos kills the dragon.	
	The Spartoi kill one another.		
			Labdacos (Laios' father) = *lame (?)*
	Oedipus kills his father, Laios.		Laios (Oedipus' father) = *left-sided (?)*
		Oedipus kills the Sphinx.	
	Oedipus kills his father, Laios.		Oedipus = *swollen-foot (?)*
Oedipus marries his mother, Jocasta.			
	Eteocles kills his brother, Polynices.		
Antigone buries her brother, Polynices, despite prohibition.			

Table 1 Lévi-Strauss's analysis of the Oedipus myth

goes on to explain that in myths, autochthonous creatures (creatures that are directly born from the earth) are often characterized by their difficulties with walking straight. Hence, the monsters in column 3 represent the chthonian element of the world. Columns 3 and 4, then, can be understood as being defined by an overrating or underrating of the chthonian nature of humanity, i. e., the belief that humans originated from the earth. The relation between columns 3 and 4 is analogous to the relation between columns 1 and 2: Lévi-Strauss claims that the myth is an expression of doubts that must arise in a human society which, on the one hand, is convinced that mankind has a chthonian origin, yet on the other hand is aware that every human being is born from the sexual union between a woman and a man. Hence, the narration offers a mytho-logical answer to the question "Is man born from one or born from two?"

Lévi-Strauss ends his article with a look at future developments of the study of myth. He thinks it will be necessary to arrange the single elements of myths into various rows and columns and experiment with such arrangements; in order to do so, he continues, we will need a complex apparatus of "vertical boards about six feet long and four and a half feet high" [238.229] and pigeonholes (this detail makes it abundantly clear to the modern reader that the article was written long before the advent of the computer). The aim of such research will be to discover in which ways "mythical thought" perceives the world. It may very well be, as Lévi-Strauss writes (and the general tone of his writing suggests that he thinks this is highy probable), that we will thus find out that the human mind in general can only perform a limited number of mental operations and that "mythical" and "scientific" thought are less unlike each other than we all tend to assume.

Lévi-Strauss's methodology has often, and rightly, been criticized by later scholars. The results of his interpretation of the Oedipus myth do not hold water. I have nevertheless presented his approach here because it is exemplary in demonstrating the strengths and weaknesses of structuralist methodology. First and foremost, Lévi-Strauss leaves himself open to the censure that on the one hand, he seems to be claiming a high degree of scientific precision for the analysis of myths (this becomes particularly clear at the end of his article); on the other hand, his own analysis does not take scientific criteria very seriously. His narration of the Oedipus myth is highly selective. While he emphasizes that there is no single authentic version of a myth, but that a myth must be considered to be the sum of all its different versions, he selects just a few elements from the various transmitted versions of the Oedipus myth without bothering to tell us by which criteria he chose what to include and what to neglect. His own answer to this challenge might be that he has chosen the significant elements, but how could a scholar decide which elements are significant and which ones aren't *before* she has analyzed the myth? Think of the example we have mentioned above, p. 31: if I look at a stream of cars running by on a busy street, I will be unable to recognize any pattern or structure because of the sheer number of possible criteria (color, marque, speed) – unless I know beforehand which qualities are significant in the system of my observation. It is hardly possible to construct the system from the observed facts themselves (from the automobiles, in our case). At least it would be the most important task of the structuralists to tell us how this can be achieved. However, this has never been explained in a satisfactory manner.

Similar problems occur when we look at the way in which the elements that Lévi-Strauss "found" are arranged into columns. When Lévi-Strauss writes "that we thus find ourselves confronted with four vertical columns, each of which includes several relations belonging to the same bundle" [238.214], and that the elements of each column bear similarities that the scholar has to elucidate, this is indeed just the clever trick of a prestidigitator: he himself had arranged these columns beforehand; again, knowledge of the system must precede analysis of the myth. If myths occurred naturally in tabular form, this approach might prove fruitful; as it is, we have to wonder why these elements have been arranged in exactly this set of columns and not any other order. And this is the fundamental difference between the semiotic system "language" and the system "myth": for a linguistic utterance, we can indeed explain why elements are arranged and analyzed according to certain criteria for we all know what a well-formed sentence in our native language signifies. It is this exterior, previous knowledge that enables structuralist linguistics to isolate and analyze the significant elements of words and sentences, to arrange them along axes of syntactic and paradigmatic value. Do we have a comparably certain knowledge of what a myth "means"? In Lévi-Strauss's structural analysis, we have to infer both the meaning of the myth and the way in which this meaning is produced from the raw material, the narration of events. This seems an impossible task, and that explains the difficulties of the structural analysis of myths.

Is Structuralist Interpretation Possible?

The problems we have found in the structuralist analysis of myths are of a general nature; we will encounter similar issues when we now turn to those branches of literary criticism that were influenced by structuralism. As we have seen, structuralist scholars do not deal with single utterances or facts (these would be on the level of *parole* and hence outside of the field of enquiry); instead, they try to analyze the functioning of entire systems of signs. Structuralist analyses, then, tend to be most successful when they do not ask *what* this or that means but *how* it can work as a sign within a certain system and how it produces meaning. These fundamental tenets help explain why structuralism has difficulties interpreting single texts. Surmounting these problems would be possible if we could regard the single text as a system in itself, a system that produces meaning by the nature of its structure and the differing elements it contains.

There is indeed a well-known effort to proceed this way. In 1962, Jakobson and Lévi-Strauss published a collaborative interpretation of a poem by Charles Baudelaire (1821–67) entitled "Les Chats" "The Cats" ([198], English translation in [197.180–97]). The Franco-American critic Michael Riffaterre (1924–2006) wrote a famous reply to this essay [306] in which he proposed a fundamental critique of their methodology and offered an interpretation of his own.

In his essay, Riffaterre emphasizes that there are two main problems with the interpretation published by Jakobson and Lévi-Strauss:

- In Jakobson's and Lévi-Strauss's article, an accurate description of the linguistic material of the poem abruptly turns into a highly speculative, philosophical interpretation. What the critics overlook, however, is that this transfer necessitates leaving the closed system of the text. They confuse, for instance, the grammatical gender "feminine" and the technical use of the term "feminine rhyme" (within the poem's linguistic system) with an idea of actual "femininity" (outside of the system). "No grammatical analysis of a poem can give us more than the grammar of the poem," as Riffaterre writes [306.201].

- The authors had given an admirably precise analysis of the syntactic structures, sound effects, and rhythmical patterns of the poem. But Riffaterre rightly points out that most of these details are imperceptible to the reader and that some of them do not contribute to the text's poetical effect. Again, we remember the distinction between functional and non-functional differences: in order to understand single utterances, I have to grasp the way in which the system works, I have to know which differences are functional. This, however, is a piece of information that cannot be found in a single poem, but has to be extracted from the entirety of the system – maybe from poetry as a whole.

This attempt to provide a structuralist interpretation, then, reveals the same problems that we have already observed in Lévi-Strauss's structuralist analysis of myth. If we want to sum up our appraisal of this use of structuralist methodology, we have to be quite critical: structuralist analyses can help us understand the ways in which texts are organized and convey their meaning, but they are incapable of actually interpreting a text for us. Or, to quote Eagleton's sarcastic words [90.95]: "Having characterized the underlying rule-systems of a literary text, all the structuralists could do was sit back and wonder what to do next."

Structuralist Definitions of Literary Genres

A somewhat different approach to the use of structuralism in literary criticism seems more promising. This method does not regard the single literary work a system and object of investigation, but sees single works as instances of *parole* and applies the methodology of structuralism to the higher level of *langue*. Narratology, to be discussed in the next chapter, is the field where this approach has probably been most productive. Here, I want to present another area where structuralist approaches have been very succesful, the analysis of literary genres.

Attempts to categorize literary texts into specific classes are as old as scholarly interest in literature; they start in antiquity with Plato (especially in the *Republic*) and Aristole (especially the *Poetics*). Structuralist attempts at the definition of genres represent but a small portion of this field. We will now give a very brief overview of structuralist analyses of genre and pay special attention to genres in classical literature. An important representative of this approach is the Bulgarian critic Tzvetan Todorov (b. 1939). In a book first published in 1970 [354], he tried to define fantastic literature as a genre in its own right. Todorov first discusses the system of genres developed by the American scholar Northrop Frye (1912–91). Frye tried to provide a psychological and anthropological basis for a theory of genres (see below, p. 200). Todorov uses a structuralist methodology: for him, the fantastic is defined by its difference to the "uncanny" on the one hand and to the "marvelous" on the other. The term "fantastic" thus has a relational value and is defined by the other elements of the same system.

The most systematic attempt to use structuralist analyses of literary genres for classical antiquity can be found in the work of the Italian Latinist Gian Biagio Conte (b. 1941; a convenient collection of English translations can be found in [59] and [61]). Here, we will take as our point of departure his brief and fundamental discussion of literary genres in an article published in 1992 [60]. Conte makes the convincing argument that genres can neither be defined along purely formal criteria (e.g., texts written in hexameters) nor with regard to their subject matter (the theme "love" can be the subject of quite different texts, such as Terence's comedies, Catullus's poems, Tibullus's elegies, or even the fourth book of Virgil's *Aeneid*). For Conte, in a reasoning that is typical of a structuralist approach, literary genres in Roman literature form a system whose elements define and elucidate each other [60.107]: "A genre is not made up by 'stuffing' it with isolated fragments of content, but by a total system of reciprocal, structured relations: the single element must enter into a constellation with others if it is to be transvalued and redefined until it too is able to connote, by itself, the presence of a whole genre." Conte argues that poets and readers in Augustan Rome already held this view of genre because Latin writers were aware of the fact that this system offered certain positions and had "gaps" that could be filled [60.113]: "The very awareness of these lacunas indirectly confirms that by this time the system of genres has become a fully constituted reality which contemporaries have begun to realize."

This attitude toward literary genres becomes most obvious when texts play with different genres or bring them into contact with each other. This is the case, e.g., in Virgil's tenth *Eclogue* where love elegy and bucolic poetry meet (on this poem, see Conte [59.100–29]), but above all in Ovid's poetry where such playful juxtapositions are common: in the first book of the *Metamorphoses*, Mercurius is told to kill Argus, a monster with a hundred eyes. Argus is the guardian of Io, who has been transformed into a cow, so he plays the role of a cattleman. This brings a different genre into play: "At once the scene is transformed from epic to bucolic, and Mercury starts to speak in a bucolic style" [60.107]. This "relational" (above, p. 31) nature of literary genres becomes understandable when we take into account structuralist positions about the relational value of elements in a system. Another structuralist aspect of Conte's work is his emphasis that genres have a real, factual existence in literary texts [60.122]: "nothing would be more useless than to conceive of genres as simple immobile abstractions, or as lifeless specimens to be collected in sterile bell jars: genre lives only in individual works."

As is clear from these remarks, Conte and other structuralist analyses look for the systematic aspect (which is necessary for every structuralist approach to work) not in single literary texts, but in the interplay between several genres and styles. Finally, I can only hint at Conte's view that genres bear concrete meanings: they are not merely artificial games played by learned poets; instead, they signify certain attitudes to reality and the world [60.120]: "Genre functions as a mediator, permitting certain models of reality to be selected and to enter into

the language of literature; it gives them the possibility of being 'represented.' "
This means that genres have certain characteristics of a language.

However, this would seem to take us to the borders of what is possible within a structuralist approach. As was the case in Jakobson's and Lévi-Strauss's structuralist interpretation (above, p. 39), the connection between the linguistic/literary system and outside reality remains somewhat vague in Conte's work. Nonetheless, his contributions are among the most thought-provoking and fascinating in contemporary Latin studies.

Further Reading

Derek Attridge's article, published in 1995 [11], is an excellent introduction to structuralist linguistics. Robert Scholes's book [321] is a brief and helpful account, as is Jonathan Culler's more thorough, yet clear and understandable treatment [67]. Culler's book has become a classic in its own right; it is widely read, especially in the USA, and has contributed to the importance of literary theory in American universities. However, some colleagues (such as Frank Lentricchia [235.103–12]) have criticized Culler and claimed that the clarity of his account has been achieved at the expense of making structuralist thought appear banal and harmless. François Dosse [86] provides a lively and highly entertaining history of the French protagonists of structuralism.

Chapter 3
Narratology

In the previous chapter, our account of the positive contribution of structuralism to literary criticism had to be somewhat vague. Structuralist theories about the definitions of literary genres are certainly impressive, yet they offer only limited help in understanding individual texts. When we now start looking at narratology, we are entering an area where structuralist methodologies have been most valuable and where structuralism has begun to provide a framework that allows the proper analysis of (narrative) texts. It is hardly an exaggeration when Robert Scholes, in his book *Structuralism in Literature* (1974), writes [321.60]: "Structuralism and formalism have given us virtually all the poetics of fiction that we have." Narratology is not a position of literary theory properly speaking, but given the importance of analyzing narrative texts in literary studies, it will nonetheless have its own chapter in this book.

The following pages will concentrate on structuralist contributions to narratology (as we have just seen, they constitute the majority of all narratological studies); this chapter can thus be read as a supplement to chapter 2. I will not present narratological approaches coming from different angles in detail; however, at the end of the chapter (p. 62), I will list some of the most important ones.

It will be easier for us to gain an understanding of the vast area of narratology if we take into account a distinction which the Russian Formalists first introduced into literary criticism. If we look at narrative texts, we distinguish between the "plot" on the one hand and the "story" on the other (these terms are the equivalents of the original Russian terms *fabula* and *sjužet*). Roughly speaking, the story is the sequence of events narrated as if they had really taken place; the plot is the form in which a given concrete narrative presents ("emplots") these events. Let us look at an example: the story of the *Aeneid* begins with the earliest of the depicted events, the destruction of Troy, and it reaches, in an uninterrupted chain, down to the latest events, the death of Turnus. The plot as presented in Virgil's text, on the other hand, starts at a later point in time: in the first book, Aeneas and his Trojans are sailing on the open sea when they are surprised by a storm; earlier events are narrated in flashbacks and speeches by the characters. We should keep in mind that the distinction between both levels is not without problems: when we are talking about a historiographical text, we can indeed say that there exists a line of events (such as the Peloponnesian War), a story that precedes its "emplotment" and is then narrated by the historian in a certain manner. The case is different for a fictional text: what we have before us is just the text itself, i. e., the plot, the story has to be constructed (by the audience) from this text. Thus, the distinction, which suggests a temporal and logical priority of the story over the plot, is somewhat misleading. Nevertheless, it is still useful even in the case of fictional texts: reading the narrative makes us (re-)construct the story – when we look at the *Aeneid*, we have a mental image (albeit a somewhat vague and hazy one) of the temporal sequence of events; we calculate (at least roughly) the time it takes Aeneas to finish the different portions of his long journey.

When we keep this distinction in mind, we will easily see that there are two main strands of narratology: one is primarily interested in the logic that connects and hierarchizes the events on the level of the story; the other looks at their representation on the level of the plot. We will now look at the ways in which this schematic distinction can help us understand narratology.

Vladimir Propp's Analysis of the Folk Tale

The Russian scholar Vladimir Propp (1895–1970) can be called the founding father of Formalist narratology. He was one of the members of the Formalist "school," yet he was able to continue his research after the end of the movement. His study of a well-defined corpus of folktales, the so-called Russian folkloric fairy tale, suggested to him that all these narratives, despite being different in their details, bear a striking resemblance on the functional level [296.23]: "All fairy tales are of one type in regard to their structure." His analysis pierces through the surface level of these texts and explores their deeper structure. Propp identifies a number of "functions," stereotypical elements of the action that occur in all tales, in an unchanging order. He distinguishes 31 such functions; as an example, here are numbers 23 through 27:

23 The hero, unrecognized, arrives home or in another country.

24 A false hero presents unfounded claims.

25 A difficult task is proposed to the hero.

26 The task is resolved.

27 The hero is recognized.

We must remember that these functions are meant to represent the deep structure of the narrative, not the concrete steps which the action involves. Every single tale will provide an individual version of how these functions are realized. Nevertheless, on the level of structural analysis, we can speak of identical elements. Not every element will occur in every folk tale, but the folk tales never change the fixed order in which these actions take place. This unchanging order explains why Propp's method of analysis can be called structuralist: the single elements define each other by virtue of their position in this order; they provide relations and correspondences with each other.

The actions of these functions are performed by various characters. Propp claims that there is a relatively limited number of actors such as the hero, the villain, the helper, the donor, and others. Again, we must be careful not to confuse these categories (which belong to the deep structure of the narrative) with the actual characters on the surface of the text: one character can, in the course of the folk tale, fulfill several roles (such as being, at the same time, donor and helper), or one such role can in turn be acted out by several characters.

It should be evident why we can say that Propp's structural analysis treats the level of the story: Propp abstracts completely from the linguistic form in which these folktales are narrated; his analyses would be as valid and possible if we translated the tales into a foreign language or turned them into a movie. This allows a clear vision of the possibilities and limitations of structural narratology:

- As we saw in the previous chapter, structuralism has its strength not on the level of single concrete texts, but rather in entire classes or series of texts. Propp's analysis, however, demonstrates that it is capable of providing a toolbox that will facilitate the interpretation of concrete narratives.

- We may still legitimately wonder what criteria Propp employed to isolate his functions: how did he decide which actions should be awarded the status of a function and which ones are mere ornaments? Again, as in the case of Lévi-Strauss's analysis of myths (above, pp. 35–38), we receive no satisfactory answer: apparently, readers of and listeners to folk tales have an intuitive knowledge of what these narratives "mean," and hence, they can name the elements that contribute to this meaning. It would be a great advance in methodology, however, if this intuitive knowledge could be made conscious and verifiable.

- Propp's analyses are only made possible by the fact that he reduces the colorful variety of the text surface to a naked outline of abstract functions. He himself is clear in stating this [296.113]: "From the point of view of composition, it does not matter whether a dragon kidnaps a princess or whether a devil makes off with either a priest's or a peasant's daughter." This is hard to swallow, especially for all those who love literature: a table listing functions and actors is not as fascinating to read as the folk tale itself because it eliminates precisely those elements that make a text aesthetically pleasing. On the other hand, we must avoid asking a methodology to provide what it cannot provide, and we should not eschew what it *can* provide. A structural analysis is meant as a tool that will help us understand the way in which such texts work; it is neither a substitute for the text nor an interpretation of it.

While these critical remarks are entirely justified, we should also take into account that Propp was careful to counter the dangers of being too abstract and theoretical by the object and the methodology of his investigations: on the one hand, he restricted his studies to a relatively small and homogeneous corpus of short and rather simple texts. Even readers who do not have Propp's structuralist toolbox at their disposal will have an intuitive understanding that a fairly uniform structure is hidden beneath the surface of these tales, so they may be prepared to accept the abstractions of his analyses. Furthermore, Propp's "functions" are immediately recognizable as elements of the narratives themselves. But narratologists after Propp did not fail to apply his methodology to greater corpora of more complex texts, and hence saw themselves obliged to replace his quite straightforward functions with more abstract elements. It is therefore permitted to raise the question of whether such abstract analyses are useful. Many readers will find it interesting to see that a number of fairy tales can be reduced to a common model of functions. But does it make sense to say, e.g., that narratives such as the *Odyssey*, the *Divine Comedy*, and *War and Peace* "really are" variations on an identical deep structure?

Structuralist narratology has given two replies to this question. The first one is pragmatic: if we want to recognize what is unique in a narrative, it is useful or even necessary to see in which respects it resembles other tales. Even literary critics who are not close to structuralism will be willing to accept this argument, but they may object that too abstract notions may not be of great help in this task. The second answer reveals larger ambitions: narratives are one of the most important means by which human beings make sense of the world that surrounds them and construct a meaningful history out of their past experiences. If it could be shown that, in the end, all narratives conform to a relatively small number of types and models, this would be a clear argument for the view that the human mind has only a limited number of mental operations at its disposal. This goal, to explore the basic principles of the functioning of the human mind, had been formulated by Lévi-Strauss in his structural analysis of myth (above, p. 37). Scholarship is certainly not even close to reaching this goal, but it would be a mistake to claim that it must be foolish to pursue this aim.

Greimas's Actantial Theory of Narrative

The Franco-Lithuanian scholar Algirdas Julien Greimas (1917–92) was one literary critic who adopted Propp's methodology most vigorously, but detractors may object that he also took its tendency to abstraction too far. His contribution to narratology is part of a bigger project of which his 1966 book *Structural Semantics* [152] gave a first outline. Before we can actually turn to his ideas about narratology, we must at least get a superficial view of this project. As we saw earlier, (above, p. 30), structuralism has a tendency to neglect the content of linguistic utterances in its inquiries. Greimas attempts the impossible: to make a structuralist analysis of linguistic meaning. First, he examines the oppositions that, according to Saussure, produce significance in language. If we restrict ourselves to structuralist linguistics, we can discover such an opposition between, say, "pack" and "back" (voiceless vs. voiced). The difference between "light" and "dark," on the other hand, is outside of language and hence outside of the scope of structuralist linguistics. If we think we see a binary opposition here, we must be aware that it cannot be analyzed with the same degree of scientific and linguistic precision; here, we have to rely on our human experience and on common sense. Greimas here focuses on a problem that we have already encountered in Propp's analyses: every narratological approach that deals with the level of the story has to make a number of presuppositions that it cannot deduct within the boundaries of its own discipline. This becomes clear when Greimas analyzes the different ways in which the French word "tête" ("head") can be used [152.46–55]: he has to rely on common sense and use rhetorical formulas such as "one glance is enough" or "without any doubt" that just disguise the fact that these assumptions cannot be proven. This is the source of an unsolvable dilemma which we have to recognize if we want to understand why some problems and difficulties in interpretation will never be solved in a manner satisfactory to all: interpretation necessitates applying knowledge that cannot be extracted, falsified, or verified from the text itself.

Yet Greimas is not content with this purely negative result. He asks what makes texts comprehensible and coherent, and he emphasizes the importance of isotopy [152.78–81]. In linguistics, this term refers to the fact that in texts, certain semantic elements are repeated in different variants; hence, texts have a certain degree of redundancy. If we take the English sentences (1) "the dog barked at me" and (2) "my boss barked at me," we will try to make sense of them by looking for such repetitions, for isotopy. The verb "bark" means (among other things) "the sound certain animals such as dogs emit." The element "dog" had already been present in the subject of the sentence "the dog," so we conclude that in sentence (1), bark has the meaning we just quoted. But "bark" can also mean "to speak aggressively, especially to utter commands in an unpleasant manner." In this case, "command" will evoke the isotopy "hierarchically superior" which had already been present in the word "my boss," so for sentence (2), isotopy will lead us to the conclusion that this second meaning of "bark" is implied. This concept of isotopy is probably not quite sufficient to explain the ways in which we make sense of texts, but it could provide a means to make, for example, investigations such as Lévi-Strauss's analysis of the Oedipus myth (above, p. 35–38) more convincing.

I hope that these preliminary remarks will help us get a better understanding of the narratological categories developed by Greimas. According to him, every sentence can be compared to a drama. The roles in this imaginary play are always the same: a subject acts upon an object. These roles are acted by different actors, but the program of this grammatical theater never really changes, regardless of whether Aeneas kills Turnus or Apollon pursues Daphne. Greimas then goes on to transfer this picture from the level of the grammatical structure of the sentence (intra-linguistic) to the level of the events that are expressed in the sentence (extra-linguistic). The "roles" in the imaginary drama are now acted by so-called "actants." These are fundamental, abstract functions of which Greimas believed there were six; two of them are always in opposition to each other:

- subject   –   object
- sender   –   receiver
- helper   –   opponent

It should be obvious that we are here dealing with events on the level of the events; the story, not the textual level of the plot. This becomes clear when Greimas emphasizes [152.148] that sentences such as "Eve gives Adam an apple" and "Adam receives an apple from Eve" are identical from the point of view of actantial analysis. If we apply the categories of grammar, we have completely different functions here (in the first sentence, Adam is the subject; in the second, he is an indirect object). From the perspective of the story, however, Eve is the subject and the sender in both sentences, the apple is always the object, and Adam is the receiver, irrespective of the syntactical functions they fulfill.

Using these six actants, Greimas arrives at the model of mythical narratives [152.207] shown in figure 1.

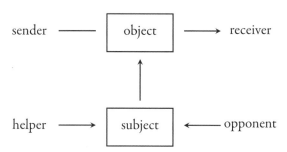

Figure 1   Greimas's definition of actants

Greimas repeatedly stresses the importance of Propp's work for his own model. Yet there is a momentous difference between both scholars: Propp arrives at his suggestion by inductive reasoning; he tries to form general rules by extrapolating from a limited number of actual narratives. Greimas, on the other hand, attempts to extract general laws of narrative from the structure of single sentences by starting from observations on the fundamental principles of language. He then goes on to test the validity of these general laws by looking at actual narratives (this procedure, which infers particular instances from general rules, is called deductive). Hence, his model has a wider range of applicability than Propp's analyses. Greimas suggests, for example, to analyze Marxist ideology along these lines (subject: man; object: classless society; sender: history; receiver: mankind; opponent: bourgeois class; helper: working class), or the investment of capitalists. It is clear that the actantial model can be used to analyze narrative texts; this is Greimas's point of departure, and in an article published a few years after his book [153.249–70], he used it to analyze the fairy tale "The Story of a Boy Who Went Forth to Learn Fear" ("Von einem, der auszog, das Fürchten zu lernen"), claiming that he had improved upon Propp's method of analyzing fairy tales and that novel results could be obtained with his new methodology.

Scholars in literary criticism soon pointed out that Greimas's model had a number of weaknesses that make it difficult to accept in its totality. However,

I have chosen to present it here because Greimas's methodology is representative of structuralist narratology in general. It sharply raises a question (again) that we have already asked (above, p. 46): Is it legitimate to reduce narratives to some bare structural formula? In Greimas's case, critics can also point out that his analyses (like those of Lévi-Strauss) disregard one element of narrative which undoubtedly is paramount: Greimas neglects the temporal dimension of narrative texts; his structural formulae do not express that narratives develop in time because they transform them into static constellations of actants. When we think about this problem, we will see that this critique is sound – in part. When we listen to a narrative, we intuitively tend to rearrange the temporal sequence of its events into non-temporal structures; one could even say that narratives themselves often do so. When the narrator in Virgil's *Aeneid* tells us, in the epic's proem, about Aeneas ("Long labors, both by sea and land, he bore, and in the doubtful war"), he is indeed summarizing long sequences of events into logical categories that neglect temporal serialization. In my opinion, there can be no doubt that such reductions are legitimate and necessary – if we want to avoid them completely, the interpretation of a narrative would necessarily be nothing more than a plot summary. The decisive question is which degree of reduction we are prepared to accept, and answering this question will always be left to the taste of every single literary critic and every single reader. Greimas's idea that it might be possible to discover some sort of "theory of everything" to which every narrative can be reduced, however, will probably be unacceptable to a majority of scholars. Nonetheless, I think that further research along the lines suggested by Greimas is legitimate and fascinating, even if we are still far from discovering such a theory. But the more we know about the common deep structure of narratives, the more we will be able to appreciate their individual differences; hence, every attempt at generalization will also teach us something about individual narratives.

Roland Barthes and the Study of Narrative Texts

In Propp's and Greimas's contributions, we have seen two narratological approaches that work on the level of the story. We will now turn to two French scholars whose work analyzes the level of the plot of narrative; hence, we will be looking at more "literary" and less abstract positions than before. First, I want to present two narratological contributions by Roland Barthes (1915–80). The first, with the programmatic title "Introduction to the Structural Analysis of Narratives," was first published in 1966, opening a special issue of the journal

Communications (English translation in [25.79–124] and in [27.95–135]). In a manner characteristic of structuralism, it attempts to provide a "grammar" of narrative. Barthes distinguishes between a syntagmatic/metonymic and a paradigmatic/metaphorical (see above, p. 32) level of narratives. As we have seen, this means that elements on the syntagmatic level (which Barthes calls "function," like Propp) connect to other, equivalent elements on the same level, while paradigmatic elements (or "indices") connect with elements on a different level.

ə➤ Functions are the single events of the action whose sequence produces the outline of the story. Barthes distinguishes between, on the one hand, core functions whose omission would change the story significantly: in the sequence "Aeneas leaves Troy, sails the seas, reaches Italy, and has to fight there," every element is necessary. Yet in the narrative itself, these core functions are usually dissolved into a series of smaller elements (such as the various parts of Aeneas's wanderings) that merely modify the progress of the action without having a decisive influence on its outcome; Barthes calls these minor elements "catalysts." Both core functions and catalysts are connected in a temporal and causal manner; hence, they are syntagmatic: if someone leaves, she will at some time arrive somewhere; if someone makes enemies, he will have to be reconciled with them or fight them.

ə➤ On the paradigmatic level, Barthes distinguishes between "informants" and "indices." Informants provide the necessary factual information knowledge of which is essential for understanding the narrative, such as the fact that Anchises is Aeneas's father and Ascanius his son. Indices, on the other hand, depict the atmosphere where the action takes place, describe the characters, and help us judge the narrative: at the beginning of the *Aeneid*, we hear that Juno is hostile to Aeneas, and this will remain a constant fact throughout the narrative.

Of course, these categories are merely tools of analysis; in reality, most elements of a narrative usually fulfill more than one function. When we read, for instance, that Aeneas carries his father Anchises on his back out of the burning battlefield of Troy, this works, on the one hand, on the syntagmatic level, as a catalyst (it is a sub-element of the core function "Aeneas leaves Troy"). On the other hand, it is also functional on the paradigmatic level because it is an index of his *pietas*, his filial devotion, that is a constant element of characterization throughout the entire narrative.

Overall, Barthes's essay is marked by an enthusiastic optimism that categories such as these will shortly provide a general system applicable to the analysis of all narrative texts, which will allow us to describe all narratives in a scientifically accurate manner and to better understand them. This optimism has not been fulfilled, and Barthes himself was to give up on it a few years later – or rather, he no longer believed that such a general system was desirable. The fundamental change in his approach can be seen best when we now turn to the second contribution to narratology that we will present here. In 1970, Barthes published a short book under the somewhat mysterious title *S/Z* [23]. It analyzed the novella "Sarrasine" by the French writer Honoré de Balzac (1799–1850). But before we turn to Barthes's contribution itself, it is worthwhile to dwell a little on the change in his methodology, for two reasons: on the one hand, as we will see later, this change is symptomatic of a general development in literary criticism; on the other, Barthes is undoubtedly one of the most important and most quoted critics of the twentieth century. A minimal knowledge of his career and development can help us understand in what sense later critics made use of his work.

It could be argued that Barthes was not so much important because his writings were so groundbreaking and masterly but because those who opposed the developing new methodologies took him as the target of their attacks – and some of those attacks were quite heavy-handed and unfair. Barthes himself was always reluctant to accept tendencies which claimed he was a pioneer or even some sort of guru of these new developments, and especially during his later years, he became increasingly skeptical about all forms of intellectual authority. This skepticism is reflected in his later work: Barthes consciously dispenses with big coherent theories, and renounces forms that have historically been signposts of scholarly authority such as the big book or the lengthy article; instead, he prefers short aphorisms or a style that eschews the marks of scholarly discourse (such as footnotes or painstaking argumentation against opponents), highlighting a more literary, "dilettantish" mode of writing. However, such an attitude is prone to misunderstanding: dispensing with scholarly evidence can mean that I am not claiming any authority for my words – or it can mean that I deem my own personal authority so commanding that I do not need these petty paraphernalia. And Barthes was masterful at letting this superficial dilettantism subtly hint at an elitist arrogance. Nor could he prevent his students (or those who claimed to be his students) from taking his style as a model and imitating this attitude, and this was certainly not to the advantage of literary criticism and an everlasting irritation to all those who had been used to the conventional modes of scholarly debate. This explains why, in the writings of some postmodern critics, Barthes could paradoxically be transformed into an indisputable author-ity and why quoting him could be seen as an argument that would supersede all rational discussion.

Moreover, what is typical of Barthes's way of working is a constant hesita-tion, an emphasis that all his results are just provisional, and a willingness to utilize new methods. Some scholars have seen this as a deplorable unsteadi-ness. Barthes himself described the development of his outlook in the short es-say "The Semiological Adventure," published in 1974 [27.3–8], and he described several stages: after an initial enthusiasm for Saussure's structuralism, in the late 1960s, Barthes lost his confidence in the exaggerated claims of scientific preci-sion expressed by structuralism. He described this change as a transition from a methodology that was inspired by systematic structuralist linguistics back to the sheer variety of the text. In this repudiation of his own earlier positions, Barthes was heavily influenced by a number of younger scholars, especially Julia Kristeva, who was then a student in his seminar and who was developing, in the late 1960s, the concept of intertextuality (see chapter 5).

S/Z [23] is a work that can in many respects be said to be on the border be-tween two periods of Barthes's development. In it, Barthes explicitly states that he is turning away from an ideal of scientific rigor characteristic of structural-ism [23.3–4]. He subdivides Balzac's novella into 561 rather arbitrary sections (which he calls "lexies") that he then analyzes. Again in a rather arbitrary man-ner, he intersperses these commentaries with 93 chapters that treat problems of methodology or fundamental concepts of literary theory – or just consti-tute interesting digressions. Chapter XLI is about "the proper name"; chapter LXVII is entitled "How an Orgy Is Created." On the other hand, it is possible to transform these fragments into a relatively coherent theory, and scholars writ-ing about Barthes have seldom resisted the temptation to force his imaginative disorder into an imaginary system. At the beginning of the book, Barthes places his thoughts about the difference between "writerly" (*scriptibles*) and "readerly" (*lisibles*) texts. Writerly texts, we are told, are not mere commodities ready for consumption by passive readers; they require the readers' collaboration. Their sense can never be fixed definitively; they always remain open to further writ-ing. The entire classical literature, on the other hand, consists of readerly texts. While they cannot be confined to one single meaning, they restrict the plural-ity of possibilities. Barthes's distinction between these categories remains vague. He never says clearly whether writerly texts already exist, whether they can ex-ist at all, or whether this quality merely represents an ideal that can never be reached. And Barthes never asks, in spite of all his declarations of openness and collaboration, whether we as readers agree with his judgments – in this respect, his own text is merely readerly, as Detering [83.878] has rightly emphasized.

S/Z is an analysis of a classical, readerly text. Barthes proposes to use five different "codes" to analyze this novella; they are meant to help analyze the single voices of a polyphonous text:

- ❧ The hermeneutic code ("the voice of truth") raises questions that will be answered in the course of the narrative. In the *Aeneid*, one such general question could be "Will Aeneas reach Italy and be able to found a city?" In the narrative, we could look for elements that refer to this question: postpone the answer, seemingly negate it, and finally deliver the "right" answer. In detective novels, this voice usually is dominant: we keep reading because we want to know "whodunit."
- ❧ We can think of the "semes" (or "connotative signifieds") as adjectives that qualify places, objects, and especially characters. By gathering information about the characters in the text throughout our reading experience, we transform them into "personalities" with certain character traits: the "piety" of *pius Aeneas* is qualified by all actions that demonstrate this feature, such as rescuing his father from the burning city of Troy.
- ❧ The "symbolic field" provides a grid of themes and oppositions that extend through the entire narrative, such as "male vs. female," "death vs. life," or "nature vs. civilization." This category remains the vaguest of all, and one may legitimately wonder whether Barthes is here utilizing a too subjective and impressionistic manner.
- ❧ The "code of actions" refers to the actions depicted in the narrative (this can be compared to the "functions" and "catalysts" in Barthes's earlier article). All these actions have a beginning and an ending, they are somehow connected to each other, and at the end of a classical text, all actions are concluded.
- ❧ The cultural code ("voice of science") brings the text into contact with a thesaurus of knowledge, proverbs, experiences, prejudices, etc. This code can be compared to a gigantic encyclopedia in which all these elements have been fixed; the narrative text contains, as it were, quotations from this encyclopedia that the reader is supposed to recognize and accept as correct, as "common knowledge."

In establishing these codes, Barthes makes no claim at comprehensiveness because he does not believe (anymore) in a toolbox that will do justice to each and every narrative (hence, we would have to ask which new codes we need to establish every time we analyze a text). This is another example of Barthes's skepticism about the totalizing claims of structuralist "science" and a sign of his respect for the sheer diversity of individual texts. However, it should be obvious that these insights and his codes are immensely useful for analyzing narratives and can be transferred to other texts without difficulty.

I have described the structure and methodology of *S/Z* in great detail in order to help you understand why different readers have seen different things in this book. Literary critics who are interested in having a toolbox for analyzing narrative texts have especially employed Barthes's five codes. Others find his distinction of readerly and writerly texts particularly inspiring. The subdivision of the book into numerous small units and the conscious lack of a visible order also have provoked different reactions: for some readers, this was a more than welcome breaking away from worn-out paths; others saw it as an annoying or at least inconvenient obstacle to scholarly work. Whatever one feels about these questions: when we reread this book today, more than three decades after its first publication, we consider Barthes's enthusiasm about "writerly" texts somewhat dated. A plurality of readers was less than eager to be liberated from "writerly" texts and their oppressively closed meaning, as the excited atmosphere of innovation in the late 1960s had anticipated. We will have to return to these questions (which we could merely touch upon here) in chapter 8.

Structuralist Plot-Analysis: Gérard Genette

If for your taste, Barthes was lacking in systematical rigor, you will probably find that the next contribution to narratology makes up for that lack. The French narratologist Gérard Genette (b. 1930), whom we will later find again in another context (below, chapter 5), has repeatedly and successfully opened up complex fields of literary criticism by providing a clear and logical structure and a coherent and precise terminology in his books and articles. His analyses have certainly not remained unchallenged and a number of details can be (and have been) improved, but at least, his contributions always constitute a solid basis on which further work can be built. If you take into account that he is also good at interspersing his terminologically accurate writing with a wry sense of humor, it makes sense to suggest Genette's books as an ideal point of departure in many fields of literary criticism.

Genette's contributions to narratology ([133] and [134]) appeared first in 1972 and 1983. They take Marcel Proust's (1871–1922) great novel *À la recherche du temps perdu* (*In Search of Lost Time*), first published in 1913–27, as their object, but they intend to do more than analyze this extended narrative: Genette wants to provide a general theory of the ways in which narrative presents its story. Accordingly, he uses a great many narrative texts, from antiquity up to modern literature, as examples. Genette's narratological system is arguably the most important one today because even narratologists who do not simply accept and follow it often take it as the starting point of their own approaches.

Genette tries to improve the opposition story vs. plot by adding a further element. He distinguishes three levels [133.27]:

1   narrative (*récit*): the signifier, the narrative text itself;
2   story (*histoire*): the signified, the narrative content, the events;
3   narrating (*narration*): the producing narrative action.

Only the level of the narrative can be the object of narratological analysis, or to be more precise, the level of the narrative in its relation to the other two levels, which, in literary texts, are *produced* by the narrative (see above, p. 44). Genette states that the smallest possible narrative consists of just one minimal sentence and that all longer narratives can be understood as amplifications of such minimal cores. One could reduce the *Odyssey* to the core sentence "Odysseus returns home." Hence, Genette believes that we can analyze the various aspects of a narrative in analogy with the various grammatical categories of the verb. Genette distinguishes between time, mood, and "voice" of a narrative. (This last aspect is, on the one hand, an analogy to the tone of a human voice, but it is also a grammatical category: the Greek "voices" active, medium, and passive define to what extent the subject is involved in the action expressed by the verb.)

It is not possible to present Genette's analysis of narrative in its totality here, even if this were desirable: it is a system the elements of which define and necessitate each other in a manner typical of structuralism. By way of example, we will present two aspects, one from the area of mood, the other from the area of voice. One subsection of mood in Genette's system is perspective [133.185–211]. He is very careful to distinguish between two categories: "who is perceiving" on the one hand and "who is speaking" on the other. The significance of this distinction, which is generally acknowledged in modern narratology, becomes clear when we look at first-person autobiographical narratives: here, the narrator can describe circumstances in the way that he perceived them long time ago (e.g, as a child) whereas now, at the time of narrating these events, he knows much more than his former self. Genette calls the "perception" of events narrated "focalization." There are several kinds of focalization which can be distinguished according to the amount of information that the narrative provides:

ᢀ In a zero focalization, the narrator assumes the position of an omniscient god: he is in possession of complete knowledge about all emotions, plans, and actions of the characters.

ᢀ Internal focalization looks at events in the perspective of one of the narrative's characters, without necessarily using this character's voice. The reader is merely told what this character knows and sees; things that the character did not witness herself or himself need to be told by other characters or added in other ways. This internal focalization becomes especially clear when we read a sentence such as "Bond believed he could see fear in Goldfinger's eyes." Here, the narrative is in the third person, yet this sentence gives us Bond's perspective of the scene: we are certain about Bond's thoughts only and can merely speculate (with Bond) on Goldfinger's feelings. The focalizing character can change in the course of a narrative; the clearest example for this case is the epistolary novel in which events are perceived (and narrated) by various letter writers in turn.

ᢀ In external focalization, readers perceive all characters from an external perspective; hence, they have no knowledge of their thoughts and emotions. Some experimental modernist novels have played with this external focalization and used it throughout the text. In "classical" narratives, it is sometimes used to introduce a new characters. In this case, we are first given a mere external description ("a young woman of around twenty years, blond, thin," etc.); later, more details that require more than a mere external perspective will be supplied. In this case, it is evident that the narrating voice was already in possession of this supplementary information but that the focalization presupposes a perspective which does not have this information.

The narrative instance (the answer to the question "who is speaking?") is treated in the section on "voice" [133.212–62]. Genette distinguishes different possibilities of the temporal relation between story and narrating:

ᢀ The subsequent narrative is the normal case: events are narrated after they have taken place.

ᢀ In prior narrative, the relation is exactly opposite: events are narrated before they take place. This is the case, e.g., in prophecies: in the *Aeneid*, 1.267–71, Jupiter predicts that Aeneas's son Ascanius will reign in Alba Longa for 30 years; this is a period of time which exceeds the narrative period presented in the *Aeneid*. However, science fiction does not usually utilize prior narrative: while the narrated events take place in the future as seen from the reader's point of view, the narrator's voice relates them in the past tense because the act of narrating is placed even further into the future and "looks back" on the events.

ᐳ As an example of simultaneous narrative, we can think of the live coverage of a baseball match on the radio: everything is narrated exactly at the moment when it is happening. Modern novels (such as the *Nouveau Roman* in France) have sometimes played with this form of narrative.

ᐳ In interpolated narrative, narrating and events alternate; good examples for this form would be epistolary novels or diaries: when the narrating begins, the events are not yet finished.

Genette [133.227–62] invents a number of (sometimes rather complicated) terms for the analysis of narrative levels. It is comprehensible that some scholars with a more traditional background have criticized these neologisms as unnecessarily inelegant, yet they have the advantage of being accurate and free from unwanted associations. Genette distinguishes an extradiegetical and an intradiegetic level. Narrative texts tell of events, situations, and characters; all these elements are located *within* the narrative, so they are intradiegetical. The act of narrating, on the other hand, usually takes place *outside of* this narrated universe, so it is extradiegetic: the narrator who, in the first line of the *Aeneid*, announces "Arms and the man I sing," and his "singing" itself do not exist in the same world as Aeneas's wanderings and battles. Of course, such levels can continue and be embedded within a narration; Ovid's *Metamorphoses*, for instance, display a highly complex system of nested narratives within the main narrative.

This fundamental difference between intradiegetical and extradiegetical elements has always been clear to most readers of narrative, even if it was not conscious. Its importance is highlighted when narratives, in a parodic or playful manner, break the boundary between the intradiegetical and extradiegetical levels. For example, in Woody Allen's 1997 movie *Deconstructing Harry*, novelist Harry Block one day has an encounter with one of the characters of his novels (and gets an earful about his messed-up life). The joke here lies in the fact that an inviolable border is transgressed: as an author, Block is not on the same level of the narrative as his characters; in regard to the world of his novels, he is extradiegetical. Genette calls such transgressions "metalepses."

Genette then analyzes the relation between the narrator and the narrative. A narrator can either be a character in her or his own narrative and have a minor or a major part in it, or (s)he can relate events in which (s)he had no active role. Genette calls the first case an homodiegetic, the second an heterodiegetic narrator. He makes these terms more understandable by providing a helpful table [133.248] (such tables are typical of his terminological precision). This table is here modified (table 2) so as to use examples from Latin literature.

Level ⟍ Relationship	Extradiegetic	Intradiegetic
Heterodiegetic	Virgil	Aristaeus
Homodiegetic	Apuleius	Aeneas

Table 2   Narrator and narrative according to Genette

What follows is a very brief explanation of the items in table 2.

- "Virgil" here means the narrator who enters the stage in the first line of the *Aeneid* and says "I sing" (*cano*); he is also occasionally present in later parts of the epic, e.g. 6.266 "permit me to relate" *sit mihi fas* or 7.41 "I will tell" *dicam*. This narrator is heterodiegetic because he is not present in the events of the epic as a character; he is extradiegetic because his "I will sing" is addressed to the audience and readership of the *Aeneid*, not at characters within the epic text.
- In the fourth book of Virgil's *Georgics* (453–527), the god Proteus narrates the story of Orpheus and Eurydice to his listener Aristaeus. Both are characters within the poem, so the entire narrative is intradiegetic. However, Proteus himself is not a character in the story he tells, so he is a heterodiegetic narrator.
- The narrator in Apuleius's *Metamorphoses* is homodiegetic because he plays an important role in his own narrative (he relates that he was transformed into an ass and could regain his human features only after long and exciting adventures). On the other hand, his narrative is addressed to the novel's readers, so it is extradiegetic.
- When Aeneas narrates his own adventures in Carthage in the second and third books of the *Aeneid*, he clearly is a homodiegetic narrator. Since his narrative takes place within the *Aeneid* and is addressed to a public in this fictional world (Queen Dido and her court), it is intradiegetic.

If you want to see examples for every imaginable situation and combination, you could analyze the complex and nested narratives in Ovid's *Metamorphoses* (as Stephen M. Wheeler [376.207–10] has done). This section has just presented a small part of Genette's narratological system to give an example of the sensitive methodology he provides for the analysis of narratives. Every critic who has a serious interest in narrative should in any case have a look at Genette's contributions themselves and get an impression of their use, but also of their limitations.

Irene de Jong's Narratological Analysis of the Homeric Epics

As an example of a fruitful use of narratological methods to an ancient text, we will here take a look at the analysis of the Homeric epics proposed by the Dutch philologist Irene J. F. de Jong in a book first published in 1987 [209]. For her work, de Jong uses the narratological methodology developed by Mieke Bal in her *Narratology* [20].

Bal and de Jong accept Genette's distinction of the categories "who speaks" and "who perceives"; de Jong calls these instances the "narrator" (abbreviation N) and the "focalizer" (abbreviation F). This distinction is not particularly interesting as long as the instance of narration is continuous throughout a narrative. In reality, however, most narratives introduce several narrators and focalizers. To quote one simple example: in the *Iliad*, the main story line is related by a narrator who is not a character in the plot of the epic. He has only a few appearances in the text, e.g., when he speaks of himself in the first person at the beginning of the long catalog which introduces the armies of the Achaeans and of the Trojans (2.493): "I will tell the leaders of the ships." This narrator relates the events which Achilles's anger entails in his own perspective; he decides which actions will be described at length and which ones will be mentioned briefly. Unlike, say, many novels of the nineteenth century, the *Iliad* does not characterize this narrator in regard to name, age, sex, or social status, nor is he completely indeterminate. We know, for instance, that he lives a rather long time after the events of the Trojan War because he repeatedly compares the Heroes of this period with people "as they are now" and claims that the heroes were much stronger (e.g. 5.202–4, 12.378–85, etc.). When the narrator laments that "it is difficult for me to tell about all those things like a god" (12.276), this implies that he is himself a human being, not a god. De Jong is certainly right to see this as a clear signal that we should not imagine the text of the *Iliad* as sung by the Muse, but as a text produced by a human singer who is inspired by the Muses. This narrator/focalizer who perceives, chooses, structures, and (at least in part) judges the events of the epic is called the "primary narrator-focalizer" (NF_1) by de Jong. It is he who puts the action of the *Iliad* into a certain perspective by providing flashbacks and predictions of events that are outside of the temporal scope of the *Iliad*; e.g., he tells us (12.3–35) that the wall which the Achaeans built around their camp was destroyed by the gods after Troy had been captured (prolepsis), or he provides the genealogy of heroes when they die in battle (analepsis).

This kind of analysis becomes really fascinating when we observe that repeatedly, a second focalizer introduces her or his own point of view into the text of the NF_1 (embedded focalization). This is made explicit when we see verbs of perception or of emotion: when we as Homer's audience are told that a character sees or hears something, we see through her or his eyes for a moment; when we hear that a character desires or loathes something, her or his emotion is embedded into the relatively objective narrative of the NF_1. De Jong describes the effect of this device in these words [209.113]: "the narrator-text does not consist of a succession of events only, but is interspersed with short 'peeps' into the minds of the characters participating in those events."

There are more complex forms of embedded focalization when there is no explicit hint at this different perspective. When, e.g., Thetis sprinkles Patroclus's dead body with Ambrosia "that his skin remain unharmed" (19.39), this final clause tells us what she intended with her action. Other examples refer to emotional judgments. In the last book of the *Iliad*, Priam visits Achilleus to ransom the body of his son Hector whom Achilleus has killed in battle. While Priam is imploring Achilleus, he kisses his hands, "the dread murderous hands that had slain so many of his sons" (24.479). De Jong plausibly suggests that these adjectives are uttered from Priam's perspective: these are the very thoughts that occur to him while he is kissing these hands [209.119]. De Jong give the term "complex narrator-text" to passages such as this one in which perceptions and emotions of characters of the narrative are embedded into the text of the primary narrator-focalizer. Her interpretation of such passages is supported by one important observation: a number of adjectives expressing emotional judgments only occur in direct speeches and in complex narrator-text; they are thus a signal that here, it is not the NF_1 who is expressing his view of things, but one of the epic characters.

This observation is an important advance in Homeric studies. Interpreters used to claim that the style of Homeric narrative was "objective." By using an advanced methodology derived from modern narratology, de Jong has convincingly demonstrated that this view is inaccurate. As a matter of fact, in complex narrator-text, the Homeric epics contain quite a number of "subjective" elements. The surface is of the text is not uniformly shaped by an invisible, om-

niscient, detached narrator; much rather, it provides a number of different vistas
and allows us to see the events from many different perspectives. The Homeric
epics demonstrate a masterful skill in handling such narrative techniques; they
are by no means creations of a "primitive" mind, but products of a sophisticated
art. Hence, modern narratology is a good way of analyzing these narratives.

Further Reading

A regrettable trend of literary studies is particularly visible in the field of narratology: the different philologies of modern literatures are working in splendid isolation; hence, scholarly traditions exist that have almost no contact with
each other. My own competence is least in the field of German studies, so I will
at least name a few books that are often quoted and referred to in this tradition: Eberhard Lämmert's *Bauformen des Erzählens* [227], Käte Hamburger's
The Logic of Literature [170], and Franz K. Stanzel's *A Theory of Narrative* [337].
In the English-speaking world, Wayne C. Booth's (1921–2005) *The Rhetoric of
Fiction* [39] is a classic in its own right. I would recommend this book to everybody interested in narrative texts, especially those with little previous knowledge of narratology: not only is it a good read because of Booth's pleasant style,
but it is also a wonderful testimony to the author's infectious love for narrative
texts. Some of the terms coined by Booth (such as "implied author" and "unre-
liable narrator") have become generally accepted in literary criticism and are in
common use. Gerald Prince's *A Dictionary of Narratology* [295] is an immensely
useful reference on all aspects of narratology. Finally, when we look at the analysis of the Homeric epic, it is worth mentioning that Irene J. F. de Jong has also
published *A Narratological Commentary on the* Odyssey [208], which uses and
develops many of the ideas in her book.

Chapter 4
Mikhail Bakhtin

The influence of the literary theory proposed by the Russian scholar Mikhail Bakhtin has been experiencing a steady growth in the last 25 years or so, and it is likely to continue growing in the near future – some scholars are convinced that Bakhtin is "the greatest theoretician of literature in the twentieth century," as Todorov [355.ix] put it. But if you begin to develop an interest in Bakhtin and his work, soon you are quite likely to encounter a number of difficulties: on the one hand, his impressive influence makes itself felt in a number of concepts that are all but ubiquitous in modern literary theory and that are employed by many literary critics, key terms such as carnival and carnivalization, heteroglossia, polyphony, or dialogism. On the other hand, you will soon realize that Bakhtin's own thinking was much more comprehensive than these inspiring and multifaceted, yet somewhat isolated concepts suggest. Bakhtin's writings contain a philosophy that argues with and against several strands of contemporary thinking such as Neokantian esthetics, the structuralist linguistics proposed by Saussure, or Marxism. Bakhtin's philosophy aimed at providing explanations for human language and human behavior in general. The key concepts, which have been so influential in literary theory, are merely details in the vaster frame of these comprehensive endeavors.

But it is this vastness of Bakhtin's thinking that makes understanding him problematic and engenders a number of questions: to what extent can his thinking be considered systematic and consistent? Did Bakhtin change his opinions over the course of his long career, or are we invited to harmonize all his ideas? Is the system of his thought so tightly consistent and integrated that taking single ideas out of it amounts to giving a wrong impression? We have to admit that Bakhtin himself did not make it easy for his readers to find answers to these questions, and the reasons for these difficulties are only partly due to factors he could control. He lived during one of the most unstable and changeable periods of Russian history, and it can only be expected that his writings reflect the circumstances of their genesis (which, in some cases, was riddled with extreme difficulties). Hence, it is necessary to take a brief look at Bakhtin's life before we can turn to his writings.

Bakhtin's Life and the Problem of His Writings

Mikhail Mikhailovich Bakhtin was born in 1895, in Orel, a town southwest of Moscow. He grew up in Vilnius, the capital of what today is Lithuania, and in Odessa on the Black Sea, hence in unusually multicultural and cosmopolitan surroundings. He was raised by a German nanny who appears to have been a very erudite and impressive woman, so he was bilingual from an early age. In 1913, Bakhtin began to study classics, first in Odessa, then in St. Petersburg in Russia. Already during his time at high school, he had demonstrated great enthusiasm for ancient literature. This admiration for classical, especially Greek texts, and a stupendous knowledge of even the most remote authors, periods, and genres are typical of Bakhtin's entire work. Another trait that was to be characteristic of his entire intellectual life also took shape during his years at the university: Bakhtin soon became member of a circle of intellectuals interested in philosophy and theology who met regularly to discuss problems and recent developments in these fields. Bakthin was to take part in such circles at virtually all stages of his later life, and he was often the center of these gatherings. Hence, not only did he get in contact with many eminent scholars and intellectuals of his time, he also stayed in touch with discoveries and problems out of his own area of specialization.

Bakhtin graduated in St. Petersburg amid the chaos of the October Revolution of 1917 and the ensuing civil wars. In the following years, Russia suffered from tremendous economic difficulties that led to several revolts and famines. During this period, Bakhtin too suffered from food shortages and ill health and barely managed to survive. He taught in schools in several small provincial towns, and his wife had to accept odd jobs to contribute to their living expenses. In spite of these sometimes depressing circumstances, he wrote a number of important works. In 1929, Bakhtin was arrested because of his religious commitments; one year later, he was banished to Kazakhstan. In the following years he had to support himself with several menial jobs and, partly because he had to fear further prosecutions, was forced, to move house time and again. Nevertheless, he still managed to finish a number of important manuscripts, but World War II prevented their publication: a book which he had finished in 1938 seems lost forever because the publishing house that was typesetting it was destroyed in a German bombing raid; in the dire straits of wartime, Bakhtin had made cigarette paper of his own copy of the manuscript. Because of the political and ideological climate of the postwar years, a book on François Rabelais which he had submitted as a PhD dissertation in 1941 could not be published until 1965. At least, Bakhtin received tenure at the Pedagogical Institute in Saransk, a town around 300 miles southeast of Moscow, where he taught and wrote in a remote and quiet atmosphere. He was all but forgotten by the Russian and international public; only at the end of his life did he receive some sort of fame. Younger scholars in Moscow had read and admired his books on Dostoevsky and Rabelais and had managed to ensure their publication or republication; translations into Western languages were quick to follow. During the last years of his life, Bakhtin's state of health continued to decline, he was taken care of in several hospitals and nursing homes in the vicinities of Moscow. Bakhtin died in 1979.

Bakhtin's eventful life and his own personality help to explain some particularities that make it more difficult for readers to obtain a clear picture of this ideas:

- ই Bakhtin kept changing his residence and his jobs; accordingly, a number of his writings remained unfinished. It seems that some of them still have not been published, let alone translated into Western languages, so Western literary critics have to rely on the judgment of their colleagues who read Russian, some of whom claim that these texts contain some of his most important ideas.

- ই Bakhtin was unusually free from any kind of ambition and did not care much about publishing his work. When he was already living in Moscow, his friends retrieved a number of his manuscripts in Saransk, where they had been lying in a shed, forgotten and neglected. It is possible that somewhere at one of the multiple residences that Bakhtin took up during his turbulent life there still exist some hitherto unknown manuscripts that await discovery and that would change our view of his ideas.

- ই By far the biggest and most difficult problem, however, is created by the so-called disputed texts. In particular, these are three books published in the late 1920s under the names of two friends of Bakhtin's, Pavel Nikolaevich Medvedev (1891–1938) and Valentin Nikolaevich Voloshinov (1895–1936). Since the 1970s, a number of scholars working on Bakhtin's ideas have maintained that these books, *The Formal Method in Literary Scholarship* [252] and *Marxism and the Philosophy of Language* [368], had in effect been written by Bakhtin. At this point, he was himself considered to be politically suspect, so it would make sense to assume that he published his work under the name of friends who were less liable to political pressure (ironically, both these friends were later killed in the Stalinist purges of the 1930s while Bakhtin lived on into old age). Unfortunately, Bakhtin himself later never stated quite clearly whether he was the author or coauthor of these books, and scholarship has not yet reached a definitive conclusion (and will probably not reach such a conclusion in the near future). Above all, these writings have a more pronounced Marxist outlook than the rest of Bakhtin's work. This raises the question of whether this Marxism was a mere façade in order to appease the vigilant and, at the time of their publication, particularly dangerous ideological censorship in the Stalinist Soviet Union; however, we also have to wonder whether Bakhtin's other work should be read in the light of Marxism.

This chapter will attempt to present and explain Bakhtin's contributions to the field of literary theory properly speaking. I want to avoid the impression that the key concepts mentioned above are, as it were, free radicals that float around and can be used in any context, yet we have to admit that Bakhtin's far-reaching influence is precisely due to a certain ambivalence and multidimensionality of his ideas. My own reading of Bakhtin's work has not found support for the claim made by some scholars that this thought can only be understood if we take his entire system into account. Hence, his anthropological and philosophical speculations will be presented in a very brief manner only, by way of background; the main part of the chapter will be an exposition of his well-known key categories.

Dialogism and the Novel

Bakhtin expounded his thoughts on the functioning of human communication and interaction (of which he believed literature to be a part) by discussing a number of positions put forward by other scholars. We will be using his critique of Saussure's structuralist linguistics (which we encountered in Chapter 2) as our point of departure. In Saussure's definition, only the system of language, the *langue*, not single utterances, could be the proper object of linguistic investigation. Bakhtin argues against this abstraction. Unlike Saussure's methodology, he opts for a science of utterances, not of abstractions, and he emphasizes the dialogical and contextual character of linguistic utterances. Language always works within certain situations, and utterances produce their significance within this context. The linguistic material alone is not enough to determine whether a word or a sound is enthusiastic, gloomy, ironical, threatening, or deferential; rather, this depends on a number of factors such as intonation, volume, the interlocutor, and prior utterances in the dialogue. Bakhtin is right to draw attention to the fact that linguistic utterances never occur in isolation, but are always part of a dialogue – even if this is an imaginary dialogue with a partner who is absent. Our words reply to past utterances and bear the traces of this past. We don't reinvent the signification of our language every time we speak, but we connect our own words with what preceded them. Hence, every utterance we make is "dialogical": "Only the mythical Adam, who approached a virginal and as yet verbally unqualified world with the first word, could really have escaped from start to finish this dialogic inter-orientation with the alien word that occurs in the object" [16.279]. While it is true that there are tendencies in language which silence this dialogical aspect and strip words of their multidimensionality (Bakhtin calls these forces "centripetal"), they are bound to fail in view of the living diversity of human speech and dialogue, which always makes every utterance resonate with things said and written previously, which anticipates replies and objections, and which lets words have different meanings in different contexts and situations [16.271–2]. What we call by the abstract name of "language" really is a variety of different levels: literary and everyday usage, different forms of language used in different professions and social strata, forms of language used in different historical periods [16.288–91]. Bakhtin called this aspect of language "heteroglossia."

We can stop here and reflect to what extent this view of language opposes Bakhtin on the one hand and Saussure and the structuralists on the other. Bakhtin's insistence on linguistic context, which cannot be explored in a simple and systematic way, sets him apart from Saussure, who favored the abstract system of *langue* over the living variety of utterances. Moreover, when Bakhtin claims that in language, there are no "neutral words" that "can belong to no one," he again distances himself clearly from Saussure's ideas [16.293]:

> For any individual consciousness living in it, language is not an abstract system of normative forms but rather a concrete heteroglot conception of the world. All words have the "taste" of a profession, a genre, a tendency, a party, a particular work, a particular person, a generation, an age group, the day and hour. ... Contextual overtones (generic, tendentious, individualistic) are inevitable in the word.

According to Bakhtin, the literary form which represents this linguistic diversity, in which it can even be said to be the proper object of artistic representation, is the novel [16.416]. He holds that the aim of the novel consists in orchestrating the heteroglossia of language in an artistic system. Every single instance of the heterogeneous styles and languages does not merely provide a pleasant effect of linguistic diversity, but represents an entire perspective on the world [16.333]: "It is precisely as ideologemes that discourse becomes the object of representation in the novel, and it is for the same reason novels are never in danger of becoming a mere aimless verbal play." In this orchestrated arrangement, all forms of language are in a dialogue not only with each other, but also with the language and the perspective of the author; every utterance in a novel is always "double-voiced," serving the author as well as her or his characters [16.324].

Bakhtin's theory of the novel presented here is extracted from his lengthy essay "Discourse in the Novel," which was written in 1934–5, but not published until 1975 (in [16.259–422]). This article can be read as a continuation, but also as an implied correction of his book *Problems of Dostoevsky's Poetics*, which first appeared in 1929 (a second, modified edition was printed in 1963; this was the basis for the translation in [17]). There is an unmistakable similarity between the 1929 book and the 1935 article, with one major difference: many of the aspects that Bakhtin later said were typical for the novel in general are still said to be particular characteristics of the works of the Russian novelist Fyodor Mikhailovich Dostoevsky (1821–81) in this book. Above all, attributes such as the "double-voiced" discourse, the "dialogism," and the heteroglossia of language are said to be achievements of Dostoevsky, whose "polyphonous" novels are compared to and contrasted with the "monologic" novels of Leo Tolstoy (1828–1910) (e.g., [17.69–73]). In his book, Bakhtin called Dostoevsky's texts a "Copernican revolution" [17.49]; in the later essay, he would say that novel in general is an "expression of a Galilean perception of language" [16.366]. Both metaphors refer to the same quality of discourse: language in the novel cannot be homogenized by centripetal tendencies. Since the groundbreaking discoveries of Nicolaus Copernicus (1473–1543) and Galileo Galilei (1564–1642), our view of the universe no longer admits that there is any privileged place, any center. In the same way, the novel's polyphonous structure does not admit reduction to any unequivocal ("monologic") view of the world.

Bakhtin quietly omitted one idea of his book that posed a number of grave problems in modern scholarship. He had claimed that in Dostoevsky's novels, the author did not set himself above the characters but was entering into a dialogue with them on an equal footing: "For the author the hero is not 'he' and not 'I' but a fully valid 'thou,' that is, another and other autonomous 'I' ('thou art')" [17.63]. We can leave unanswered the question of whether this interpretation of Dostoevsky's novels holds water. Yet there is room for serious doubts if such a relation between an author and the characters (s)he creates is possible at all. There are certainly marked differences in the amount of independence that authors are willing to concede their characters – some novelists use their characters as mere mouthpieces of their own convictions, and everything in the novel is inevitably subordinated to the task of proclaiming these apparent truths (see [16.327]); others are more prepared to let their characters "live their own lives" and let points of view be heard with which the authors themselves do not agree. But overall, every character is a creation of the author, and the extreme that Bakhtin thought he had found in Dostoevsky's novels can hardly be realized at all.

Bakhtin emphasized the dialogic element of language in general and of the novel in particular because this view originated in certain convictions he held and which he called his "philosophical anthropology." I cannot dwell on this system here and will merely outline it very succinctly: for Bakhtin, human beings are never able to fully know themselves. He illustrates this by means of a simple picture: I will never be able to look at my own forehead or to see myself within the scene that I am part of. In order to do so, I need a person opposite myself, even if this person is imaginary. Her or his "exotopy" ("place without") enables her to have a more complete view of me than I can ever have myself. To achieve this surplus of perception, to see ourselves as human subjects in the full sense of the word, we human beings need to dialogue with each other. For Bakhtin, dialogue, the use of language, and the self-knowledge achieved by these means are more than interesting, but unnecessary amusements; instead, they are an essentially vital form to make sense of the world we live in. This is a conviction that Bakhtin expressed in his earliest writings and which he maintained till the end of his life (see [355.94–107]). It led him to repudiate Saussure's view of language and to develop his own theory of discourse in the novel. We will have to return to both points later.

The Carnivalization of Literature

Before doing so, however, I want to introduce another concept coined by Bakhtin that has been connected with his name even more intimately than the term "dialogism" and that has had a wide-ranging influence in literary criticism: "carnivalization." Already in his 1929 book on Dostoevsky, Bakhtin had included thoughts on carnivalesque festivals and their influence on literary language and genres; he then went on to give a systematical account of these ideas in the second edition of his book on Dostoevsky, published in 1963 [17], and in his book

on Rabelais, published in 1965 [18]. We will begin here with a short summary of
the book on Rabelais because it provides a general presentation of the essence
and influence of carnival, using a specific case study.

Between 1532 and 1552, François Rabelais (ca. 1494–1553) published four
books in which he described, with a unique power of expression and grotesque
humor, the fantastic adventures of the giant Pantagruel and of his father Gar-
gantua. As Bakhtin explains, interpreters up to his time had provided two contradictory explanations of the comic elements in these books: either they saw
them as part of jolly and innocent entertainment, or they claimed it was a satirical means of social criticism. Bakhtin maintained that these works must be
understood against the backdrop of the "carnivalesque" of his times. Rabelais
wrote at a time when the humanists in France were rediscovering antiquity but
when medieval ideologies and institutions were still powerful and continued
to resist the new spirit of the Renaissance. Bakhtin's analyses clearly show that
medieval carnivalesque festivals exerted a strong influence on the form and content of Rabelais's work. Such festivals held an eminent place in the lives of medieval people [18.96]: "The men of the Middle Ages participated in two lives:
the official and the carnival life. Two aspects of the world, the serious and the
laughing aspect, coexisted in their consciousness." A characteristic of such festivals was a temporary suspension of the norms and hierarchies that were valid
in normal circumstances. This reversal of usual norms was symbolized by a variety of gestures that would make things topsy-turvy: wearing your pants on your
head, choosing a beggar as a carnival king, etc.: "during carnival there is a temporary suspension of all hierarchic distinctions and barriers among men and of
certain norms and prohibitions of usual life. ... an ideal and at the same time real
type of communication, impossible in ordinary life, is established" [18.16–17].
A number of elements that are characteristic of Rabelais's novels, such as profan-
ities and swear words, long lists of humorous items, parodies and puns, insults
that are not meant seriously, all of these are typical aspects of the style of language used in such carnivalesque festivals. One aspect that is particularly worth
mentioning is the irreverent parody of everything that is sacred and sublime;
this parody does not even stop short of the prayers and rituals of the Christian
church.

According to Bakhtin, such festivals do not merely have the function of providing a break from the rigor of everyday rules to a society ossified in its customs
and hierarchies; rather, they symbolized the moment of transition that was essential for the entirety of the people: "destruction and uncrowning are related
to birth and renewal. The death of the old is linked with the contradictory one-

ness of the dying and reborn world" [18.217]. This connection of the old and the new is symbolized by the picture of the earth which is, at the same time, the life-giving producer of plants and crops and the place where the dead are given their final place of rest. It is also visualized in the vision of a "hell" that swallows the old and spews out the new. Moreover, it is at the origin of the carnivalesque predilection for the "grotesque body." Unlike the classical, beautiful body, "it is never finished, never completed; it is continually built, created, and builds and creates another body. Moreover, the body swallows the world and is itself swallowed by the world" [18.317]. In this grotesque body, emphasis is placed on orifices and bodily functions such as eating and digesting, copulation, pregnancy, giving birth, and death. This close connection between death and coming-to-be explains why laughter and mockery in carnival can never be exclusively negative: they not only attempt to destroy the old, but at the same time they also provide for the coming-to-be of the new. The transient nature of this moment also helps us understand why the utopian, anti-hierarchical society created by carnival can never be enduring: carnival always embodies what is being born and becoming, not what exists in a static way.

Bakhtin emphasizes that this close connection between death and birth only applies to society as a whole, not to its single members. It is the entirety of the people that celebrates carnival, hence its rejuvenation and renewal; "the individual feels that he is an indissoluble part of the collectivity, a member of the people's mass body. In this whole the individual body ceases to a certain extent to be itself" [18.255]. Such carnivalesque festivals remained popular all through the Middle Ages. According to Bakhtin, it is no coincidence that it was especially during the Renaissance that their influence was felt all the way from the counter-culture of the marketplace to high literature: the humanists desired that the rigid, inflexible medieval world (embodied above all in the complex system of rules of scholasticism) give way to the innovations of their own ideology. "This is the reason why in all great writings of the Renaissance we clearly sense the carnival atmosphere, the free winds blowing from the marketplace" [18.275]. Bakhtin names, e.g., Giovanni Boccaccio (1313–75), Miguel de Cervantes (1547–1616), or William Shakespeare (1564–1616) as further representatives of such carnivalesque literature.

Menippean Satire and Ancient Carnivalesque Literature

From the very start, then, Bakhtin wanted his analysis of carnivalesque forms, topics, and themes in Rabelais to be more than merely a contribution to the

understanding of a single text. This becomes clear when we read the closing remarks of his book on Rabelais: "his work sheds its light on the folk culture of
humor belonging to other ages" [18.474]. One attempt at systematizing these
insights into the connection between carnival and literature can be seen in the
chapter "Characteristics of Genre and Plot Composition in Dostoevsky's Works"
in his book on Dostoevsky [17.101–80]. It should be especially interesting to
classicists because here, Bakhtin tries to trace the history of carnivalesque literary genres back to antiquity.

Bakhtin sees the origin of such literary texts in carnivalesque festivals such
as the Roman Saturnalia; he had already given a clear and vivid analysis of their
medieval avatars in his book on Rabelais. In the chapter of his book on Dostoevsky, Bakhtin defines the nature of such festivals by naming the following
characteristics [17.122–6]:

- During carnival, the rules that normally govern normal life are temporarily
  abolished. In particular, the usual hierarchical barriers between upper and
  lower classes or older and younger people are removed. Carnival is certainly
  a show, but it is a show without a division into performers and spectators.
  What is characteristic for carnival is the free and familiar contact among
  people.
- This contact will juxtapose and reconcile persons and things that are normally separate; Bakhtin uses the term "misalliance" for this aspect of carnival: "Carnival brings together, unifies, weds, and combines the sacred with
  the profane, the lofty with the low, the great with the insignificant, the wise
  with the stupid" [17.123].
- This misalliance applies especially to everything that, under normal circumstances, is sublime, powerful, or sacred: it is desecrated and derided by being
  combined with the obscene or the scatological. Hence, parody, mockery,
  and debasement are the means of expression most typical for carnival.
- The effect of this misalliance is a topsy-turvy world in which the logic of
  normal life is not valid anymore: carnival is marked by "eccentricity," by
  "life turned inside out."
- One playful event that is especially characteristic of the carnivalesque spirit
  is "the mock crowning and subsequent decrowning of the carnival king"
  [17.124]; it provides a vivid and impressive staging of death and rebirth.

It is not difficult to recognize the features of medieval carnivalesque festivals in these traits. Bakhtin, however, goes one step further in maintaining that

there is a fundamental statement made by carnival's juxtaposition of death and rebirth, viz. "the joyful relativity of everything" [17.126]. Here, we immediately perceive a parallel to Bakhtin's thoughts about language: heteroglossia, which never allows for a "final word," is an especially appropriate means to express this relativity. Heteroglossia is in opposition to the centripetal, unifying, hierarchical forces of language in exactly the same manner that carnival resists social hierarchies and demonstrates that the established order is not the only imaginable form of society, as it claims to be.

The perception of this relativity and the "creative ambivalent carnival laughter, in which mockery and triumph, praise and abuse are inseparably fused" [17.164], have wide-ranging effects on literature and philosophy. This cheerful relativity penetrates a number of literary genres. It is at first conveyed by immediate contact with carnivalesque customs: "Carnival was, as it were, *reincarnated in literature*" [17.157; emphasis in the original]. This reincarnation can take a variety of forms. At a later stage, laughter can, e.g., be "reduced": "we see, as it were, the track left by the laughter in the structure of represented reality, but we do not see the laughter itself" [17.164]. This carnivalization permits literature to depict opposites such as death and birth as mirror images of each other and thus to prevent either of such positions from becoming absolutized. In this sense, carnivalization can be said to prepare the way for Dostoevsky's polyphonous novel because its open, relativistic structure hints at the fundamental principles of dialogism [17.177]: "A single person, remaining alone with himself, cannot make ends meet even in the deepest and most intimate spheres of his own spiritual life, he cannot manage without *another* consciousness. One person can never find complete fullness in himself alone."

According to Bakhtin [17.106–7], Dostoevsky's polyphonous novel is just one link in a long chain of "serio-comical" literature that began in antiquity. Bakhtin claims that antiquity subsumed a number of genres under the term "serio-comical" (σπουδογέλοιον), e.g., "the mimes of Sophron, the 'Socratic dialogue' (as a special genre), the voluminous literature of the Symposiasts (also a special genre), early memoir literature (Ion of Chios, Critias), pamphlets, the whole of bucolic literature, 'Menippean satire' (as a special genre) and several other genres as well." In this general form, Bakhtin's statement is incorrect: as a matter of fact, we have no accurate knowledge of what the word σπουδογέλοιον signified in antiquity, but the number of texts to which it is indeed applied is certainly smaller than Bakhtin suggests. However, when he gives this long list of genres, Bakhtin is not interested in their totality; instead, he zeroes in on one particular instance, the so-called Menippean satire. Menippus of Gadara, a philosopher who lived in the third century BCE, is indeed called σπουδογέλοιος in ancient testimonies (such as Strabo's geographical handbook, 16.2.29). We have very few fragments of his own works, but the Greek writer Lucian (ca. 120–80 CE) and the Roman scholar M. Terentius Varro (116–27 BCE) wrote "Menippean satires" in his wake. These writings, in a fantastic, sometimes exuberant comical vein, mock human flaws and weaknesses. Their form is characterized by the fact that their prose is, time and again, interspersed with poetical lines in different meters; this is why texts such as Seneca's († 65 CE) *Apocolocyntosis*, Petronius's (first century CE) *Satyrica* or, from late antiquity, Boethius's (480–524) *Consolatio Philosophiae* are called Menippean satires.

In the following pages, we will take Petronius's novel as an example of a Menippean satire. The *Satyrica* is a vivid and immensely funny first-person narrative; its main characters are the narrator Encolpius and his companions Ascyltus and Giton. Unfortunately, only part of it has been transmitted, so our judgment on the text and its characteristics must sometimes remain inconclusive. Nevertheless, it is possible to examine to what extent Bakhtin's definition of the Menippean satire is valid for antiquity. Bakhtin lists 14 traits typical for Menippean satire; we will scrutinize only the most important ones. What, then, are the most important characteristics of Menippean satire as a carnivalesque genre?

- The comical aspect is paramount. This is undoubtedly true for Petronius's text.
- The quest for truth, on the other hand, does not to have an important part in the *Satyrica*, nor an interest in the ultimate, decisive problems of human life. These aspects are more prominent in some of Lucian's works, e.g., the *Icaromenippus* which has Menippus fly on birds' wings up to Mount Olympus to perform a philosophical interview with Zeus.
- A crude naturalism is a prominent feature of Petronius's novel; it is especially visible in the longest stretch of text that has been preserved, the so-called *Cena Trimalchionis* in which food, bodily (especially digestive) functions, and sex are treated in a conspicuously vulgar language and perspective and form the main subject of the narrative.
- The fragmentary state of preservation makes it difficult to decide to what extent the motif of the philosophical journey throughout the entirety of the universe, "from heaven, through the world, to hell" (as Goethe said in his *Faust*), was an important feature of the *Satyrica*. Here, too, it is safer to refer to Lucian's works: in his *True Stories*, the first-person narrator travels

the oceans, the heavens, the moon, and even goes to the beyond.

ᵃᵛ The depiction of abnormal psychological experiences occurs certainly in Petronius's text, but it is not a very prominent feature; we can point to the poetical "inspiration" of Eumolpus that is depicted as a sort of ecstasy (90.4 *coeperis a te exire*, "you begin to go out of your head"), or to the way Trimalchio's dinner party degenerates into a wild orgy.

ᵃᵛ Breaches of usual conventions, especially linguistic lapsus, are a prominent feature of the *Satyrica*; this is especially clear in the *Cena Trimalchionis* which is, from beginning to end, one uninterrupted depiction of vulgarity and tastelessness in which the uneducated and ungrammatical Latin of the guests is the main source of the readers' entertainment. At the end of the *Satyrica*, we find a description of the customs in the city of Croton, which is a representation of a topsy-turvy world.

ᵃᵛ A mixture of different styles, linguistic levels, and literary genres is a characteristic of Petronius's work: in the *Satyrica*, we find everything from the sublime style of Roman epic to the vulgarity of street slang. Several metrical forms are embedded in the prose narrative; novellas and short stories (such as the famous "Widow of Ephesus") are related. Moreover, we can observe that those different levels of style and language are more than merely means of expression: they become themselves the subject of the text when, e.g., Eumolpus accompanies his recitation of an epic about the Roman civil wars with lengthy elaborations on poetical theory (118).

Comparing Bakhtin's definition of the serio-comical genre with Petronius's text demonstrates that Bakhtin has indeed found qualities which are common to a number of literary texts whose close connection had not been observed beforehand. Another penetrating analysis of a classical text which takes Bakhtin's hypothesis of the carnivalization of literature as its point of departure is Bernhard Teuber's article on Apuleius's *Metamorphoses*, published in 1993 [346]. In his interpretation, Teuber makes a convincing argument that Apuleius's novel displays numerous features of carnivalization such as obscenity, the recurring motif of the topsy-turvy world, the depiction of a "laughing ritual" for the god *Risus* (Laughter) in the second book of the novel, and the motif of theatricality that is ubiquitous in the text. Such contributions (to which Möllendorff's analysis of Aristophanic comedy along the lines of Bakhtin's theories [263] can be added) demonstrate the fruitfulness of Bakhtin's categories. However, one needs to be careful about their use: if a term such as "carnivalesque" is employed in an undiscriminating manner, it will lose its selectivity. If all literary works are considered to be polyphonous, heteroglot, and carnivalesque, these categories cease to be useful for literary criticism.

Further Reading

Undoubtedly, the best starting point for getting in touch with Bakhtin's theories are his own writings. As I have written above, all his major ideas can already be found in his 1929 book on Dostoevsky [17]. For classicists, an English collection with four important essays [16] will be of special interest; most contributions cover classical texts extensively. There are a number of clear and helpful introductions into Bakhtin's work: the 1984 book by Clark and Holquist [56] is more thorough, the 1990 book by Holquist [186] is briefer. For those who read German, Möllendorff's 1995 book on Aristophanes [263] may be useful: the first hundred pages or so give an introduction to Bakhtin, and they are among the most thorough and comprehensive treatments of Bakhtin that have been published yet. The volume *Karnevaleske Phänomene in antiken und nachantiken Kulturen und Literaturen* [85] contains a number of articles dealing with the question of whether Bakhtin's theories can and should be applied to classical literature. Moreover, there is an article by W. Rösler published in 1986 [312]. Volume 26.2 of the journal *Arethusa* is a theme issue on "Bakhtin and Ancient Studies: Dialogues and Dialogics": in it, you will find, e.g., an interesting article by C. Platter [289].

Chapter 5
Intertextuality

As we saw in Chapter 4, the dialogical character of language has a decisive role: all utterances are marked by the fact that they belong to certain discourses and display traces of their origins. This is the part of Bakhtin's work that inspired the Bulgarian psychoanalyst and literary critic Julia Kristeva (b. 1941) to develop her own theory of the use of language, for which she coined the term "intertextuality." The word soon became popular and was widely used, and as happens often, it began to lose its precision and before long was no more than a newfangled catchword to express phenomena that had been known and analyzed long before Bakhtin and Kristeva, viz. quotations and allusions in literary texts (hence Kristeva [221.59–60] soon abandoned the term; cf. the critique in Karlheinz Stierle's article [338]). Kristeva's original use of the word, however, had meant more than merely "quotation," and it is worthwhile examining this original use closely in order to better understand the different branches of studies on intertextuality.

Leading the Way: Julia Kristeva

In late 1965, Julia Kristeva arrived in Paris as a student. She took classes with some of the important structuralists, in particular with Roland Barthes. She had read and admired Bakhtin's work in Bulgaria, and now she began translating it into French. It is through her that readers in the West first became aware of Bakhtin's ideas. But Kristeva was not content with merely being the translator and prophet of a thinker who had hitherto been unknown; rather, taking Bakhtin's positions as her point of departure, she started to develop her own thoughts on literary theory. In particular, she made use of Bakhtin's concept of the polyphonous novel. Let us recapitulate (above, p. 67–69): with this term, Bakhtin had expressed his conviction that in the novel, different discourses, i.e., different perspectives on the world are in dialogue with each other. For Bakhtin, it was especially important that the novel had no controlling mechanism (such as the author) which would be the uncontested center of this universe and regulate this variety of discourses; instead, he saw this diversity as consisting of a multitude of discourses on an equal footing.

Kristeva had her own particular way of developing these thoughts. I want to mention one detail before we take a closer look at her theoretical project: Kristeva's writings are not always easy to read. She loves a rather cryptic style with obscure mathematical formulas; this does not facilitate comprehension (and seems completely superfluous in many instances). With that said, let us look at Kristeva's critical approach. She reformulates Bakhtin's theory of heteroglossia and polyphony by claiming that the literary word is no fixed point; instead, it is "an intersection of word (texts) where at least one other word (text) can be read" [220.66]. Every word, then, must be analyzed on two axes:

- horizontally, as a relation between the writing subject and the addressee;
- vertically, as directed toward anterior or synchronic text.

We have already seen (above, p. 33–34) that for structuralism, the human subject could not be the fixed point of communication which would guarantee the meaning of the message. Kristeva draws our attention to one consequence of this structuralist decentering of the human subject: I am the sum of everything I have heard and read, and I define myself by what I say and write. This is one decisive step beyond Bakhtin: for him, the polyphonous novel was the interplay between various discourses; for Kristeva, this is true for literature in its totality, even for any use of human language. According to her [220.66], every text has to be understood as a "mosaic of quotations." This accounts for her famous statement that intertextuality now replaces intersubjectivity [*ibid.*]. Kristeva thus makes fundamental statements in the field of philosophical linguistics or psychology rather than providing tools for the analysis of literary texts. Her main point is this key position which is precisely in the wake of the structuralist decentering of the subject: every human being is nothing more than an intersection of preexistent discourses. It is not we who create texts; instead, we are created by them.

Further Developments of Intertextuality

Kristeva's thoughts are fascinating, but literary criticism is not only interested in fundamental ideas about the human mind and human language, but also in the ways specific texts work. Hence, it was a logical step to ask how Kristeva's "intersection of texts" functions in specific literary works. This does not necessarily mean that we are interested in naming single texts which are quoted or alluded to. As we have seen (above, p. 54), Roland Barthes defined a number of different "codes" in his book *S/Z* [23], among them what he called the "cultural code." This code was the result of the accumulated wisdom of several discourses such as science, history, or philosophy. Even though Barthes does not mention the name Kristeva in *S/Z* and does not use the term "intertextuality," he later emphasized repeatedly how much his approach here owed to his young student.

Barthes's analysis of the cultural code can be described as a first step toward a more focused, literary use of the concept of intertextuality. With it, we are leaving the abstract level of linguistic and philosophical speculation and turning to the question of how intertextuality manifests itself in specific literary texts. This provides a more immediate use of the concept in literary criticism. At the same time, however, there is also an inherent danger. When the term intertextuality is used for this kind of work, what we find is often no more than a fashionable version of pretty old-fashioned studies such as have been undertaken for centuries: which prior texts does a specific author quote, in which way does he imitate his models, and how does he highlight his allusions, imitations, and parodies? Undoubtedly, the use of the modern term can be a mere fad, especially when such studies are not so much interested in the text itself, but in its author, and when categories such as "influence" or "sources" are highlighted. But one does not have to go to such extremes to make the concept of intertextuality fruitful for the analysis of specific texts, as we will see shortly.

We already encountered Michael Riffaterre when we looked at his critique of the structuralist interpretation of a Baudelaire's poem (above, p. 39). Riffaterre has used the term intertextuality in a number of contributions to develop his own theory of how poetic texts are understood, and he has repeatedly demonstrated the working of this theory by analyzing specific texts. Riffaterre distinguishes two acts of reading [307.1–7]:

- The heuristic reading provides an understanding of the text at the level of the linguistic material, as if this text were conventional speech referring to objects outside of itself. This kind of reading will deliver a level of comprehension that Riffaterre calls "meaning."
- This first stage is followed by a hermeneutic reading, which is retroactive: as readers progress through a literary text, they discover that the text signifies something beyond the pure meaning, that it says more than becomes evi-

dent during a first reading. This level is called "significance." In structuralist terms, what we have here is a signifying system of a higher level in which the signs of the first level are now in turn signifiers (s. above, p. 35).

While decoding and understanding a text on the level of meaning requires only linguistic competence, which every speaker of a language possesses, one needs literary competence to decode the significance. We wonder, then: how does this literary competence decide that a statement in a poem must not be taken literally, but has a significance beyond its immediately perceivable verbal meaning? Riffaterre's answer is: every reading of a poem will detect "ungrammaticalities," utterances that make no sense on the level of verbal meaning. Let us look at a simple example: when Horace, in his *carmen* 3.11.3–4, mentions "the tortoise, clever at resounding on seven strings" (*testudo resonare septem / callida neruis*), this is nonsensical on the level of a purely referential reading (i.e., a reading which refers words immediately to real objects). The reader has to see that *testudo*, "tortoise," here is a metonymy that refers to the resonant body of the lyre, made from the tortoise's carapace, and thus to the musical instrument itself.

Maybe the most important manner in which such "ungrammaticalities" are solved during the hermeneutical reading is the realization that a poem is alluding to prior texts. Interpreting a text by Jules Laforgue (1860–87), Riffaterre reaches the following conclusion [307.149–50]: "the correct, that is, the complete interpretation of the poem is made possible for the reader only by the intertext. This neatly frees us of any temptation to believe that in such a poem there can be referentiality to a nonverbal universe: the poem carries meaning only by referring from text to text." Like symbols or clichés, intertexts can constitute the "matrix" of a poem, an underlying idea that is expressed by the text (without being mentioned explicitly) and knowledge of which is necessary in order to understand the poem.

Gérard Genette's Model of Hypertextuality

As in the field of narratology, Genette also has made an admirable effort to map and structure the wide and difficult area of intertextuality. Of course, one may be tempted to smile at some of his finer distinctions (as he has already done himself, with a good sense of irony and humor), but it is quite obvious that again, his contribution offers an excellent starting point for further discussion. Without any ideological axe to grind, Genette takes an entirely pragmatical approach

to what he calls "literature in the second degree" in his book *Palimpsests* [136].
Unlike Kristeva, he does not consider the reference to other texts to be a general
trait of language and literature; instead, he sees it as a characteristic of certain
texts. Genette calls this general quality "hypertextuality" and distinguishes five
types [136.2–6]:

- The term *intertextuality* denotes the effective presence of text A within text
  B, e.g., in the form of quotations or allusions.
- *Paratexts* are parts of a literary work that are grouped around the text proper,
  such as title, notes, prefaces, mottos, etc.
- The phenomenon of *metatextuality* should be familiar to classicists: here,
  text B is a commentary on text A.
- In Genette's system, *architextuality* refers to the fact that texts belong to
  certain literary genres and denotes the text's relation to the genre's rules.
- Finally, Genette defines *hypertextuality* as the derivation of text B (the "hypertext") from text A (the "hypotext") without text B being a commentary
  on A. Examples he mentions are, among others, Virgil's *Aeneid* and James
  Joyce's (1882–1941) novel *Ulysses* (1922), both of which are hypertexts to a
  common hypotext, the Homeric *Odyssey*.

Genette's book is only concerned with the last-mentioned kind of textual
relations, with hypertextuality (so that, if we apply his own terminology in a narrow way, we are no longer dealing with intertextuality). As in his contributions
to the study of narratology, Genette is above all careful to examine the phenomena and to give a systematic structure to this field; again, we will only be able to
examine a small section of his systematic study. Genette distinguishes between
several "hypertextual practices," depending on the relation between hypotext
and hypertext and on the mood in which these relations are activated [136.28]
(Table 3).

relation \\ mood	playful	satirical	serious
transformation	PARODY	TRAVESTY	TRANSPOSITION
imitation	PASTICHE	CARICATURE	FORGERY

Table 3 Hypertextual relations

We will try to understand the meaning of these terms by taking examples from classical texts and their reception in Western literature.

- According to Genette, parody must always refer to a single text. This underlying text is changed minimally but transferred to an unserious subject matter. As an example, we can look at a classical poem from the so-called *Appendix Vergiliana* (*Catalepton* 10). It transforms, line by line, a poem that Catullus had written on a boat (*carm.* 4). While the subject of Catullus's poem was a fast boat, the poem in the *Appendix Vergiliana*, by making minimal adjustments to the text, transforms it into an invective against a good-for-nothing muleteer.

- Travesty is, as it were, an inversion of parody: it is also always targeted at a single text; however, in this case, the same subject matter is treated in a low, vulgar style. As an example, we can quote the numerous travesties of Virgil's *Aeneid* which became very popular in seventeenth-century France (e.g., the *Virgil Travestied* by Paul Scarron, 1610–60). In these texts, Aeneas and his Trojans are forever using foul language and acting as unheroically as possible. The genre reached its pinnacle in Johann Aloys Blumauer's (1755–98) *Adventures of the Pious Hero Aeneas*.

- The transposition is a "serious parody," the transformation of a single text without satirical intent. This is the main focus of Genette's book because it is such an important feature in literary texts. First of all, every translation or free adaptation can be considered a transposition (e.g., Seneca's tragedies in their relation to Attic tragedy). Moreover, there is an abundance of ways of transposing a text: it can be transposed into a different genre (e.g., Epicurus's philosophical treatises can be rewritten as a didactic poem, as in Lucretius's work), or a poet can treat the same subject matter as a predecessor and introduce subtle differences into the manner in which (s)he forms this material (such as Ovid who, in the thirteenth and fourteenth books of the *Metamorphoses*, narrates the adventures of Aeneas). As a matter of fact, a high percentage of classical literature can be decribed as belonging to this category because imitating and surpassing predecessors played such an important role for ancient authors.

- Caricature does not imitate a single text but an entire style, in a satirical vein. This category, then, would encompass all texts written "in the style of …." In classical literature, we could refer to Aristophanes, whose comedies imitate and mock, e.g., the high-flown lyrical style of his fellow poets.

- Pastiche uses a very similar procedure, but in its case, there is no satirical intent, just a playful manner. In antiquity, we have the epic *Battle of Frogs and Mice* which narrates, in Homeric language and lofty epic style, the battles of these little animals.

෬ If this kind of imitation is performed with serious intent, Genette speaks of "forgery." In antiquity, we can refer to Quintus of Smyrna who narrates the events that happened after the end of the *Iliad*, in serious Homeric style. In the Renaissance, so-called supplements to the *Aeneid* were an immensely popular genre; they related what happened after the twelfth book of the classical epic.

Genette offers painstaking analyses of all these forms, and his book, which is as entertaining as it is meticulous, can only be recommended as a first encounter with these phenomena of "literature in the second degree."

Intertextuality in Virgil

It is easy to understand why approaches that analyze phenomena such as inter-textuality and hypertextuality have been very welcome in the study of ancient, especially Latin, literature. Already in antiquity, it was a well-known fact that Rome, since its first encounters with the Greeks, had been quite impressed by their advanced civilization and that Latin authors had been inspired by Greek literature since the very beginnings of Latin culture. Horace's famous line from his *Epistle to Augustus* is often quoted as evidence for this view (*epist.* 2.1.156 *Graecia capta ferum uictorem cepit et artes / intulit agresti Latio*, "Conquered Greece conquered her savage victor and brought culture to rustic Latium"). Of course, the relationship between Greek and Latin literature has been an object of scholarly research for a very long time. However, for a long period, scholars studied these questions exclusively from the perspective of the author (below, p. 87); they examined which "sources" and "models" poets such such as Horace and Virgil followed.

A different approach has begun to develop since the 1970s. Scholars began to become aware of the fact that Latin texts expect their readers to recognize the models they transform and that they constantly challenge their audience to compare the orginial version and its new form. In an article first published in 1942, the Italian scholar Giorgio Pasquali (1885–1952) drew our attention to this phenomenon, which he called "the art of allusion" (*arte allusiva*) [284.275–82]. This aspect of Latin literature has seen a steady stream of scholarly work since the mid-1980s, and theories of intertextuality have helped shed new light on Latin texts. As an example, we will have a brief look at some recent contributions to the study of Virgil.

As in other branches of classics, until the first half of the twentieth century, the main focus of Virgilian scholarship had been on the question of the poet's sources. More recent contributions, on the other hand, emphasize that Virgil was an immensely learned poet whose references to predecessors, especially to Greek literature, must not be considered as a lack of genuine inspiration; instead, they presuppose a readership that is familiar with the literary tradition and that can savor the double perspective that such allusions offer. In an important article, Richard F. Thomas distinguishes the various kinds of intertextual allusions (which he calls "references") in the *Georgics* and has analyzed examples of their function [349.114–41]. One instance will suffice here: in the fourth book of the *Georgics* (104–10), Virgil describes farmers irrigating a field. The language of the passage clearly refers to lines in the *Iliad* (21.257–62). In this model, however, the irrigation is used as a simile to describe Achilles's battle against the river god Scamandrus. Thomas convincingly argues that Virgil's readers are meant to recognize the context of the model and to interpret the lines in the *Georgics* from this perspective: like Achilles, the farmers are fighting against the forces of nature.

Another scholar who has contributed a number of publications to the study of Virgilian intertextuality is Oliver Lyne (1944–2005). In his book *Further Voices in Vergil's* Aeneid, first published in 1987, he emphasizes [243.103]: "To read the *Aeneid* is to be constantly aware of other texts in and behind the new creation." We will look at one impressive example of the ways in which intertextual phenomena inform Lyne's reading of the *Aeneid*. In the epic's last book, Turnus decides to face his superior enemy Aeneas in battle. Amata, the Queen of Latium, attempts to dissuade him from doing this (54–63); her daughter Lavinia, who had originally been engaged to Turnus, sheds tears and blushes, "as when someone stains Indian ivory with blood-red dye, | or when white lilies blush with many a rose: such colors did the maiden's face display" (12.67–9). The simile clearly alludes to a passage in the *Iliad*: "as when a woman stains ivory with scarlet" (4.141–2). This Homeric simile, however, describes a wound that the hero Menelaus receives and which stains his white leg with blood. Lyne argues that Virgil's readers heard the model's wider context in his simile, and, taking other evidence into account, he reaches the conclusion that Virgil wanted to suggest that Lavinia, too, is wounded, namely by love (we can think of the way in which the word *saucia* "wounded" is used in the first line of the fourth book of the *Aeneid* to depict Dido's love for Aeneas). Lyne concludes that Lavinia is depicted as being in love with Turnus, and this renders the morality of Aeneas's fight against him doubtful. This is never mentioned explicitly in the text of the *Aeneid*, but Virgil's use of such allusions makes such "further voices" resonate in the epic: the text's polyphony allows other perspectives, under the dominant surface of the epic narration, to be expressed. Joseph Farrell has formulated his similar interpretation of Virgil's *Georgics* as follows [101.237]: "the intertext presents vistas and possibilities that would otherwise remain unglimpsed and inaccessible."

Not all studies that analyze the "art of allusion" in Latin literature in these ways explicitly refer to the theory of intertextuality; instead, the last few years have witnessed an animated debate as to whether this theory is really helpful in understanding classical texts. One of the most substantial contributions is the book *Allusion and Intertext*, published in 1998 by the Irish-American scholar Stephen Hinds. He criticizes that concepts such as "allusion" and "reference" are apt to limit the potentially indefinite play of intertextuality. His own position is radically different [181.199]: "There is no discursive element in a Roman poem, no matter how unremarkable in itself, and no matter how frequently repeated in the tradition, that cannot in some imaginable circumstance mobilize a specific allusion." In a number of penetrating analyses, Hinds has demonstrated that the notion of intertextuality has deeply changed our understanding of the history of Latin literature.

Further Reading

Graham Allen's book *Intertextuality* [3] provides a comprehensible introduction to the field, but it is not always clearly focused on its main topic. The collection *Intertextuality: Theories and Practices*, edited by Michael Worton and Judith Still [385], offers a number of important papers with a good introduction; moreover, some of the articles in the collection *Dialog der Texte* [317] (in German) can be recommended. When we turn to the possibilities and limitations of applying this approach to classical texts, apart from Stephen Hind's book *Allusion and Intertext* [181], one can turn to a paper by Don Fowler [121.115–37], with a very useful bibliography.

Chapter 6
Reader-Response Criticism

The theoretical positions we have seen so far were, by and large, approaches that developed out of Saussure's linguistic structuralism or engaged in a discussion with it. This chapter will leave this straightforward line of development behind, at least temporarily. In Germany, structuralist ideas and the reactions to these developments that are often referred to by the somewhat vague term of "poststructuralism" have never played as important a role as in the intellectual debate in France or the USA. There are a number of social, political, academic, and intellectual reasons for this difference about which one could speculate at length (there is a fascinating account in Robert C. Holub's book [188]). One of them is rather simple: around the time when structuralism became so important in other countries, a different strand of literary criticism became dominant in Germany and monopolized the public's attention, the so-called "theory of reception." Its origin can be dated with a great deal of precision: in 1967, Hans Robert Jauss (1921–97), who worked in the field of French literature, delivered his inaugural lecture at the University of Constance; it was entitled "Literary History as a Challenge to Literary Theory" (English translation in [203.3–45]). In the same year, Wolfgang Iser (1926–2007) accepted a position in the English department at Constance, and Harald Weinrich (b. 1927) published his article "Towards a Literary History of the Reader" (in German; reprinted in [373.21–36]). Hence, for a number of years, Constance became the center of this approach to literary studies which is often referred to as the "Constance school."

Occasionally, reception theory made polemical arguments against other positions and was attacked in its own turn, yet these debates were always relatively tame, compared to the embittered war of words that was provoked by some varieties of poststructuralism such as deconstruction (see below, chapter 8). One reason why reception theory was less controversial and contentious among more traditional philologists in Germany and elsewhere may be that it can be considered some sort of bland, "low-fat" theory: it is less rooted in philosophical speculations, and its language is less rich in specialized technological vocabulary than the idiom of poststructuralism. Moreover, it could lay claim to a series of illustrious forebears. Its main argument, to put the audience (in most cases, this means the reader, but see below, chapter 7) into the focus of interpretive attention, can be traced back to antiquity. When Aristotle, in chapter 6 of his *Poetics* (1449 b 27), sees the main aim of tragedy in providing a purification from excessive emotions by means of "fear and pity," or when Horace, in his *ars poetica* 333, defines that poets attempt to "enlighten or delight," this is a clear signal that for them, the audience is the most important part of literary communication, where author and text have to follow its lead. If we are willing to accept sweeping generalizations, we can say that this was the dominant view of literature until well into the eighteenth century. It was only Romanticism which emphasized the "genius" and individual creativity in literature and all artistic activity and thus foregrounded the producers of literature to the detriment of its receivers. And it was precisely during Romanticism's heyday, in the nineteenth century, that philology and literary criticism emerged as academic disciplines and developed their methodology. Hence, the Romantic view of literature prevailed in these fields and was hardly ever challenged. Reception studies criticized this bias and postulated that the reader be restored in her or his rights. A literary work, its adepts argued, cannot be said to exist in the same manner as a material object such as a table; much rather, it can be compared to a musical score which will only be transformed into music when it is performed. Analogously, a literary text has only a virtual existence until a reader picks it up and concretizes it in her or his reading.

Empirical Reception Studies

The idea that literary texts do not become "real" until they are actualized in the experience of a reader's mind and that accordingly, the reader should be at the center of literary studies can be pursued in two quite distinct directions. The first current can be described as a pragmatical approach: it asks in which ways literary texts have been concretized by different readers, in different periods, in different social classes, or in different national contexts. Scholars following its lead have, for example, explored the ways in which texts were read in certain periods and areas: Who read novels? How was such reading seen and judged by society? How were texts understood and interpreted? Classical studies have been engaged in this kind of research for a long time; for example, Birger Munk-Olsen has examined who read classical texts during the Middle

Ages and how these texts were studied [272]. There are numerous studies of
the history of transmission and reception of single authors (such as Monique
Mund-Dopchie's book on Aeschylus [271]). However, concerning classical antiquity itself, we are in a much more difficult situation than students of modern
literature: we do not have contemporary evidence such as diaries, private letters, or published reviews at our disposal for studying the attitudes and criteria
of readers in antiquity (what we do have, however, are the texts of ancient commentators, but they are rather difficult to use for this sort of research).

Another avenue of reception studies is closed to classicists as well: we cannot conduct psychological experiments to test and assess the reactions and responses of readers in antiquity. Such experiments have been at the basis of some
branches of modern reader-response studies such as Norman N. Holland's research (below, p. 201, but cf. Jauss's well-founded criticism of this approach in
[202]). When we have access to evidence documenting the experience of ancient readers, these are, in general, productive readers, i.e., authors who read
and reacted to their predecessors' works. Virgil was a reader of the Homeric
epics; Ovid was in turn a reader of Virgil's texts, and we can see their works as
witnesses of their reception of classical texts. In general, however, this kind of
evidence is rather treated as examples of intertextuality (above, p. 83–85).

Aesthetics of Reception

The Constance School, however, was not primarily interested in this empirical
approach; instead, they developed a position called "aesthetics of reception." Its
main focus is not individual (or collective) historical readers, but rather the ways
in which literary texts interact with their recipients, and deploy their potential
meanings and the roles they assign to their readers. In his inaugural lecture,
Jauss himself had criticized the methods of conventional literary history: without really providing a sustained argument for its choices or writing a continuous historical account, he claimed, it merely produced a hodgepodge of short
biographical notices, descriptions of individual works, and literary assessments,
which, as Jauss said, quoting a line by the Austrian poet Rainer Maria Rilke,
"pop up in some accidental spot here" [203.4]. Jauss himself proposed a new
way of writing literary history which ought to take into account that literary
works do not magically appear on an empty stage but are framed by the literary
context of their period. When a reader opens a new novel, (s)he has already read
other novels and developed certain assumptions of what a novel is and should
be; the new text will be read and understood against the backdrop of these as-

sumptions. This is what Jauss called the "horizon of expectations," which he defined as "the objectifiable system of expectations that arises for each work in the historical moment of its appearance, from a pre-understanding of the genre, from the form and themes of already familiar works, and from the opposition between poetic and practical language" [203.22]. It is only by comparing an individual work to this historical background that we can judge its position in the poetical, literary, and aesthetical system of its period: what is its relation to these preexisting assumptions? Does it fulfill them, does it contradict them, thus modifying and extending the horizon of expectation for future works?

According to Jauss, it is precisely the horizon of expectation which provides criteria for aesthetical judgments about literature [203.25]: "to the degree that this distance decreases, and no turn toward the horizon of yet unknown experience is demanded of the receiving consciousness, the closer the work comes to the sphere of 'culinary' art or entertainment art [*Unterhaltungskunst*]." Only works which breach and modify the readers' expectations can be considered great literature; texts that merely gratify preexistent assumptions belong to the realm of good workmanship, but not art. Jauss explicitly quotes the contributions of the Russian Formalists whose ideas about the function of parody in the course of literary history are quite similar to his own (above, p. 24).

This aspect of Jauss's contributions has been discussed intensely; the problems it entails are easy to see. On the one hand, it betrays a marked bias for literature that we might call unconventional, revolutionary, or belonging to the "vanguard." But is it really justified to say that these are the only texts which possess aesthetical value? On the other hand, Jauss remains somewhat vague about the methodology for reconstructing the horizon of expectations which makes such a judgment possible: has not every individual reader made her or his own experiences; can we pretend that there is a way of measuring and assessing the audience's expecations with any degree of objectivity? It may not least be due to such problems that Jauss is considered a great influence on the development of an esthetics of reception but that his calls for a new kind of literary history have not been followed (not even by himself).

Unlike Jauss, his colleague Wolfgang Iser tried to make consistent use of a receptionist approach for the interpretation of individual texts. He also drew up a methodological program in his inaugural lecture at Constance, entitled "Die Appellstruktur der Texte," English translation "Indeterminacy and the Reader's Response in Prose Fiction" [257.1–45]. Moreover, he published two further books ([195] and [196]) which demonstrated a practical use of his ideas. Iser is not interested in individual historical readers either; instead, he establishes the role of the "implied reader" [196.34–8]. This concept describes the role of the reader such as it is inscribed into the text; any individual reader must assume this role in order to realize the potential offered by the text.

Iser is serious in claiming that texts become alive only through being read; before their reception, they are merely black spots on white paper. They need to be concretized in the "act of reading," which, in the case of literary texts, is characterized by the fact that they contain *Leerstellen*, "empty places" which need to be filled by the reader. Hence, readers are motivated into participating and embracing the view produced by the text. Iser has called this aspect of literary texts *Appellstruktur* (the English translation "indeterminacy" does not convey the idea that in Iser's diction, it is the text itself which "appeals" to the reader). Here are some possibilities of what such indeterminacies can be:

- by omitting elements which are self-evident, narratives create gaps which the reader has to fill;
- texts provoke readers to think about possible continuations (this is especially visible in the case of novels which are published in several installments);
- modern literary works often have an "open" end which does not solve all mysteries and leaves unanswered important questions which readers might have.

It is the interplay between textual elements which provide explicit information and thus lead readers in a certain direction, and such indeterminacies which give them (some degree of) freedom from narratorial constraints that motivate readers to make assumptions about the continuation of the narrative, to revise what they thought they knew about the story and its characters, to accept new perspectives even while they are reading. For Iser, what constitutes a literary text is not "the words on the page," but rather this picture which is constantly changing during the act of reading, this concretization of what is merely hinted at in the text, and the interaction between the reader and the raw data of the text. If, while reading the *Aeneid*, we infer, from clues given in Virgil's text, that Aeneas will not continue his voyage to Italy but stay in Carthage, this assumption (and its final refutation by the text when he does indeed travel on) is part of the text of the *Aeneid* as concretized in our act of reading.

Iser's hypotheses about the ways in which the act of reading works have provoked lively discussions, especially in the USA, and these debates have demonstrated that there are some open questions in his account. Stanley Fish (whose own version of reader-response criticism we will examine later, below p. 92) has argued that Iser's concept is based on a distinction between clear, explicit data provided by the text and places where the reader is at greater liberty to react to the text; according to Fish, however, this distinction does not hold water [108.78]: "there can be no category of the 'given' if by given one means what is there before interpretation begins." If Iser were to take seriously his own assumption that texts can be concretized only through reading, i.e., through interpretation, his optimistic belief that there are stable parts which control and govern this interpretation would break down. A related problem can be seen in the fact that Iser's reader is merely a stance that we produce by interpreting the text. But this entails that this reader's role is bare of any claim to be a binding force; if we look closer, we realize that this reader is no more than a construct which allows Iser to bolster his own interpretation. This difficulty has been expressed with special liveliness in Eagleton's words [90.73]: "If one considers the 'text in itself' as a kind of skeleton, a set of 'schemata' waiting to be concretized in various ways by various readers, how can one discuss these schemata at all without having already concretized them? ... It is a version, in other words, of the old problem of how one can know the light in the refrigerator is off when the door is closed." Other critics such as Susan R. Suleiman have cricized Iser for his unclear position with regard to the reader's freedom [343.22–6]: are readers' reactions predetermined by the text and the data it provides or do they have an ample margin in concretizing what is merely hinted at?

American Reader-Response Criticism

This lively discussion of Iser's work in the USA was provoked by the fact that at around the same period when the Constance School was defining its position in Germany, a similar movement in America was pleading for a more prominent role of the act of reading in the interpretation of literature. We have to take a short glimpse at the history of literary criticism in the USA in order to understand why this approach was considered so exciting. From the end of World War II, the practice of literary interpretation in American schools and universities had been dominated by an approach which is called "New Criticism." Its origins date back to the 1920s and 1930s of the last century. New Criticism emphatically claims that a literary work of art must be considered an organic unity whose different parts are in a relation of harmonious tension to each other. It is the interpreter's task to recognize and express this harmony. In order to achieve this aim, the new critics utilize a manner of scrutiny of and immersion in the text that can almost be labeled religious and contemplative in nature; this is the famous "close reading" of New Criticism: the text is isolated from all its surroundings and circumstances, be they historical, biographical, social, or political. This isolation has often been summarized in the slogan "just the words on the page." In this point (and in several other aspects) New Criticism can be compared to the practice of "immanent interpretation" which was dominant in Germany after the end of World War II; its most well-known proponent was the Swiss scholar Emil Staiger (1908–87).

New Criticism firmly believed that unmediated and intense encounters with texts of great poetry can be fruitful and rewarding for our mental life: we are faced with possibilities and experiences that are otherwise inaccessible to us, and by contemplating works of art, we learn to sustain the tension between opposite poles that are irreconcilable in everyday life and to find a balance between such oppositions. In order for this striking and enriching encounter to take place, however, we have to be careful to approach the text itself. Hence, the New Critics caution us against

- ෂ attempts to paraphrase a work of art (termed the "heresy of paraphrase" in chapter 11 of Cleanth Brooks's book *The Well Wrought Urn* [47.192–214]),
- ෂ making the assumption that a text is identical with its author's intentions (this mistake is called the "intentional fallacy"; see below, p. 124),
- ෂ failing to distinguish between the text itself and the psychological effects it exerts on its readers ("affective fallacy").

It is this last point which will be of special interest to us here. The essay in which William K. Wimsatt (1907–75) and Monroe Beardsley (1915–85) defined and condemned this "affective fallacy" [379.21–39], became a classic of literary criticism in the USA; it was often read and quoted. Wimsatt and Beardsley write [379.21]: "The Affective Fallacy is a confusion between the poem and its results .... It begins by trying to derive the standard of criticism from the psychological causes of the poem and ends in biography and relativism."

Yet this orthodoxy began to crumble at the end of the 1960s: a number of scholars began to pay more and more attention to the reader's role in literary texts. As an example, we will have a look at an article published in 1980 by Stanley Fish (b. 1938), who was then a young scholar. Fish argues against the positions of Wimsatt and Beardsley, and he develops his own methodology for interpreting literary texts which he provocatively calls "affective stylistics." By analyzing a single sentence in a poem by Thomas Browne (1605–82),

Fish demonstrates the ways in which the reader's experience is a result of expectations generated, fulfilled or frustrated, modified and adapted as (s)he meets every single word in this sentence. Fish writes about this sentence [107.25]: "It is no longer an object, a thing-in-itself, but an event, something that happens to, and with the participation of, the reader. And it is this event, this happening ... that is, I would argue, the meaning of the sentence." Fish's methodology consists in an extreme deceleration of this reading process, which is usually imperceptible to readers themselves; in this slow motion, it becomes visible and analyzable.

However, Fish's approach does not escape difficulties that we have already seen in Iser's position: when thus reading in slow motion, can he ever be certain that he is describing more than his own quite subjective impressions that are not valid for other readers? And when he claims that a text's meaning is identical to its reader's experiences in the course of reading it, can he avoid a total relativism in which a text can mean anything any reader sees (or hallucinates) in it? Fish's reply to these objections was not too convincing at this point in time [107.52]: "Most literary quarrels are not disagreements about response, but about a response to a response. What happens to one informed reader will happen, within a range of nonessential variation, to another." In a short while (below, p. 127–130), we will see how Fish tried to bolster up this position by developing his concept of interpretive communities.

Overall, the attempts made by Fish and other literary critics to attack the New Critical orthodoxy that the "affective fallacy" must be avoided at all costs, were soon to be successful, and they caused a steady rise in interest for the instance of the reader and the act of reading. However, this development led to different consequences than on the German scene because precisely at the same time, different theoretical positions were monopolizing the public's attention in the USA: instead of advancing a full-blown aesthetics of reception, most American strands of reader-response criticism joined forces with these approaches, as will be seen in some examples: in one of his most well-known contributions, Barthes had written about the "death of the author" and claimed that this death was necessary for liberating the reader (below, p. 126); this was at the core of a connection between reader-response criticism and deconstruction (such as has been proposed by Culler [69.31–83]). Feminist strands of literary criticism were interested in examining aspects of a feminine readership (below, p. 185–186). Psychological and psychoanalytical approaches explored connections between reading experience and the creation of personal identity (below, p. 201). We have already seen the ways in which Riffaterre combined aspects of a receptionist reading of literary texts with the tenets of intertextuality (above, p. 79). Finally, we can briefly mention Culler's attempt to mediate between the extreme opposites of overly subjective interpretation in reader-response criticism and the danger of hypostatizing the "text in itself" to some solid, unmoving object: he tries to define a "literary competence" (for the concept of competence see above, pp. 27, 80) which is meant to navigate between Scylla and Charybdis.

This development helps us understand why there was not a single unified movement such as the Constance School: "Audience-oriented criticism is not one field but many, not a single widely trodden path but a multiplicity of criss-crossing, often divergent tracks," as Suleiman writes [343.6]. In a paradoxical manner, one could argue that reader-oriented approaches have been killed by their very success: many of their aspects and concepts have been integrated into the frameworks of several different strands of literary criticism; they have become so evidently useful for the daily work of critics that the necessity to have a "school" of its own for these concepts is not felt any longer.

Wheeler's Analysis of Ovid's *Metamorphoses*

The development we have just seen can be observed in classical scholarship as well: concepts such as the "implied reader" or the "horizon of expectations" have become part of the normal analytical toolbox of many scholars, even when they do not explicitly refer to the theories and hypotheses of reader-response criticism. As we have already seen (above, p. 86), this adoption of critical terms was facilitated by the fact that in ancient rhetoric and poetics, this orientation toward the reader was quite common. Furthermore, there are a large number of studies which try to utilize the strategies and key concepts of reader-response criticism in a more consistent and systematic manner (to quote just a few examples: Niall W. Slater on Petronius [331]; James Morrison on Homer [268]; Thomas A. Schmitz on Callimachus [320]; in connection with the methodology of narratology, John J. Winkler on Apuleius [380]). Here, we will look at a new interpretation of Ovid's *Metamorphoses* which makes fascinating use of the methodology of reader-response criticism.

When we see Stephen M. Wheeler dedicate the entire first chapter of his study *A Discourse of Wonders* [376] to a detailed examination of the first four lines of Ovid's poem, this can be understood as a clear hint that he is following Fish's lead. In particular, he concentrates on an ambivalence in the first sentence (which had already been noticed before): readers seeing the words *in noua fert animus* will at first tend to regard them as a syntactic unit and understand them as saying "my mind carries me into new, unknown realms." When reading on, however, they will correct this first impression and realize that *noua* is, in fact, an adjective belonging to *corpora* which depends on the participle *mutatas*: "My mind wants to tell about forms which have been transformed into new bodies." Yet our first interpretation does not become completely invalidated by this new reading; much rather, it remains part of our reading experience. The first metamorphosis in the *Metamorphoses* is this linguistic game [376.13]: "The experience of reading the sentence thus exemplifies and confirms Ovid's claim: transformation is the innovative incorporation of two statements into one."

In his analysis, Wheeler is careful to distinguish between the real author (the historical person P. Ouidius Naso), the implied author (the authorial instance as we construct it while reading the text), and the narrator of the story in the *Metamorphoses* [376.78]:

> In writing the *Metamorphoses*, the implied author adopts a narratorial persona: in this case, an epic poet "singing" a continuous song. When the Ovidian poet says in the proem that his inspiration moves him to tell of metamorphosis and he prays to the gods for help, this is not meant to be the record of a real event, but rather a fictional rendition, or imitation, of a bard (*vates*) beginning to rhapsodize. This pretense necessitates the involvement of a second type of audience, a narratorial audience, which is the fictional counterpart to the narrator.

Wheeler demonstrates that Ovid is extremely clever at playing with his public's reactions. On the one hand, readers are invited to adopt the role of the fictional audience that is listening to an oral bard improvising stories; on the other, they know that they are reading a book composed by a highly learned and refined poet. Wheeler points out, for instance, that Ovid's narrative contains a number of chronological inconsistencies. The public is thus provoked to compare two points of view: that of the audience who is listening to an oral narrator and is naively giving credence to his story, and that of the cultured reader who has a thorough knowledge of the narrated myths from other sources and is therefore able to recognize anachronisms.

Wheeler suggests that Ovid depicted this ambivalence explicitly in the numerous narratives which are inserted into the poem, some of them in complex frames. The reaction of the homodiegetic public (see above, p. 58) often oscillates between acceptance and skeptical rejection. Within the fictional world of the *Metamorphoses*, however, the skeptics are often punished for their behavior.

This becomes especially significant when we take into account that the emperor Augustus himself is depicted as being part of the audience of the *Metamorphoses* (this becomes clear, e.g., when the narrator addresses him with *tibi* "you" in 1.204–5). Thus, the tension between singing and writing, between acceptance and skepticism becomes a question of political ideology [376.185]: "What Ovid represents, in effect, is a model for how dissent is controlled in the early principate: he makes his audience complicit in accepting myths that enshrine the imperatives of a new social order." One could extend Wheeler's idea by pointing out that Ovid is at the same time undermining this process by drawing his public's attention to the fact that only a voluntary action of the audience, the acceptance of a certain point of view, bestows authority on these "noble" myths.

It is a difficult task for interpreters to come to grips with Ovid's ironical way of narrating which constantly wavers between apparent naiveté and superficial credulity on the one hand and tongue-in-cheek sophistication on the other. Wheeler's analysis of the way we read the *Metamorphoses* and of the role of the audience helps us gain a better understanding of these fascinating and important aspects of Ovid's text.

Further Reading

There are a number of excellent collections of articles for those who are interested in the various strands of reader-response crticism. If you read German and want to learn more about the Constance School and the German aesthetics of reception, you will find a collection of the most important programmatic statements as well as a very knowledgeable and helpful introduction by the editor in Rainer Warning's volume [370]. There are two fine collections of articles mainly of American reader-response criticism: the volume edited by Susan R. Suleiman and Inge Crosman [344] as well as the one by Jane P. Tompkins [357]; both also contain immensely useful annotated bibliographies. Harald Weinrich's slim volume *Literature for Readers* [373] is highly recommended, if you read German (no English translation is available). Concerning the application of reader-response criticism to classical literature, one can refer to volume 19.2 (1986) of the journal *Arethusa* which is a special issue on the topic "Audience-Oriented Criticism and the Classics." The German scholar Wilfried Barner has given a number of suggestions to classicists [21] which are still worth consulting. Lowell Edmunds refers explicitly to Jauss and Iser in his interpretation of Horace's Soracte Ode (*carm.* 1.9), but the results are not entirely convincing (see the discussion of Edmunds's approach in Ruurd R. Nauta's contribution [273]), and there is no consistent application or discussion of the methodology of the Constance School.

Chapter 7
Orality – Literacy

The field which is the subject of this chapter cannot be called a theoretical position or a methodology in the narrow sense of the word. Nevertheless, scholarship in this area has had profound and far-reaching effects on our understanding of literature. Moreover, this is an interesting case, where an approach was orginally developed in the field of classical literature and is still extremely important in our own discipline. Hence, it seems justified to dedicate a chapter of its own to these questions and problems. We will start by looking at the general theoretical positions and their implications for literary criticism at large before turning to their origin and implications in classics in particular.

Most of the time, scholars active in the field of literary criticism regarded it as self-evident that they were dealing with texts which were available in written form, most often as printed books. It is true that those in some areas (such as classics or the study of medieval literatures) were aware that because of the special conditions of transmission, the texts they were looking at could not simply be considered as fixed and reliable, but had to be reconstructed through painstaking work. Some scholars were also keenly aware that dramatic texts such as tragedies or comedies were not meant for silent reading in an armchair, but were recited and sung by actors and chorists who were acting and dancing on a stage, accompanied by musical instruments. It was even acknowledged that, for example, ancient lyric was composed for such musical performances and that the text alone, which in general is all that a modern reader still has before her or him, represents, very much like the libretto of a modern opera, merely part of the original audience's experience. Nonetheless, these qualities were most often considered mere details; scholars paid lip service to these aspects without really taking them into account for their interpretations. In the end, ancient drama or lyric was interpreted in pretty much the same manner as, for example, a poem by Rilke which was from the start composed with a view to appearing in print.

Oral Cultures: The Theses of Goody and Watt

From the early 1950s, a number of scholars found this state of affairs unsatisfactory. Some of the reasons which contributed to this feeling of uneasiness were:

- In the field of ancient texts, an ever growing number of classicists pointed out that long periods of antiquity had not known writing or had at least not used it in the same way as we do today. Until the end of the fifth century BCE, literature was not primarily composed for reading, but for oral performance and for listening. These scholars insisted that this observation should play a more prominent part in our interpretations of these texts.
- Even in the modern world, scholarship detected numerous cultures which either did not know writing and reading at all or used it much less extensively than our own Western civilization. In these cultures, we often encounter great bodies of oral poetry. Comparative studies of such cultures (such as Yugoslavia in the 1930s, tribes in Africa, or the Aborigines in Australia) demonstrated that these different bodies of oral texts, despite their complete isolation, had a surprising number of common features. This fact could most easily be explained by the assumption that there is a specifically oral mode of poetry and narrative.
- Finally, this thesis was elaborated and extended in the 1960s and 1970s. One of the main hypotheses proposed by the Canadian intellectual Marshall McLuhan (1911–80), who was especially influential in the USA, was that messages transmitted in some form of communication are not independent from the manner in which they are communicated; rather, the means of transmission will have profound and far-reaching effects on the content of the message (this idea is often referred to in the aphoristic statement "the medium is the message"). A number of scholars argued that this principle is especially important for orality: it shapes the minds of listeners and speakers in an essential manner; one can even speak of a specifically oral mindset.

This approach draws a sharp distinction between orality (which is prevalent in a great number of societies) and our modern fixation with reading and writing; it considers the introduction of literacy as perhaps the most important intellectual innovation in human history. This position found its most pointed and most provocative formulation in an essay published jointly by the British anthropologist Jack Goody (b. 1919) and the American literary critic Ian Watt (1917–99) [144]. They proposed the hypothesis of "strong" orality which they argued had a decisive influence on a number of social and cultural factors; this thesis was soon adopted and elaborated by other scholars. According to these thinkers, writing is not just one among several tools used by humans, but determines our entire mental activity. Our modern world is so much accustomed to and dominated by texts, i.e., by writing, that people today find it immensely difficult and laborious to imagine what an oral society and its specific outlook on the world is like. But historically speaking, this "literal" orientation is an exception, not the rule. Seen over the long course of human history, writing is a late invention that had little or no bearing on most human civilizations. Scholars of this school argue that most qualities which we ascribe to so-called primitive societies really are consequences of this orality which influenced and shaped all intellectual activities. They insist, however, that this "oral thought" is by no means underdeveloped or inferior to literacy. Much rather, we are dealing with a fundamentally different mode of functioning of the human mind which needs to be explored and understood in its own right. Here are some of the numerous characteristics which these scholars think define this oral mode of thinking:

- The isolated word, the isolated text do not exist in oral societies. Every communication takes place in a precise context which is common to both speaker and listener. Behind every utterance stands a speaker who is clearly identifiable and who warrants his words with his person and his authority. The idea of the "autonomous text," so important to formalism and structuralism (above, pp. 20–23), is, according to this hypothesis, a clear instance of "literal thinking" which cannot be applied to oral societies.

- In oral societies, there is no means of conserving and transmitting knowledge and the results of mental activities other than constant repetition. If you have any kind of complex philosophical insight in such a society, you cannot simply write it down for further reflection the next day, but have to formulate it in a way which will allow you to reproduce it later. If such a culture wants to transmit information or laws, this has to be done in oral performances and continual reiterations. These factors make it paramount for all kinds of important texts to be formulated in a way which will ensure that they are easy to memorize. Hence, they are characterized by a number of qualities which will facilitate memorization (mnemonic qualities). Among other things, this can be a preference for rhythm (a long series of metrical lines is much easier to memorize than an equally long passage of prose), a high degree of redundancy, and formularity which tends to use the same words and combinations for the same content (whereas literal language is marked by an avoidance of such repetition and a striving for variation).

꣠ While for members of a literate society, words have a fixed form because of their unchanging appearance in writing, members of oral societies perceive language in a profoundly different manner. They cannot look up words in a dictionary; instead, their meaning is always exclusively determined by their context; they are a volatile linguistic phenomenon that does not leave unchanging traces. Therefore, oral cultures tend to preserve only words which are useful and relevant in their immediate circumstances; everything else falls into disuse and is soon forgotten. Changes in these circumstances trigger changes in language, but these changes usually go unnoticed because there are no controlling authorities (such as historical dictionaries or preserved ancient texts).

꣠ The same is true for the perception of the past in general: oral societies do not have historical documents available. They derive knowledge of the past from the living memories of the oldest members of their groups on the one hand and from oral traditions handed down through the generations on the other. But since such traditions are primarily targeted at being relevant for the present, such cultures tend to transform past traditions so that they conform to present expectations. One particularly instructive example can be found in the essay published by Goody and Watt [144.32–3]: for members of the Tiv in modern Nigeria, genealogical ties are an important criterion for deciding competing claims and legal issues. Hence, oral tradition constantly repeats such genealogical information. British colonial authorities, who realized how important such historical traditions were for the tribe, therefore produced written versions of these genealogies to use them as evidence in court. But when, around 40 years later, anthropologists were doing fieldwork in this area, it turned out that the Tiv still found the evidence of these genealogies paramount, but the genealogies had, in the meantime, changed in a number of important details. The Tiv insisted that their own (oral) version was correct while the version preserved in writing simply was wrong. In the intervening years, the past had been changed to conform to the present situation. Yet the respective version of the past is always considered as the only true and reliable version, and in purely oral societies, there is generally no means for comparing several versions of past events. To make a more general statement: one can say that in oral cultures, only facts that are relevant for the present are preserved; everything else falls into oblivion. Hence, such cultures are termed to be "homeostatic": they live in an apparently unchanging world, without any consciousness of historical change. Written documents, on the other hand, facilitate perceptions of the difference between the past and the present and thus make historical change discernible.

ชิ๖ Finally, we can say that literacy has a tendency to separate texts and the knowledge preserved in them from their original authors and thereby create a detached, objectifying relation toward linguistic utterances. In oral cultures, the opposite is true: words are perceived as being intimately tied to their origin, their speaker; listeners feel invited not just to understand them rationally, but to react to them emotionally. Therefore, scholars from this strand of thought describe oral cultures as being characterized by the warmth of personal relationships.

What Does "Orality" Mean?

The last point in the preceding list will help us understand why opposition to this "strong" orality was swift to form. The attempt to define oral culture by contrasting it with our modern literate culture entails a danger of idealizing orality and seeing it as some kind of paradisal society which is free from all the aberrations and inconveniences which make life in our modern world so burdensome (such as the lack of intimate personal ties, or "cold" and objective science). This version of speculation, then, can be seen in the tradition of Romanticism and its longing for some original unity lost in the modern world, formulated by thinkers such as Jean-Jacques Rousseau (1712–78) or Johann Gottfried Herder (1744–1803). Romantic philosophy often expressed a disillusionment with the modern world and dreamed of an original natural state in which human society was still marked by unity and poetry would spontaneously spring from the voice of the people. Hence, critics of this strong version of orality argue that its adherents import their own utopian desires and fantasies into their analysis of oral cultures. Moreover, one of the arguments summarized above can be turned against this hypothesis itself: its proponents claim that many qualities which we generally consider as being characteristic of "primitive" societies really are consequences of orality. Opponents, on the other hand, argue that these scholars run the risk of subsuming numerous traits under the rubric of "orality," which are in reality effects of the state of development of these cultures. Orality, these critics suggest, is not the single cause for the qualities and attitudes we have seen above, but merely one among several aspects of societies at a certain stage.

Furthermore, more recent analyses often attempt to avoid generalizations. They do not claim to define what is typical for all sorts of orality, but try to provide in-depth explorations of concrete cases which often show how problematic general statements are. The use of writing, for instance, can fulfill extremely different social functions in different societies. Cultures in which writing is primarily used by merchants for economic purposes are quite different from societies in which it is used by officials for administrative means; priests can use writing for cultic and ritual functions, and societies in which this use dominates will again be different from ones in which writing is mastered by a very small elite only for their own artistic and cultural production. Only in a few societies is writing used by the majority of people for everyday purposes. Factors which seem quite unimportant indeed can produce momentous differences: is the writing system easy to learn and handle (such as an alphabetic script), or is it a complex system, like Chinese writing with its thousands of characters? Are writing materials very expensive, or cheap and easy to obtain? Are they easy to handle, or do they require a great amount of manual dexterity and extensive training? These material factors can play a decisive role in shaping the entire attitude of a culture toward writing and reading. If we consider how different the use of writing in cultures can be, it becomes almost impossible to speak of literacy in general.

In a similar manner, scholars have become increasingly reluctant to give a general definition of orality. Cultures that do not know writing exhibit a much wider range of attitudes than the generalizing account given above may suggest. Hence, new studies are more interested in examining and analyzing the ways in which a given culture utilizes the written word than in making general statements about orality in itself. Moreover (and this is especially important concerning classical antiquity), more recent scholarship no longer accepts a clear-cut binary opposition of "orality vs. literacy." Even in modern societies like our own which makes intensive and extensive use of writing, there are large parts of life that are dominated by oral communication (scholars who work in universities and spend most of their waking hours with books and in libraries are likely to overestimate the importance of texts and of writing in human life). It goes without saying that this caveat is even more important for the ancient world. The use of writing did not influence the entire society immediately after it had been introduced, nor did this literacy destroy the preexisting orality. More recent studies explore the manifold aspects of this coexistence of orality and literacy by looking at concrete cases; they criticize older theories for being less accurate because of overgeneralization.

It is difficult to decide which way of exploring orality and literacy is better. There can be no doubt that we have to be careful with generalizations: very few scholars indeed possess enough knowledge to provide thorough and mean-

ingful comparisons between a representative number of different cultures and
thus distinguish what is really typical from what is coincidental. On the other
hand, the obvious differences in the use of writing and in oral societies should
not make us abandon any attempt at generalizations altogether. Of course, generalizing always means dispensing with details, but it can be argued that leaving
out irrelevant elements and teasing out structural equivalences between general
characteristics is an essential part of any scholarly or scientific activity, as much
as paying attention to fine differences. What is certain: there is still a field wide
open to future research in analyzing and comparing various cultures and the
different ways of using oral and written communication they exhibit.

Oral Poetry

This rather lengthy general introduction was necessary to demonstrate some of
the questions and problems that are inherent in research discussing the uses
of orality and literacy. We will now turn to the field of literary studies where
this approach has been most fruitful. Scholars generally avoid speaking of "oral
literature" because this juxtaposition is considered as being contradictory: the
word "literature" is etymologically derived from Latin *littera* "letter," so the idea
of writing is already inherent in it. Instead, the term "oral poetry" has gained
common acceptance. As we have mentioned (above, p. 100), oral societies have
a general predilection for metrical texts, because of their mnemonic quality.
Hence, scholarly attention has focused on oral poetry, especially in a comparative perspective which takes into account poetical texts from a great many human cultures. Yet we should be aware that in oral texts, there is no absolutely
clear boundary between prose and poetry, and it should also be noted that there
is a great amount of oral prose (such as folk tales or myths) which must not be
neglected. In the following pages, however, we will concentrate on the field of
oral poetry because it is of essential importance for ancient literature.

The first question we must ask is: What exactly are the defining qualities
of oral poetry? Scholarship has pointed out three aspects which define orality; their respective importance is a matter of discussion: (1) oral composition;
(2) oral transmission; (3) oral performance. Each of these criteria brings its own
set of questions and problems:

1   It has often been argued that the term "oral poetry" should be reserved for
    poets who improvise their texts while declaiming (composing) them. How-
    ever, comparative studies of several oral poets across different cultures seem

to suggest that there is a much wider range of possibilities: some poets, for instance, need a rather long period of time for preparation and then declaim their text from memory, as it were.

2   When can transmission be called oral? Is it sufficient for a text to be written down at some arbitrary point in its transmission for its oral status to be destroyed, even if there is some other branch of oral transmission, completely independent from this written version? Anthropological research has often had a certain tendency to regard everything written with a certain amount of contempt because it is no longer "purely" oral.

3   Even for written texts, oral performance can be the only or at least the predominant mode of reception. Greek tragedies, for instance, existed in written form – poets had to submit a copy of the play to participate in the Dionysiac contests. Yet for author and audience alike, it was the actual performance that was regarded as important, not this written copy (only at the end of the fifth century BCE do we hear of people who actually read these scripts). Are tragedies oral poetry, then?

What is particularly impressive about research in oral poetry is the breadth of comparative studies. Scholars have analyzed numerous cultures across the entire world and explored the poetic texts they produce, and there can be no doubt that this broadening of our horizon has been especially helpful for classics as a discipline: comparing our material with more exotic traditions has helped us understand the specificities of classical texts. A more thorough discussion is beyond the scope of this book; I can only refer readers to studies such as Cecil M. Bowra's book *Heroic Poetry* [44].

Overall, it can be said that the study of oral poetry has undergone a development comparable to scholarship on orality in general: in a first phase, scholars were enthusiastic about the material available for comparison, most of which had hitherto been unknown. The common features between cultures which were geographically and temporally remote from each other impressed them, so many attempts were made to give a unifying theory of oral poetry as a whole or at least of a genre such as oral epic as a whole. Later scholars became increasingly skeptical about such generalizations; they tend to emphasize how various oral traditions across the world really are. However, there is a certain danger that scholars will withdraw into their own special subfields and thus waste the opportunities that a truly comparable approach may offer.

Finally, it should be clear that analyzing oral poetry will necessarily involve giving up an approach which concentrates exclusively on the text itself. For scholars active in this field, the object which they study is not primarily "the words on the page" (see above, p. 90), but instead the actual, living performance with all its details: the voice, the facial expression and body movements of the performer, the interaction of performer and audience, the social situation in which the performance takes place, the rank and roles of all those who take part in them, and many other aspects need to be taken into account. Hence, there are not only literary critics doing research in this field, but also scholars from other disciplines such as anthropology, sociology, or the study of religion. These questions concerning the social function of poetry, the social position of poets, and the interaction between poet and public are certainly not restricted to oral poetry, but because of the immediate presence of this social context, they impose themselves with particular clarity and intensity.

The Homeric Epics as a Test Case

After examining the general theses and problems about orality, we will now turn to an example from classical literature. This procedure puts things in a reverse chronological order: the debate about the nature of the Homeric epics, which will be our ancient example in this chapter, was what motivated interest in oral poetry in the first place. Whoever reads the *Iliad* and the *Odyssey* cannot but realize that this poetry exhibits a number of features which make it quite different from the epic works of, say, Virgil or Ovid. Scholarly work on the Homeric poems had already begun in antiquity itself, yet the beginning of the problem which will interest us here can be dated to the modern period with a great deal of accuracy: the "Homeric question" was triggered by the publication, in 1795, of the *Prolegomena ad Homerum* by the German scholar Friedrich August Wolf (1759–1824). Wolf tried to explain the peculiarities of the epics by proposing a number of hypotheses that were revolutionary in his time. He conjectured that the poet Homer lived in a period when writing was as yet unknown in Greece. Wolf believed that therefore, it was impossible for the epics to have been composed in the form and size as we know them; poems of such length, he thought, exceeded the capabilities of a poet working in an oral environment. Instead, he argued that a number of smaller, independent epic songs had at first been composed and transmitted orally; it was only some centuries later that some editor, with the help of writing, collected them into the form as we know it today. This long period of oral transmission was the cause of numerous additions, transformations, and adaptations which radically changed the original shape of the epics.

As we can see, Wolf's suggestion made Homer into a representative of some oral mode of poetry, but neither Wolf himself nor his successors, who took up his hypothesis and developed it further, had any clear view of what was special about oral poetry. Instead, research about the Homeric epics attempted to isolate these older songs from the transmitted poems. Scholars were quite optimistic in believing that it was possible to recognize, with a great deal of precision, where exactly later editors had patched these songs together. However, when we think about it, we see that this approach presupposed something which is alien to the epics' oral origin: it takes for granted that the older songs, in spite of transformations and patches, were still quite stable and possessed a fixed text. It is obvious that modern literacy here prevented these scholars from imagining what orality really meant: for an oral poet, there is no fixed text; instead, the epic is created anew at every performance. But scholars imbibed in a modern literate culture could not conceive of this radically different status of an oral poem, and this contradiction went unnoticed. Hence, for a long time, there were two opposing camps in Homeric scholarship: while the "analytics" tried to isolate and define older strata of the text of the Homeric epics and were convinced that the transmitted form of the text is a hodgepodge of songs put together by inept editors at a later stage, the "unitarians" defended the transmitted text as a perfectly organic whole and tried to demonstrate its artistic unity.

It is rather unusual for the work of a single scholar to be so influential, but the American philologist Milman Parry (1902–35) changed the discussion about the Homeric epics fundamentally with his contributions. He created an entirely new way of looking at and interpreting these texts, and our image of the *Iliad* and the *Odyssey* will never be the same again. It is certainly not the case that all scholars after Parry have accepted his theses at face value, but scholarly discussion of the Homeric epics is absolutely impossible without a profound grasp of this new approach (there is a convenient collection and translation of Parry's writings with an excellent introduction by his son, in his *Collected Papers* [283]). Parry's main thesis was that the peculiarities of Homeric style become explicable only if we suppose that the poet improvised his epic texts in oral performances. The oral singer certainly had some rather rough plan of events and scenes he wanted to deal with, but the text itself was the momentary creation of the performance. This explains a number of salient features that no reader can fail to realize. What is striking in the Homeric epics is repetition on all levels:

ᛒ The main characters of the epics receive stereotyped attributes that recur again and again, such as "swift-footed Achilleus" or "much-enduring divine

Odysseus."

ॐ Parts of lines or entire lines are repeated several times, such as the introduction of a speech ("and addressing him (s)he spoke") or the description of
   dawn ("when appeared the early-born rosy-fingered dawn").

ॐ Certain typical scenes recur several times and are described in lines that are
   nearly identical; this is true, e.g., for sacrifice, eating, or arrival.

In all these repetitions, Parry sees a system which is meant to facilitate the
task of a poet who is orally improvising his text. If you want to extemporize
an extended narrative or even a whole epic, you will need some tools of this
sort which will allow you to think about what and how to tell next while you
are almost mechanically declaiming the current scene. According to Parry, it
is impossible for this extended system to have been invented by a single poet;
instead, it must be the product of many generations of oral bards improvising
epic poetry.

Parry claims this system is marked by two qualities, economy and depth. In
order to fit the name of his main character, Odysseus, into the metrical lines, the
oral poet has a wide range of combinations of different forms of the name and
attributes (so-called noun-epithet formulae) available, but there is exactly one
form for every metrical position – so the bard did not have to take any decision
at all as to which combination to utilize in a given line; he could proceed quite
mechanically. This is what Parry called the "economy" of the system. "Depth"
is his term for the fact that for the main characters of the epics, there is a wide
range of formulae ready for use, for different metrical positions and different
grammatical cases. This entails important consequences for our interpretation
of the Homeric epics: the choice of a particular attribute for an epic character is not an expression of a specific meaning, but is exclusively determined by
the metrical conditions of the line in which the character is named; basically,
all these combinations mean nothing more than just "Odysseus," "Achilleus," or
"Agamemnon." In Virgil, we are invited to wonder why Aeneas is called *pius* in
a certain line, in a certain situation; in the Homeric epics, it is only a question
of metrical convenience whether Odysseus, in a certain scene, will be called "divine," or "son of Laërtes," or "crafty." An interpretation of these attributes, then,
is impossible.

Parry's new approach explains a number of characteristics of the Homeric
language which had been difficult to understand before, such as the fact that
his language uses words and forms from several Greek dialects. For a long time,
scholars had wondered whether this was a mark of a certain geographical origin,

a region where dialects overlapped and mixed, or whether Homer lived in a period where rapid linguistic change occurred, but this seemed difficult to imagine because there was such a wild mixture of forms. According to Parry, this variety was used because the improvising bards kept whichever form had proved to be metrically convenient.

At first, Parry emphasized that this formulaic system was a clear mark of a long poetic tradition. It became increasingly clear to him that it was a specific characteristic of orally improvising bards when he performed fieldwork in what was then Yugoslavia in 1933–5. There was still a vivid tradition of oral epic in this area then. Parry recorded a number of such songs and observed striking structural similarities to the Homeric epics: there were recurring metrical formulae, stereotypical introductory lines for direct speech, and fixed noun-epithet combinations. After Parry's untimely death, his research assistant Albert Lord (1912–91) continued his work. It was Lord who published, in 1960, the most systematic account of this hypothesis in his book *The Singer of Tales* [241]: Homer, so this book claimed, was an oral bard improvising his narrative and quite similar in nature to the singers who are still active in some cultures in the modern world. Generations of such bards had learned from each other the difficult trade of extemporizing lines in the complex form system of the dactylic hexameter; in the course of many centuries, they have thus produced a complicated system of formulae and recurring elements. The *Iliad* and the *Odyssey* are merely a small part of this tradition, transmitted by chance, which consisted of a large number of oral epic narratives, similar to the Homeric epics, that were sung in Homer's time.

These "Parry–Lord theses" have fundamentally changed the direction of Homeric scholarship. Discussing older songs and miniature epics, analyzing their boundaries, and dissecting their contradictions, as the "analytics" had done for such a long time, now became completely meaningless, if these epics really are orally improvised texts. Parry's hypothesis has found wide acceptance, especially in the English-speaking world, where a great number of scholars today are convinced that the *Iliad* and the *Odyssey* are examples of oral poetry. It took longer for this momentous change to become acknowledged and discussed in Germany (which was, after all, the origin of the older analytical school), but a few key concepts and arguments seem universally accepted today:

- The Homeric language is an artificial dialect that has never and nowhere been used for normal communication; its origins are the metrical requirements of the epic verse.

ə♦ The style of the Homeric epics is profoundly influenced by the traditions of orally improvising poets; many peculiarities can be explained by this influence.

However, this does not mean that the Parry–Lord theses as a whole are accepted by all scholars. Even if we admit the main arguments, there are a number of questions to which satisfactory answers are still to be found: when exactly was the text of the *Iliad* and the *Odyssey* fixed in writing? Which circumstances induced this fixation? Are these epics, with their complex structure and their system of preparation and flashbacks, really comparable in artistic quality to the products of other oral traditions? Can the apparent stability of their text be reconciled with the assumption of a relatively long period of oral transmission?

Moreover, there are a number of serious objections against Parry's hypotheses. First, we now know that Greek culture before Homer had not been completely ignorant of writing, as had been assumed for a long time. The excavations at Mycenaean sites had produced a large number of inscribed clay tablets, but it was not until 1953 that two English scholars, Michael Ventris and John Chadwick, succeeded in demonstrating that the language written in this syllabic script (which is called "Linear B") is not some unknown pre-Hellenic idiom but an early form of Greek [365]. However, this early literate culture seems to have been destroyed together with the palaces in the twelfth century BCE, in circumstances that are still mysterious. Hence, the Greeks had to learn writing a second time some centuries later; however, this time they adopted an alphabetic script which they took over from the Phoenicians. The exact date when this new system was introduced in Greece is still debated, but it looks as if this must have been at the beginning of the eighth century BCE at the latest, possibly some time before that. Hence it is clear that the composition of the Homeric epics did not take place in an exclusively oral society; we have to take into account the possibility that their poet knew and made use of the new technique of writing when he conceived of these works.

Moreover, more thorough studies of the style of the epics have produced further evidence which call the Parry–Lord theses into question. The epics, it has been shown, do not use all noun-epithet formulae for the characters without any distinction, but reserve some of them exclusively for speeches of the characters, others for the text of the main narrator – can we believe that an orally improvising bard would have been capable of making such a fine distinction? Recent studies criticize Parry for relying on concordances when he analyzed

Homer's use of names and epithets. Parry failed to take into account that characters are also referred to by way of circumlocutions or pronouns. Scholars, especially in Germany, have pointed out that there are subtle correspondences between passages separated by many thousands of lines, and have argued that this can only have been achieved if the poet used writing for composing his work.

An end to this debate is not in sight. It is clear that the *Iliad* and the *Odyssey* are intimately linked to a very ancient oral tradition, but it remains a matter of contention in which relation our epics stand to this tradition. Every possible position has its own share of difficulties and open questions:

ех The *Iliad* and the *Odyssey* are themselves products of oral poetry. Does this mean that the form of the text as we have it is merely fortuitous? But why were these particular poems in this particular form preserved; why does their text appear to have been pretty stable from the very beginning?

ех Our epics are related to this oral tradition, but their composer knew and made use of writing. But how are we to imagine the composition of such a long text in this early period? Which writing material did the poet use (animal skins?), why do we have no further written documents of comparable size, and what motivated someone to write these poems down?

It may be true that there will never be a definitive answer to such questions, but I hope the fundamental change in Homeric scholarship induced by the discussion of orality and literacy has become more comprehensible. For us, Homer is the beginning of Greek and hence of European literary history, yet paradoxically, he stands at the same time at the end of a long poetical tradition.

Finally, I can do no more than merely mention that not only the Homeric epics, but Greek culture until the fourth century BCE as a whole has been regarded as an example of a predominantly oral society by some scholars. Accordingly, they have used the theses of a strong orality as described by Goody and Watt in order to understand and explain Greek culture. There is an intense and fruitful discussion of these matters in our discipline, and we have certainly learned a great deal about the characteristics of archaic Greek culture.

Further Reading

As explained above, the groundbreaking and canonical exposition of the characteristics of orality can be found in the essay by Jack Goody and Ian Watt [144]. Another momentous influence have been the writings of Marshall McLuhan,

who described the fundamental consequences of a number technological innovations such as writing and printing in the vivid metaphor of the "Gutenberg
Galaxy" and who coined such well-known expressions as "the global village."
Walter J. Ong, who was a student of McLuhan's, has written a careful and comprehensible introduction into all aspects of the field of orality [282]. Rosalind
Thomas has written an excellent overview about orality and literacy in antiquity
[350]; for those who read German, there is a short and helpful introduction in
an article by Øivind Andersen [5].

Chapter 8
Deconstruction

Probably no other approach in literary theory has met with such vehement and severe, sometimes unfair and hostile criticism as deconstruction. Russian Formalism and structuralism had undoubtedly been distasteful to many traditional scholars, but it turned out that the new concepts and methodologies developed by these approaches could be assimilated and integrated into more conventional forms of literary criticism without destroying or completely overturning them. This was different with deconstruction: it claimed to possess a number of intellectual pretensions and asserted that its consequences were so radically at odds with all conventional forms of literary theory that most scholars considered either enthusiastic acceptance or bitter resistance the only choices available. Moreover, a number of tenets of deconstruction were promulgated by the mass media to a larger reading public, often in a provocative and inflated manner; this also created much hostility in the academic landscape. But it should also be noted that the adherents of deconstruction themselves had their share of guilt in making the debate more and more shrill and emotional: some of their pronouncements were clearly aimed at provoking by endorsing extreme positions and thus bluffing and ridiculing their opponents ("épater le bourgeois," "shocking middle-class attitudes" was the name given to this behavior in the nineteenth century). These opponents reacted with ad hominem attacks, some of them vehement and vitriolic: for René Wellek, deconstruction is a "new apocalyptic irrationalism" [374.99]; José G. Merquior calls it "the dismal unscience of our time" [255.236], and Wendell V. Harris simply terms it "intellectual debris" [171.5].

As we will see in this chapter, there are various reasons why deconstruction was regarded as such a threat to literary studies (or even to Western civilization as a whole) and why it split the public into ardent supporters and adamant opponents. For a (relatively short) period in the late 1970s and early 1980s, deconstruction was so dominant on the scene of literary criticism, especially in the USA, that many readers considered it representative of literary theory as a whole. A regrettable consequence of this was that for a while, any dialogue between more "progressive" theoreticians and more "traditional" interpreters was made difficult or even impossible. Only since the late 1990s has there been a cautious rapprochement of both camps.

For many traditional critics, the pedigree of deconstruction is already a cause for being suspicious about its qualities. Its main tenets are derived from the works of the French philosopher Jacques Derrida (1930–2004). But it is certainly wrong to say (as has sometimes been done) that a transfer of these philosophical concepts to the sphere of literary studies creates problems: Derrida's writings are usually situated on the boundaries of philosophy and literary studies. He develops his most important ideas by interpreting texts and by reading philosophy as literature and vice versa. Therefore, in a first step, we will examine some of Derrida's key concepts before turning to their implications for literary criticism.

Derrida often formulates his own concepts in extended discussions of the works of earlier thinkers (such as Nietzsche, Heidegger, or Rousseau, to name but a few), and most of these arguments can serve as introductions to the ideas of deconstruction. We will begin by looking at his criticism of Saussure's structuralist linguistics, because this is the area where the consequences of Derrida's idea for literary criticism are most immediately perceptible.

The Foundations: Derrida's Criticism of Logocentrism

Derrida begins his reading of Saussure's lectures with a passage that may, at first glance, appear trivial or irrelevant. Saussure claims emphatically that linguistics is not concerned with written texts, but with the spoken word, and he devotes a lengthy passage to a criticism of writing [315.23–32]. Derrida wonders to what extent this censure of writing is necessary and justified within Saussure's system. What, he asks, is the essence of writing, in abstraction from all contingent factors which may vary across different cultures and periods? Derrida sees two elementary and stable qualities in writing [75.44–6]:

- The letters of a word designate its phonetic value in an arbitrary fashion. The connection between the visible form of the letter "a" in a given script and its pronunciation is by no means "natural," but determined by the conventions of a particular culture.
- Writing makes a sign permanent. The letters "hat" serve as a signifier of

the corresponding phonetic value even though (or better: especially when) the speaking voice is absent. These letters can be retranslated into linguistic sounds by different speakers, at different occasions, and will always be perceptible as identical to themselves.

Derrida points out that according to these qualities, writing is a model of any kind of language as Saussure himself had defined it; more than that: we can imagine a sign system as described by Saussure which could dispense with phonetic utterances (above, p. 28, we have seen that a system like traffic signs is a perfectly valid example for a language according to Saussure), but no sign system can do without these essential qualities of writing. The sound of the human voice is a volatile event which lasts only a tiny fragment of a second. If these short phenomena are to be recognizable as identical in nature, if hearers are to perceive that the phonetic value "hat" as realized by two different speakers is indeed the same and evokes the same signified, a certain idea of writing must exist. Of course, Derrida does not mean to say that language could not emerge before the existence of any concrete writing system. What he wants to show is that the qualities of writing outlined above are at the core of any system of signs. Derrida terms this "writing before writing" "arche-writing" [75.56–7]; there is a clear account of what this concept entails in an essay published in his *Margins of Philosophy* [78.312–18].

Derrida's interpretation of and argumentative engagement with Saussure's ideas can serve as a model of a deconstructionist reading. We can summarize some of the strategies of deconstruction which Derrida employs in his reading:

   As we have seen (above, p. 32), structuralist thought regularly emphasizes the importance of binary oppositions. Faced with such an opposition, deconstruction sees its own task as twofold: (1) it tries to demonstrate that such an opposition is always based on a hierarchy – one of the two opposing elements is typically valued higher than its counterpart and is the center of the structure. There are numerous examples for such "violent hierarchies" [77.41–2]: good vs. bad, nature vs. culture, male vs. female. Derrida emphasizes that Saussure, in defining the opposition "orality vs. writing," makes the first term the center of his thinking and is forced to discredit writing as an object of linguistic examination. (2) Furthermore, Derrida tries to show that this seemingly inferior, excluded negative pole of the opposition really is necessary for it to function: we cannot imagine a linguistic system without writing because "there is no linguistic sign before writing" [75.14].

In a similar reading of one of Rousseau's texts, Derrida speaks of a "supplement" [75.141–57]. The term supplement has two different, contradictory meanings: on the one hand, we call supplement something added to a whole which is already complete of and by itself – an encyclopedia has covered the entire range of the alphabet from "A" to "Z"; then, a series of supplemental volumes is added. On the other hand, the fact that such an addition was possible and necessary is proof that the original completeness was only apparent: the original body already had some lacuna which had to be filled up by a supplement.

ટ્ This idea of the supplement helps us understand what is the goal of deconstruction. Derrida is not interested in overturning Saussure's hierarchy and arguing that writing is and should be the center of the linguistic system. Instead, he wants to demonstrate that every hierarchy always (or "always already," as Derrida is fond of saying, quoting a formulation by the German philosopher Edmund Husserl [1859–1938]) carries within itself the material for its own subversion – deconstruction is not something which is applied to a text from without; much rather, when looking closely at a text, interpreters will realize that it is deconstructing itself.

We now have to understand that Derrida's deconstruction of this opposition and this hierarchy in Saussure's *Course* is not a trivial footnote to an obscure aspect of structuralism, but instead regards one of the central elements not only of Saussure's work, but of large parts of Western thought in general. In his *Course*, Saussure emphasizes the importance of his criticism of writing, thus placing himself in the line of a great number of thinkers who maintain that "the letter killeth, but the spirit giveth life" (*2 Corinthians* 3:6). The earliest and most vigorous formulation of this criticism of writing can be found in one of Plato's dialogues, the *Phaedrus*. In it, Socrates has a long discussion with his young friend Phaedrus and narrates how the Egyptian god Thoth invented writing. Socrates then goes on to criticize this invention: unlike oral communication and instruction, writing can never be more than a "game" (παιδιά). Written words can never enter into an exchange with their readers; as Plato says, writing can never defend itself, but is in need of its "father" (i.e., its author) to help it. But once he has sent the written text into the world, this father will be unable to prevent it from becoming severed from the original context of its communication and running into situations where it will be misunderstood. Hence, a real philosopher will never commit his most important ideas to such a dangerous and feeble medium as writing, but will reserve them for oral instruction.

For Derrida, Plato's condemnation of writing is not a fortuitous whim or a personal predilection; he calls it [78.316] "the philosophical movement par excellence." He asks what makes writing so questionable in the eyes of Plato and a number of other philosophers, and he lists the following qualities:

- A written message does not presuppose the presence of its creator and its origin (its author) nor of its addressee; it is produced in a way that ensures it will function in their absence.
- Similarly, writing functions in the absence of its context: the objects it refers to, the situation in which it was uttered, etc. A written word is always liable to be "taken out of context," to be quoted, repeated, uprooted, and transplanted.
- Because of this double absence, the meaning of something expressed in writing is not immediately present, but has to be reconstructed by its addressee (through interpretation); this can induce misunderstandings.

As for Saussure's attempt to exclude writing from his structural analysis of language, Derrida claims that these criticisms do not concern writing alone, but language in general. Language can only be imagined as a social meaning shared by a group of speakers and listeners. Every linguistic utterance can always (already) be repeated in the absence of its author and its context (an aspect which Derrida terms "iterability"); without this "citability," it would be impossible to use language. Every linguistic utterance can be misunderstood by being severed from its origin and its context.

Behind this disparagement of writing, then, Derrida sees a general fear of linguistic iterability, or, to put it in positive terms: a desire to fix the meaning of linguistic utterances once and for all by tying them to their origin, to guarantee the fullness of their sense by recurring to their author's presence. Derrida calls this desire phonocentrism: the living voice (Greek φωνή) appears as an assurance that this fullness of sense is possible because we can always perceive the living speaker behind this voice. And the speaker, while he hears herself or himself speaking (Derrida's succinct and elegant French formulation "s'entendre parler" receives the rather clunky translation "hearing (understanding)-oneself-speak" [75.7]), has access to her or his own ideas. (S)he perceives not only the signifiers (which may be ambivalent or even deceptive), but also the signified itself, which is unequivocal and clear in her or his mind. It was in this consciousness of our own thinking that philosophers hoped to find the ultimate ground of our intellectual activities to which language is anchored and through which it possesses a fixed and unmovable sense. However, a closer look reveals that this distrust of writing really is a distrust of language as a whole: we yearn to be confronted not with words, but with pure ideas; we hope to have immediate access, in our consciousness, to our own thoughts and reflections themselves, without any intervening medium. The clearest formulation of this centrality of the human subject which is conscious of itself and of its own mind can be found in the words of the French philosopher René Descartes (1596–1650): he claimed that even if we have radical doubts about the reality of everything surrounding us, the consciousness of our own thinking will always remain an unshakable fact which can serve as a secure ground for exploring the rest of the world. In reference to Descartes's famous sentence "cogito, ergo sum" (above, p. 33), this human subject which holds within itself the foundation of all sense has been called the "cogito" (in a manner which flies in the face of Latin grammar).

Derrida is extremely skeptical about this secure ground of all sense, not only for the reasons we have already seen when we spoke about the structuralist de-centering of the subject (above, pp. 33–34). His doubts are even more fundamental. In order to understand them, we should go back to his reading of Saussure's *Course*. Saussure had formulated the memorable sentence that in language, there are no positive terms, only differences (above, p. 31). Signifiers do not signify because they are tied in some mysterious manner to the mental concepts they designate, but because they are different from other signifiers. Derrida considers the implications of this view. Imagine we had forgotten the meaning of a word, say "hard," and had to look it up in a dictionary. We would find a series of other words which define what "hard" means – words that are similar, but also opposites, examples for using the word, and synonyms. We could then go on and look up these other words in turn. By doing so, after a long time, we could see a connection between "hard" and every other word of English – as Saussure would say: "hard" receives its meaning because it is *not* all these other words.

But this entails that the meaning of a word is not present in itself; it is not a simple and fixed given. Instead, words signify as much through what they are not, through things absent from themselves as through what they are [77.26]. If we browse our imaginary dictionary, we would look in vain for a word that would put an end to our search and that would allow us an unmovable, definitive definition of all the other words. Such an "Archimedean point" of language does not exist (Derrida [75.50] calls such an imaginary point a "*signifié transcendental*," and explains what this term means in [77.19–20]; the English translation "transcendental signified" became a catchword of sorts for some adherents of deconstruction). Hence, there is no way of limiting the absent through which words receive the capability to function as signs – basically, every other word in a language is part of defining a particular sign, plays a role in its "signness." Derrida [77.26–7], taking up ideas of Friedrich Nietzsche (1844–1900) and Emmanuel Lévinas (1905–95), calls the function of these absent elements the "trace." Absent signs leave their trace in what is present (say, in our word "hard"); they are there and not there at the same time.

It is difficult for us to speak or write about these "traces," to provide a scholarly or philosophical analysis of this concept. In the first place, it is impossible to give a definition of it in our ordinary language. Derrida, following the lead of the German philosopher Martin Heidegger (1889–1976), sees the entire tradition of Western philosophy dominated by our inability to imagine "being" in other terms than as "presence" (he calls this trait of occidental philosophy the "metaphysics of presence"). Hence, Derrida writes [75.167]: "*The trace itself does not exist.* To exist is to be, to be an entity, a being-present, *to on.*" How, then, can we speak about the trace? Even when I write "the trace is something absent, not something present," I fall into the trap of the metaphysics of presence – since the trace is never present, it cannot be said to "be" in the ordinary sense of the word. Derrida sometimes tries to face this problem by writing "under erasure," "crossing out," again following Heidegger's suggestions [176.310–1], such as "the trace X̶."

It may be easier to describe the effect of the trace in language: by its absent presence (or its present absence), it prevents sense and meaning from ever being fully present. Since every word in a language carries within it the traces of all other, absent words, it always promises to give us its full meaning, but always defers delivering it by referring us from one absent trace to the next. Like in the German folk tale "The Hare and the Hedgehog," users of language are forever pursuing the sense of language, but whenever we think we are catching up, we "meet" (another word which ought to be written "crossing out") yet another trace, yet another absence.

Derrida coined the artificial word *différance* for this play of differences which keeps deferring the presence of the sense and makes reaching its fullness impossible. In French, it differs by one (written) letter, but not by its pronunciation from the normal word *différence* "difference." The termination "-ance" makes it clear that the word is a verbal noun derived from the verb *différer* which means "to differ" as well as "to defer." The deferment of the full sense which is always promised, yet never delivered by the linguistic sign, is inherent in the language itself. *Différance* is not a mark of some shortcomings in a language, of misunderstandings that should be eliminated; instead, it is a fundamental characteristic of every linguistic utterance.

We have now come to know the main concepts of Derrida's thinking and can try to summarize: language is characterized by an immanent play of *différance* which can never be limited. It prevents the sense of a word or an utterance from ever being fully present in this utterance itself. This is true for any kind of use of language – even when we "hear ourselves speak," the meaning of our own words can never be fully present to ourselves because its deferment by means of *différance* is inherent in language itself. It is especially philosophers who find this situation hard to accept: they want to arrive at the true nature of things, using language as a tool only; they do not want to deal with words which just refer to each other, but with concepts that exist beyond the sphere of language and of *différance* and are really present. Hence, the history of Western philosophy witnesses numerous attempts to deny the existence of this *différance*, for instance by limiting its play by means of the living consciousness of the speaking subject. Derrida calls the totality of these strategies logocentrism. He himself pleads for accepting this absence and unattainableness of linguistic meaning. Hence, to conventional linguistic phonology, he opposes his own grammatology which no longer uses the living voice and its (alleged) presence as a model of philosophical exploration; instead, grammatology turns to writing in which speaker and context are always absent and require of the reader (listener) to fill this absence herself or himself.

Deconstruction in America

Derrida's attacks on Western logocentrism were quick to gain wide prominence, especially in the USA. Derrida was often invited to give guest lectures or to participate in conferences at American universities, and he taught as a visiting professor, most notably at Yale University, where he met a group of literary critics whose outlook was similar to his own. There are certainly a number of subtle (and important) differences between these scholars. Nevertheless, they were often perceived as forming one rather homogeneous school, the "Yale deconstructionists." All card-carrying members made more or less explicit use of Derrida's ideas; they all seemed to be doing work on a common project, each in her or his own way. The most influential member of this group was undoubtedly the Belgian-born scholar Paul de Man (1919–83). De Man, who taught French literature, was a close friend of Derrida's and was considered the unofficial chief of American deconstruction (or, for less well-meaning observers, the "resident

Godfather" of the "Yale Mafia"). Unlike Derrida's works, de Man's own texts generally contain very few theoretical explanations; instead, we find painstaking analyses of literary works, most often from the eigteenth and nineteenth centuries. De Man takes up the problem of the nature of poetical language which had been so prominent since the days of Formalism; he believes that the literary quality of language can be found in its rhetorical potential. Rhetorical tropes (such as metaphor or synecdoche) replace an (ordinary) word with another word – instead of saying "a brave man," we say "he was a lion"; instead of "ten ships," we say "ten sails." When used in such a rhetorical, unliteral way (as opposed to the concrete everyday use), words do not refer to objects (their referents), but instead to other words.

In a close reading of some of Nietzsche's works [72.103–18], de Man demonstrates that this German philosopher had already deconstructed the binary opposition between "literal" and "rhetorical" use. This opposition, then, is a typical example of a "violent hierarchy" in which one term (the literal use of language) is seen as superior and thus made the center of the structure while its opposing term can only play the role of a parasitical supplement. Yet according to Nietzsche [213.47], "truths are ... metaphors which are worn out and without sensuous power." Or, in de Man's terms: language can only give the impression of being referential because it denies its own rhetorical character, because this is its blind spot.

De Man goes on to apply this insight to Nietzsche's text itself: if language is always rhetorical and metaphorical, if it cannot claim to tell the truth about its referents, but only refers to itself or to other texts, how can any sentence Nietzsche writes ever lay claim to expressing a philosophical truth? The reader arrives at a paradoxical situation or, as de Man likes to say, an aporia: on its "philosophical" or "referential" level, the text pretends it is speaking about some extratextual reality; on its "literary" or "rhetorical" level, on the other hand, it seems to say that this is fundamentally impossible [72.117]: "A more rhetorically aware reading of *The Birth of the Tragedy* shows that all the authoritative claims that it seems to make can be undermined by means of statements provided by the text itself." This conclusion can be seen as typical of de Man's manner of reading and interpreting. He believes that a number of literary texts display a similar discrepancy between their rhetorical and their referential content and thus make the possibility of understanding and interpreting them deeply problematic. One example which de Man uses to demonstrate this situation is the rhetorical question [72.9–10]: "For what is the use of asking, I ask, when we cannot even authoritatively decide whether a question asks or doesn't ask?" A "rhetorical" reading of this sentence will reveal that it is attempting to make a positive statement: the use and elegance of rhetorical questions is clearly evident. A "literal" meaning, however, contradicts this positive statement since it asks the question whether the use of such questions might conceivably be doubtful.

According to de Man, similar, if much more complex paradoxes are at work in literary texts. On the one hand, they seem to be making statements about a world; they appear to be narrating a chain of events. On the other hand, they are "allegories of reading" (as de Man himself terms this aspect) and call into question whether such statements can be made at all. De Man firmly believes that texts are not waiting for readers and critics to deconstruct them from the outside, as it were; much rather, texts deconstruct themselves because they deny the possibility of understanding them [72.17]. Since interpretations can never grasp both textual aspects at the same time, they are forever doomed to be nothing but "misreadings."

De Man himself never goes so far as to assert that texts make no statements about the extratextual world at all or that they can mean anything, since every interpretation is always a "misreading." Much rather, he is content to profess a profound skepticism in this regard [74.11]: "it is not a priori certain that language functions according to principles which are those, or which are like those, of the phenomenal world. It is therefore not a priori certain that literature is a reliable source of information about anything but its own language." But he was aware that the emphasis he placed on the rhetorical dimension of language, just as Derrida's attacks on Western logocentrism, flew in the face of all conventional wisdom. We all take it for granted that language is just a transparent medium which is capable of conveying our ideas and deliver information about the extralinguistic reality. De Man, on the other hand, always emphasized the nontransparent, opaque nature of language – and he was aware that his position would meet fierce resistance [74.17].

Objections to Deconstruction

As we mentioned at the beginning of this chapter, the tenets of deconstruction provoked an intense debate, especially in the USA. The volume of this discussion was at times regrettably high so that it became difficult to perceive reasonable arguments. Nevertheless, we will first attempt to sift out the topics which are directly relevant to literary criticism before then turning to some wider implications of deconstruction. There can be no doubt that its opponents had some valid objections; the most important ones are:

ॐ The deconstructionists are not justified in adducing Saussure's structuralist linguistics as support for their claims. In particular, their attempt to sever the signifier from the signified (de Man, for example, speaks of a "pure signifier" [72.283]) is incompatible with Saussure's theories: in the linguistic sign, both terms are joined inseparably; one cannot exist without the other.

ॐ Another critical remark was especially targeted at American deconstruction: Derrida had formulated his philosophical insights as a general critique of the entire Western tradition of metaphysics, especially its logocentrism. Was it possible to derive concrete rules for reading individual texts from these philosophical endeavors? Is not de Man's attempt to see every text as an allegory of its own lack of interpretability in danger of obscuring all differences between texts? Can his hypothesis that literary texts are always deconstructing themselves really be applied to all texts from all periods and all cultures? Merquior was not entirely wrong to call American deconstruction "merely a technique for unreading texts" [255.228] and to reproach it for eternally reproducing the same predictable results.

ॐ As we have seen, Derrida is deeply wary of linguistic *différance* and doubts that signs can ever convey meaning; this has led other adherents of deconstruction to the conclusion that every interpretation must necessarily be a "misreading." Meyer Howard Abrams has called this attitude an expression of the "all-or-none-principle" [1.273–6]. Of course, it is right to say that the relation between linguistic signs and extralinguistic reality is not always evident and that some signs impose an arbitrary order on this reality (think of the way in which the perfectly continuous color spectrum is divided into discrete colors: this division varies with different cultures and languages). But does this entail that the order of language is completely detached from the order of reality and that there is no way out of textuality, as Derrida suggests in his (in)famous statement "il n'y a pas de hors-texte" "There is nothing outside of the text" ([75.158]; there is an even more radical formulation at [75.163])? Merquior summarizes this criticism nicely when he writes [255.233]: "As so often, radical scepticism, about meanings as about almost everything else, is just a disappointed absolutism." Only people who were overly optimistic in hoping that a perfectly transparent language would give us unmediated access to reality would, at the merest sign that linguistic communication might not be that smooth and unproblematic after all, jump to the conclusion that successful communication does not exist at all. There may be more than an ounce of truth to Harris's belief [171.77–8] that this disappointment with language is a direct cause of the spectacular failure of structuralism to deliver on all of its promises, most notably its hope to provide a scientifically verifiable method of interpreting literary texts (above, pp. 35–40).

ஜ Finally, it has often been said that deconstruction's theory of the unreadable text and of the fundamental *différance* of the lingustic sign is just a consequence of their tendency to "decontextualize" words and texts. When, for example, Derrida claims that words in a dictionary just refer to each other and that there is no "transcendental signified," he is not only confusing the levels of *parole* and *langue* (words only have this variety of meanings on the abstract level of the system of language; within a specific utterance, they have one specific meaning), he also disregards that we usually do not encounter isolated words, but meet them in distinct contexts which can be linguistic (determined by neighboring words in the sentence) or extralinguistic (by the situation in which something is spoken, e.g., when somebody says "give that to me!").

However, all these arguments are not sufficient to discredit the theses of deconstruction entirely. Its adherents might reply: it is true that not *every* reading is a misreading. But as long as we do not possess secure criteria to distinguish correct interpretations from misreadings, we gain little in knowing that once in a while, we may be right. And the deconstructionists are certainly right in emphasizing that there is no authoritative instance which will fix and guarantee the meaning of texts once and for all. In everyday communication, context in the widest sense, the entire situation of communication, fulfills this function – but when we interpret literature, it is much more difficult to determine what its context is. We will now have a look at this problem by examining a question which has been haunting interpreters of literature for a long time.

The Role of the Author

In 1967, Derrida's *Grammatology* was published; in the same year, the American critic Eric Donald Hirsch, jr. (b. 1928) published his book *Validity in Interpretation* [182]. Its first chapter is entitled "In Defense of the Author," and this title is meant as a programmatic statement. Hirsch proclaims forcefully that the interpretation of literary texts cannot throw out the author's intentions, but ought to put them at the center of all its endeavors. Hirsch thus argues against one of the main tenets of the New Criticism which had been virtually canonical in literary studies in the USA for a long time (see above, p. 92). In the essay

"The Intentional Fallacy" [379.3–18], which first appeared in print in 1946, the critics Wimsatt and Beardsley had argued that the meaning of literary texts is determined exclusively by factors such as grammatical, semantical, or symbolical structures of its language; hence, they claimed it was completely irrelevant for the interpreter to enquire what an author may have defined as her or his "intentions" in documents such as letters or diaries. Hirsch opposed this position and argued that an author's intention was our only criterion for determining the validity of our interpretation.

Hirsch supports his position by referring to concepts which had been developed by the German mathematician and logician Gottlob Frege (1848–1925). Frege distinguished between the "meaning" and the "significance" of an utterance (for a similar distinction in the work of Riffaterre, see above, p. 79). It is a question of significance whether we read the *Aeneid* as a tribute to the achievements of Augustus or as a subtle attack on Roman imperialism. But in order to ask such questions, we must have a secure understanding of the text's fundamental verbal meaning. For Hirsch, this meaning is identical to the author's intention. To the objection that authors sometimes change their mind about their own texts and that therefore, their intention has proven to be unstable, Hirsch replies that in this case, they are mere readers of their own texts whose verbal meaning is always identical to the author's intention when the text was written.

Yet when he tries to elaborate on this thesis, Hirsch soon encounters difficulties: an opponent could argue that authors are fallible, like all human beings, so they may not always succeed in expressing what they intended to say. In this case, what would be the meaning of the text: the (unexpressed) intention of its author or the way in which readers interpret the text? Since Hirsch is concerned with establishing a methodology of "objective intepretation," he cannot but opt for the sense as expressed in the text itself. He says [182.218]: "Verbal meaning is, by definition, that aspect of a speaker's 'intention' which, under linguistic conventions, may be shared by others." Hirsch even claims that documents such as letters or diaries may be used to obtain information about the whole personality of the author in order to determine her or his intention, but they can never be more than mere expedients, for "the speaking subject is not … identical with the subjectivity of the author as an actual historical person; it corresponds, rather, to a very limited and special aspect of the author's total subjectivity; it is, so to speak, that 'part' of the author which specifies or determines verbal meaning" [182.242].

These limitations, however, seriously undermine Hirsch's attemps to make the author's intentions the criterion of objective interpretation of texts. If we want "intention" to play the role of an Archimedean point to which we can anchor the sense of texts, this intention has to lie outside of the text itself. But as we follow Hirsch's argument, we realize that this is not the case in his theory: his author's intention is something we have to extract from the text. Hirsch's position, then, becomes theoretically empty: every interpretation of a text presupposes a belief, on the side of the interpreter, that the text does indeed intend to convey a meaning. If this "intending instance" is situated in the text itself, not without it, we enter a vicious circle: interpreting a text means filtering out its author's intention, but this can only be achieved by interpretation.

A position which we may call the exact opposite of what Hirsch tried to argue has been established by Roland Barthes in an article on "the death of the author" first published in 1968 (English translation in [26.49–55]; also in the collection *Image, Music, Text* [25.142–8]). It will be easier for us to understand this famous essay if we recall Barthes's distinction between "readerly" and "writerly" texts (above, p. 53). In his 1974 book *The Pleasure of the Text* [24], Barthes characterized these two terms as being related to "pleasure" (*plaisir*) and "bliss" (*jouissance*). Barthes asserts that regarding the author as the origin and source of all textual meaning is a modern invention unknown, e.g., to the Middle Ages. Granting the author such a predominant position was equivalent to the belief that texts possess a single, fixed meaning which it is the interpreter's task to elucidate [26.53]: "To assign an Author to a text is to impose a brake on it, to furnish it with a final signified, to close writing." But, as "we now know" (one of Barthes's favorite formulae), the author is not capable of assuming this role assigned to him because he is not in control of his own language, his own culture, and his own psyche. Hence, Barthes thinks that texts are not an expression of an intention, but much rather [26.53] "a multi-dimensional space in which are married and contested several writings, none of which is original." This vanishing of the author will cause a liberation of the reader. It now becomes clear that the focus of a text's multiplicity can only be the reader. Barthes concludes his essay with the catchy and oft-quoted slogan [26.55] that "the birth of the reader must be requited by the death of the Author."

Barthes's famous essay has a companion piece in an article by Foucault published one year later, "What Is an Author?" (English translation in [297.101–20]). Foucault's analysis disagrees with Barthes's view on a number of points, but overall, Foucault also thinks that the author will disappear. Using his method of discourse analysis (below, chapter 9), Foucault develops the concept of the "author function" and remarks that in our modern culture, only certain texts carry this function – while we expect literary texts to be signed by an author, we don't think this is necessary for, e.g., a medical textbook. Hence, Foucault does not want to regard the author as the source of all meaning; instead, he proposes to examine in which circumstances and by which means individuals can fulfill this author fuction and which constellations of power are thus created [297.118].

But Foucault's position also begs a number of important questions. Undoubtedly, his suggestions open up several interesting and rewarding avenues for approaching literary texts. But numerous literary critics have vehemently opposed Foucault's and Barthes's view that the author is dead (or at least is dying). Barthes is often criticized for being unclear about the question whether this death is already an accomplished fact and whether his thesis can only be applied to contemporary texts or if it is also valid for older literature (e.g., Harris [171.28–9]). This lack of clarity reminds us of the problems which were connected with Barthes's distinction between "readerly" and "writerly" texts (above, p. 53). I also find another reproach justified: Barthes and Foucault, critics say, are so engrossed with large structures and systems that they have an exaggerated tendency to underestimate the importance of individuals (this has been formulated, e.g., by Edward W. Said [314.186–8] or Harris [171.34]). This is a valid criticism not only against the patently absurd conclusion (which seems to follow from Barthes's and Foucault's positions) that the *Metamorphoses* would have been written by some anonymous social structures even if the individual Ovid had never lived. We also have to ask if the consequences of the "birth of the reader" are indeed as desirable as Barthes thinks. If we just leave our own mark on everything we read, if readers have to produce the meanings of texts themselves, why should we bother to read at all? Even if we mistrust the all too lofty sentence that we read literature to encounter great human beings (see, e.g., the formulation by Abrams [1.331]: "Literature has survived over the millennia by being read as a presentation of human characters and matters of human interest, delight, and concern"), we have to acknowledge that reading literature would degenerate into a pretty solipsistic business if the text were completely empty and we had to bring everything to it.

Stanley Fish's Model of "Interpretive Communities"

I have given such a lengthy explanation of this debate about the position of the author in the interpretation of texts because in its consequences, this is a discussion about the most central problem of deconstruction. Adherents of a model of interpretation which places the author and her or his intentions at the center of our attention have often reproached the deconstructionists for making interpretation quite impossible: if we sever texts from their origin, there will be no valid criteria for reading and intepreting texts (see, e.g., Hirsch [182.226]), and texts can mean anything and everything. Adherents of deconstruction have several times tried to argue against this conclusion. In a paper which discusses the structuralist methodology of Lévi-Strauss, Derrida distinguishes "two interpretations of interpretation" [76.369]. One of them, Derrida says, attempts to arrive at absolute truths and so limit the *différance*, the free play of the linguistic sign by finding its origin and tying it to this firm ground. The other emphatically accepts and welcomes *différance* and continues to play this game. As Culler [69.132] rightly says, deconstruction is often understood as advocating unequivocally this second way of interpretation. Yet Derrida, in the passage just referred to, makes it quite clear that there is no choice between these two ways of interpretation. He and other deconstructionists have often emphasized that their ideas are not meant as a justification for an out-and-out relativism, an advocacy of "anything goes" (see Derrida's remarks in [79.144–7]). But they have neglected to answer the question of what can ever be capable of limiting the free play of the linguistic sign if their theories about the ubiquitous, absent–present trace and the fundamental *différance* of every linguistic utterance caused by it are indeed correct.

It thus becomes clear why this position met with such intense criticism. One objection which is often made and which it is difficult to avoid concerns the deconstructionists' own use of language: when they give talks or publish articles, they obviously expect to be read and understood, and they defend themselves against misinterpretations of their words. If we accept that there are no correct interpretations, no working communication, such a behavior becomes utterly absurd. We can even say that, if we take seriously the deconstructionist slogan that "every reading is a misreading" (above, p. 122), if texts can mean anything or nothing (this amounts to the same, in the last consequence), the entire business of literary criticism becomes preposterous: we can no longer distinguish between right and wrong interpretations or, at the very least, between more or less plausible ones. Opponents of deconstruction have often claimed that such a relativism amounts to complete anarchy. Its adherents have tried to argue against this assumption. For example, Robert Crosman, holds that the view that texts have one single meaning which it is the interpreter's task to elucidate is just a political statement [66]. According to him, this position cannot but cause tensions and disputes, while his own opinion (the meaning of texts is produced by their readers) will lead to a tolerant pluralism.

But this matter seems more complex than his position suggests. Whoever accepts the basic tenets of deconstruction does not believe that texts have a number of different meanings, but instead that they have no fixed meaning at all, and this will make linguistic communication superfluous or impossible. There can be no doubt that Crosman is right to some extent: the claim that there is just one absolute truth has often been misused as part of authoritarian ideologies. But Crosman's own view is no more compatible with the idea of democratic society since taken to its final consequence, it will produce a mass of individuals each of whom is convinced of her or his claim to truth and thus incapable of conferring with others.

Another way of coming to terms with Derrida's ideas can be seen in the influential works of Fish (about whom see above, p. 92). Fish combines the tenets of deconstruction with the methodology of reader-response criticism. He emphatically denies that there is a difference between meaning and significance, as had been argued by Hirsch. According to Fish, it is impossible to distinguish between an immediately obvious, universally accessible textual meaning and a deeper significance that can only be extracted via interpretation. As soon as we start reading a text, we are already in the process of interpreting it [108.9]: "Meanings that seem perspicuous and literal are rendered so by forceful interpretive acts and not by the properties of language."

Such formulations demonstrate that Fish's theoretical position is quite similar to deconstructionist tenets such as "There are no facts, only assemblages. There is always only interpretation," as Vincent B. Leitch formulated it [233.58]. However, Fish does not accept the objection raised by opponents of deconstruction that in this case, everyone can read and interpret texts according to her or his own whims. Fish holds that we are not free to choose the way in which we produce facts and read texts, but that our view is predetermined by the "interpretive community" to which we belong. Fish gives an instructive example taken out of everyday life on a university campus: even here, we never encounter raw, uninterpreted facts, but everything is always perceived in a pre-interpreted, mediated manner [107.330]: "It would never occur to you, for example, to wonder if the people pouring out of that building are fleeing from a fire; you know they are exiting from a class (what could be more obvious?) and you know that because your perception of their action occurs within a knowledge of what people in a university could possibly be doing and the reasons they could have for doing it." Hence, Fish concludes that [108.331] "all objects are made and not found, and ... they are made by the interpretive strategies we set in motion." Therefore, texts can *not* mean anything, but we will always find in them only what our interpretive community allows us to perceive.

During the last three decades, Fish has defended his position in a number of brilliant and rhetorically efficient contributions (his texts are always clear and often highly entertaining, and this seems to embitter his opponents even more). Nevertheless, his thesis is open to a number of questions and objections:

- Fish has problems explaining how, given the existence of interpretive communities as postulated by him, radical change can ever occur. True, he has emphasized that the rules of interpretive communities are not monolithic and can hence produce changes [108.151], but in that case, it becomes questionable whether the term "interpretive community" is not so watered down as to become unclear and useless.
- Harris [171.42–3] rightly points out that we all are not members of one, but of several different interpretive communities whose norms and expectations influence, reinforce, or contradict each other. Religious, political, or social circumstances will determine my reading of a given text as much as the fact that I am a student of classics. This situation, then, brings opportunities to compare different points of view and thus see their relative merits and weaknesses. Hence, the norms of every individual interpretive communities are less stable and obligatory than Fish claims.

However, I would argue that the most important objection against Fish's model of interpretation is that in the end, he is as incapable of escaping the pitfalls of ethical and political irresponsibility as the deconstructionists. When all is said and done, Fish does not offer any means of choosing and mediating between the claims of different communities. With Fish's model, we would be completely helpless against the assertions of, say, a conspiracy freak who denies that the events of 9/11 ever took place – he could argue that there are no facts before interpretation, hence, in my interpretive community, my view is as valid and correct as his is in his own community. The problem of such ethical implications and consequences of deconstruction will be the topic of the next section.

The Responsibility of the Interpreter

We will explore this topic by looking at evidence which may at first glance rather trivial and circumstantial, but will soon take us to the core of the issue: Derrida's style. More traditional literary critics have often reproached deconstructionists for using obscure jargon which makes understanding and discussion needlessly difficult. This criticism is certainly too sweeping, as we have already seen (above, p. 9), and it is not entirely justified in Derrida's case: most of his earlier writings are not more difficult than any "ordinary" philosophical texts. Their complex and scrupulous argumentation demands the reader's full attention, but they don't convey the impression of glossing over intellectual hollowness by using pretentious jargon. The presentation of Derrida's thought given above relies on his works *On Grammatology* [75] and *Margins of Philosophy* [78], both of which are written in a language and style that are largely accessible and offer clear arguments.

But Derrida is also able to write in a completely different manner, and some of his texts are simply outrageous and arrogant in their narcissistic incomprehensibility. It is impossible to argue with these texts in a dispassionate scholarly way, and one can understand why many critics have reacted to this style with indignation and aggression. A good example for this side of deconstruction can be found in a debate Derrida conducted with the American philosopher of language John Rogers Searle (b. 1932). In a paper "Signature Event Context" [78.309–30] read and published in 1971, Derrida had attacked a theory proposed by Searle's teacher, the Oxford philosopher John Langshaw Austin (1911–60). Austin is the founder of the so-called "speech act theory." In a series of lectures given at Harvard University in 1955, but published only after his death under the title *How To Do Things with Words* [12], Austin had proposed some philosophical speculations about certain linguistic utterances that look like "ordinary" statements but cannot be true or false in the same way as statements. Austin was thinking of sentences such as "I promise" or "I apologize." Uttering them does not make a statement about something that exists outside of language, but constitutes an action of and by itself, namely, a speech act. Whereas real statements can be true or false, we can distinguish between "felicitous" and "infelicitous" speech acts (or "performative sentences"). If an official pronounces the words "I name this ship the *Queen Elizabeth*" during a launching ceremony while smashing a bottle of champagne against its stern, this utterance stands a good chance of being a felicitous speech act which does indeed cause an action to be fulfilled and a ship to be named. If I pronounce the same words while sitting at my desk, the speech act is certainly infelicitous or downright silly. Austin now explores the question of which circumstances are necessary for a speech act to be felicitous. In order to facilitate this examination, Austin excludes certain uses: when an actor pronounces the words "I hereby declare you husband and wife" on a stage, this is not a felicitious speech act (even if the actor pronouncing these words happens to be a minister and the other two actors responding to them happen to be unmarried), but a quotation, an unserious use which Austin calls "parasitic" [12.22] and excludes from his investigation.

It should not come as a surprise that this hierarchical opposition "serious vs. parasitic" just begs to be deconstructed, in categories which we have already seen. Derrida points out that Austin's analysis of speech acts presupposes the existence of certain conventions: the formula "I hereby declare you husband and wife" can only be successful and possess the power to perform a certain action because there are rules and laws that give it this power. This entails that the condition of the possibility of its felicitiousness is its repeatability – laws can only govern what is general and repeatable. Hence, such a formula can be cited in contexts other than the conventional ones, and its quotation on the stage cannot be excluded as being a parasitic special case; much rather, it clearly demonstrates that paradoxically, a felicitous speech act is only made possible by the existence of such an (unserious) repetition.

Again, we have to be clear that deconstruction of such an opposition is not tantamount to its destruction. Derrida is not saying that there are no felicitous speech acts at all or that the difference between felicitous and infelicitous does not exist or is irrelevant. Instead, he emphasizes that this violent hierarchy between both poles might as well be inverted. This "iterability," the possibility of being quoted even outside of its conventional context, leaves its trace in every speech act, even in felicitous ones; it is not parasitical, but a supplement which has "always already" been necessary.

Searle replied to Derrida's arguments in an article [324] written in a style which was polemical, yet clearly within the limits of academic conventions. In particular, Searle accused Derrida of misunderstanding Austin. Derrida replied in turn with the article "Limited Inc." [79]. We are not concerned here with the details of this debate; we are more interested in its style. Derrida avoids entering into any real discussion or dialogue with Searle's arguments. Instead, he sets out to "deconstruct" every concept and undermine every common ground that might have been a basis for proper understanding. In the first footnote to his article, Searle had thanked two colleagues with whom he had discussed the subject of his article. From this, Derrida concludes that the article really had been written by several authors ("3 + n") and calls this collective author "Sarl"; this is a pun on Searle's name and at the same time the French equivalent of the English term "limited inc." ("société à responsabilité limitée" = "limited incorporated company").

Overall, we get the impression that a student of philosophy is playing a prank on his professor to find out to what extent such a joke will be tolerated. (There is a strong ongoing tradition of such practical jokes, called "*canulars*," at the École normale supérieure where Derrida studied and taught.) But Derrida stubbornly refuses to take off his clown's mask and enter into a serious debate. The numerous interjections "let's be serious" [79.34, 39, 45] are just part of his game since his aim is deconstructing the opposition "serious vs. playful." But Derrida is not willing to admit this playfulness; in an afterword, "Towards an Ethics of Discussion," which was written for the republication of the paper in a book, Derrida continually claims that his reply to Searle had been serious and philosophically sincere.

Undoubtedly, Dosse was right in saying that Derrida believed that his deconstructionist stand [86.2.40] "justified his pulling out all stops and hitting below the belt." But there is more at stake here than the naughty side of a philosopher who became intoxicated by his own prominence, especially in the USA, and came to believe that the ordinary rules of academic discussion did not apply to himself. Much rather, the style of Derrida's article appears symptomatic of a set of problems caused by deconstruction: is an "ethics of discussion" possible at all if one of the discussants is convinced that language is fundamentally incomprehensible and utterances can never be interpreted in an unequivocal way? Derrida's attitude seems to confirm Eagleton's sarcastic comment [90.125]: he saw one of the main advantages of deconstruction in "that it allows you to drive a coach and horses through everybody else's beliefs while not saddling you with the inconvenience of having to adopt any yourself."

The question of such moral implications of deconstruction was to explode with much greater vehemence in 1987 during the "de Man affair," and its adherents and especially Derrida himself were asked a couple of more pressing questions. In this year, the young Belgian scholar Ortwin de Graef was researching for his dissertation in Belgian archives, and he chanced upon some articles which de Man had published in Belgian newspapers in World War II, during the German occupation of Belgium. When de Graef decided, in collaboration with Derrida and other scholars, to publish these papers in a reprint, he probably had no idea what an uproar this publication would cause. One article especially , entitled "The Jews in Current Literature" and published on March 4, 1941 in the journal *Le Soir*, prompted indignation. In it, de Man argued that modern European literature was not, as had been claimed by "vulgar anti-Semitism," "enjewished" (*enjuivé*) throughout, but had managed to preserve itself from "pernicious Jewish influences." He concludes his article with the remark that "a solution of the Jewish problem, which would plan to establish a Jewish colony isolated from Europe, would not entail any negative consequences on European literature."

The republication of the articles elicited a flurry of media coverage. Paul de Man and deconstruction had hardly been known to the general public outside of literature departments in universities; all of a sudden, they were brought into the limelight. Mass journals such as the *New York Times* or *Nation* in the USA or the *Frankfurter Allgemeine Zeitung* in Germany published lengthy articles about this affair. Of course, it is understandable, if highly regrettable, that some of these publications took a sensationalistic approach and exaggerated the importance of de Man's articles. To give one example of such a reaction: it was in Germany that the journalist Frank Schirrmacher labeled de Man "a National Socialist by conviction and an extreme anti-Semite" (*Frankfurter Allgemeine Zeitung*, February 2, 1988); on the front page of the same issue, one of the editors of the paper, Johann Georg Reissmüller, wrote an editorial entitled "The Hunt Continues" in which he defended the former Secretary-General to the United Nations and Austrian president Kurt Waldheim (b. 1918). Waldheim had served as an officer in the Nazi SA and was probably involved in war crimes; his deeds and subsequent lies about his own role during the war dwarfed de Man's wrongdoings. But conservative critics and the media were not concerned with historical judgments or the personal offenses committed by a professor of literary studies; instead, they saw a chance to tarnish, in de Man's person, deconstruction as a whole. Schirrmacher writes: "All of a sudden, one becomes aware that every argument and every thesis was just meant to serve an illusional flight from remembrance," and he goes so far as to assign a "latent fascism" to deconstruction.

These are of course self-serving gut reactions which have no place in serious discussion. As Holub has rightly remarked, whoever subscribes to such generalizations is "wholly ignorant of both the philosophical diversity and complexity of the deconstructionist enterprise and the historical forms in which German fascism proliferated" [188.149]. Moreover, rather more caution about such accusations would be appropriate, particularly in Germany: if we apply these standards and condemn every academic discipline whose proponents were Nazis or sympathized with the Nazi governement, there would not be much left to teach in German universities. Undoubtedly, de Man's articles are despicable and vile, and their existence must not be forgotten or downplayed, but such personal transgressions cannot dictate our moral judgment of an entire theoretical position with which de Man had been connected for a long time. Nevertheless, the de Man affair is more than academic gossip. The ways in which de Man's friends and colleagues dealt with this discovery was indeed a touchstone of deconstruction as a method of critical reading, and we can anticipate the result: deconstruction failed this test miserably.

After discovering these articles, de Graef got in touch with Derrida. Photocopies of the articles were made and sent out to a select group of literary critics. In October, 1987, they convened at a conference in Tuscaloosa, Alabama, to discuss these texts. It was decided that a facsimile edition of the articles should be published, accompanied by a collection of responses to these texts. The lengthy volume *Responses. On Paul de Man's Wartime Journalism* [169] was published in 1989. It does not consist entirely of contributions by friends of de Man's; some of the articles (such as the papers by Stanley Corngold and Jeffrey Mehlman) attack him vigorously. Overall, however, the book conveys the impression of being a vindication of de Man. This is most visible in Derrida's own contribution. Even if we disregard his furious and emotional attacks on colleagues such as Todorov, Jürgen Habermas, and Jon Wiener, and his insidious insinuations even against de Graef, which again demonstrate his megalomaniac and paranoid insistence on being right all the time, Derrida's reading of de Man's articles is just extraordinary. In a close reading of the article "The Jews in Current Literature" which analyzes every sentence, Derrida tries to show that this text really is a subtle criticism of antisemitism. When de Man's assertions make this strategy completely impossible, Derrida retreats to the position that de Man was forced to write the worst passages because of outside pressure or that editors inserted them into his text at a later stage. Holub [188.168] rightly characterizes Derrida's article as "a pathetic and disgraceful tirade by an arrogant and condescending man who feels that his cult of interpretation is on the wane."

The de Man affair is particularly telling; it goes a long way to demonstrate why the reading strategies of deconstruction are bound to lead to an impasse. In order to defend their friend and colleague, deconstructionists saw themselves faced with two possible routes, both of them unsatisfactory: they could either recur to conventional principles of interpretation which they usually eschewed and admit that there are correct and wrong readings of texts (Derrida himself was convinced that his reading of de Man's articles was superior to the superficial and shallow interpretations of his opponents). Or they could take their thesis of the fundamental unreadability of texts to extremes – and thus demonstrate the political and moral nihilism of deconstruction.

Deconstruction's Merits and Demerits

Since the late 1980s, these moral deficiencies of deconstruction have done more to discredit it and make it less attractive than its internal inconsistencies and problems. Some conservative literary critics, especially on the academic scene in the USA, still like to pretend that deconstruction is as powerful and dominant today as it used to be in the mid-1980s, but interest in and enthusiasm for deconstruction has continued to dwindle. This does not mean, however, that all the fundamental issues it raised have simply disappeared: philosphical positions are not invalidated in the same way as a theory in, say, physics or chemistry can be falsified by experimentation. When all is said and done, a fundamental, radical skepticism about all kinds of communication can probably never be disproved completely. In this sense, deconstruction is as valid as the positions which the sophist Gorgias formulated in the fifth century BCE. Gorgias made three provocative claims [84.2.279–83 = *fr.* B 3 DK]: (1) Nothing exists; (2) even if something existed, we would be unable to apprehend it; (3) even if we were able to apprehend it, we would be unable to communicate it. Even modern philosophy does not appear to have come up with a really convincing refutation of such radical skepticism.

Such extreme positions, then, are unassailable, but by the same token, they are unproductive. We should therefore remember the nagging doubts that deconstruction raised and be aware of their existence without letting them paralyze us. Even opponents of deconstruction are willing to concede that in this regard, it has had positive effects (see, e.g., Gerald Graff's formulation in his article "Deconstruction as Dogma" [145.421]). The debate about the status and role of the author in literary interpretation can provide us a good example for this attitude: it may sound vague to say that the truth is in the middle, between Hirsch's attempt to transmit all textual power (back) to the author and give her or him full control, and Barthes's position, which tries to get rid of the author in favor of the reader. Those who favor the view that texts have only one fixed and unmovable meaning have trouble explaining why so many literary texts have been read and interpreted in so many different ways; those who argue that texts are completely open and can mean anything at all fail to explain why there seems to be some stable core of all meaning.

It would thus appear that a "local" use of deconstructionist arguments is a possible way: deconstructionist strategies of discovering and subverting "violent hierarchies" can be immensely useful. Deconstruction, then, has its place especially "when it blended some broader project: feminism, post-colonialism, psychoanalysis," as Eagleton writes [90.196]. In the following chapters, we will see a few ways of using deconstruction in this manner.

Deconstruction in Antiquity? Socrates und Protagoras

If we consider the fundamental doubts about interpretation formulated by deconstruction, it will come as no surprise that there is no simple "application" of this methodology to ancient texts. We could certainly refer to articles which use texts from classical antiquity to demonstrate, in the wake of de Man, the ways in which texts undermine the possibilities of interpretation; we could also quote some of the numerous articles in which Derrida discusses some key texts of ancient philosophy. In all these cases, however, the interpretation is more concerned with finding more examples of the free play of language than with providing an illuminating reading of an individual text. Hence, I have chosen to look at an ancient text which seems to provide, as several scholars have pointed out, an antecedent for some of the problems and questions which deconstruction has raised.

Plato's *Protagoras* is a dialogue between Socrates and the sophist Protagoras about the question of whether "virtue" and "politics" can be taught. A first attempt at answering this question fails; both cannot agree on a common solution to the problem; their discussion seems to have arrived in an impasse. In this situation, both agree to interpret a poem by the lyric poet Simonides (556–468 BCE). Protagoras first quotes lines in which Simonides says (*fr.* 542.1–3): "To become a truly good man is difficult, foursquare in arms and feet and mind, modeled beyond reproach." When Socrates says that he knows this poem well and admires it, Protagoras goes on to demonstrate that Simonides is contradicting himself in the poem and that hence, it cannot be a good text. As evidence, he quotes a passage later in the poem in which Simonides says (ll. 11–12): "Nor do I think the word of Pittacus was said harmoniously even though it was said by a wise man. He said it was difficult to be a good man." Then, Socrates attempts to explain this apparent contradiction and refute Protagoras's claim.

In a fascinating and engrossing article, Glenn W. Most [269] has analyzed this debate between Socrates and Protagoras. He shows that the disagreement between both is caused by a fundamentally different approach to reading the poem. Protagoras finds the two contradictory passages striking because he takes Simonides's words out of their context – he decontextualizes [269.129]: "the two sentences he quotes seem to float like monads, pure citations quite free of any determinate attachments, and to collide with one another in unmediated

and windowless contradiction." When we think of this approach, we are immediately reminded of Derrida's emphasis on the "iterability" of utterances.

Socrates, on the other hand, makes a twofold effort to take the context into
account in his interpretation: on the one hand, he connects the poem to a narrative on how the Spartans philosophized (this narrative is clearly marked as being ironical); on the other hand, he attempts to elucidate the intentions of the
author Simonides by paying attention to the entire text of the poem. Hence,
Socrates's approach is the opposite of Protagoras's; he "recontextualizes." Most
holds that Socrates's attempts at analyzing the text in this way are not entirely
successful. He explains that Plato, the author of the *Protagoras*, was eminently
skeptical of literary interpretation (for some of the reasons for this skepticism,
see above, p. 116). Nevertheless, Socrates's method of reading is depicted as a
clear antithesis to Protagoras's "deconstructionist" manner [269.129]: "it provides an example of the kind of story which must be told by anyone who wants
to integrate a text plausibly into a determinate external context."

As Most argues convincingly, this discussion shows why classicists have to be
especially knowledgeable about the comparative merits of these two approaches:
because of the great historical distance, because of the cultural differences, and
because of the vicissitudes of transmission, many classical texts come to us in
an extremely decontextualized form. If we interpret them, we try (like Socrates
in the *Protagoras*) to find a context within which the statements of these texts
make sense. Yet such recontextualizations can never be supported by sufficient
evidence and proven with scientific rigor because these contexts do not simply
exist, they are produced by the activity of the interpreter; hence, they are always
open to deconstruction.

Most demonstrates that classics as a scholarly discipline has, over the course
of time, established rules and criteria which help us decide whether an individual reading is more or less convincing. For instance, an interpretation which
suceeds in integrating as many parts of the text as possible (or even all elements
of the text), which demonstrates their functionality within the structure of the
text, is seen as superior; readings which can quote parallels from classical culture
are more plausible. But remember Fish's concept of "interpretive communities"
(above, p. 127): these criteria are valid and accepted within a certain group of
interpreters; different groups may read differently – for religious fanatics, the
only acceptable interpretation of a text is one which furthers the belief in their
god. Such rules, then, do not break the vicious circle as shown by deconstructionist arguments. Certainly, it is true that the exploits of deconstruction only
work because of decontextualization. But if we take seriously their claim that

every text is always already decontextualized because there can be no real and complete presence of the context in a text, there is no reason for regarding this as a flaw. We will never be able to find a stable core meaning, a real presence of significance within the text. This consciousness of the limits of validity of all interpretation is the most important legacy that deconstruction has left.

Further Reading

In the case of deconstruction, it is especially important to quote some introductory reading because some of the most important contributions may appear difficult or forbidding at first sight. There are a number of excellent introductions: Jonathan Culler's *On Deconstruction* [69] is a logically structured, comprehensible, clear account which presents the main questions and problems of deconstruction; however, as with Culler's book on structuralism (above, p. 42), there is a danger of trivializing some issues. Christopher Norris's book *Deconstruction* [278] also is a solid and straightforward explanation, if at times too uncritical toward its topic. Vincent B. Leitch's *Deconstructive Criticism* [233] is rather more difficult to read because the author not only presents the ideas and concepts of deconstruction, but also employs the style and argumentation characteristic of it; this is an excellent introduction which I highly recommend. If you are not only interested in the tenets and ideology of deconstruction, but also in the lives and works of the most prominent French proponents of all facets of poststructuralism, you should read the immensely entertaining and at the same time informative *History of Structuralism* [86] by François Dosse. José G. Merquior [255] offers a discussion of structuralism and deconstruction which is in part quite polemical, yet well-informed and accurate. Manfred Frank [124] provides an introduction from a philosophical perspective. Howard Felperin's [103.104–46] assessment of deconstruction is more positive than the judgment given here.

Chapter 9
Michel Foucault and Discourse Analysis

Some readers may find it surprising that an entire chapter of this introduction is devoted to the French thinker Michel Foucault (1926–84; Foucault was one of the first prominent victims of AIDS) – after all, he is not primarily a literary critic or theoretician. It is extremely difficult to categorize the wide range and scope of his work under one headline: is his field the history of science, philosophy, sociology, political science, or cultural studies? Foucault's works touch all these disciplines. Only occasionally do we find him treating questions that can be defined as belonging to literary theory in the narrow sense of the word (e.g., we have seen his ideas about the "author function," above, p. 126). If Foucault is a much-quoted authority in literary studies today, this is not due to the positive results of his contributions but to the encouragement he gave to ask completely novel questions about the sciences, literature, or culture in general. His inspiration has been extremely influential since the early 1980s. It should also be noted that Foucault has often touched on topics that were to be big issues in the general opinion of the larger public just a few years later. Hence, readers will find some of the positions and theses explained in this chapter strangely familiar, even if they have probably encountered them in a slightly simplified form. This ability to sense which topics are "in the air," as it were, and to give an appropriate and appealing formulation to such questions is another factor which helps explain why Foucault became so influential (and his influence even extends to scholars who have never read a single line of his works and who would vehemently deny any such influence if we asked them).

The diversity of Foucault's writings is so great that it is sometimes difficult to imagine that they are the works of one single author. To name just a few of his most important books: he studied the history of the definition and concept of madness in the Western world [112] and the development and organization of the prison [115]. In two important books, *The Order of Things* [113] and *The Archaeology of Knowledge* [114], he laid the foundations for his project of a novel way of writing intellectual history. During the last years before his death, he embarked on a history of sexuality which he left unfinished; only the first three volumes were published, [116], [117], and [118]. I cannot present all of this voluminous work here; instead, we will concentrate on those aspects which have exerted most influence and inspiration on later scholars and which have been especially relevant for classical studies.

The Power of Discourse

It is not only the variety of Foucault's work which makes him difficult to categorize, it is also his own dislike of theoretical dogmatism. His books are often characterized by a cautious and tentative approach. Important concepts are defined and then redefined in the course of his studies; he is always ready to reject results which seem to be definitive but then turn out to be preliminary, and in the end, readers are left with more questions than answers (Foucault himself has provided descriptions of his method, e.g., in [114.17] or in [117.11–13]). This apparent lack of coherence (or better: this renunciation of dogmatism) also makes it difficult to determine Foucault's relation to deconstruction. On the one hand, he was its opponent in many regards and had a (pretty intense and polemical) debate with Derrida at one point. On the other hand, he shares a number of interests and questions with the deconstructionists. Hence, Foucault has also been called a "poststructuralist," a somewhat vague label that does not say much about his work. Like the deconstructionists, Foucault devotes much of his research to questions of language and the use of language; like them, he does not consider language a transparent medium for expressing thoughts which are produced without its help but emphasizes that language is a decisive factor in limiting our ideas and the realm of what we are able to think at all.

Moreover, Foucault's thought is an heir to structuralism in another important aspect, which has often been regarded as scandalous, and thus is related to Derrida's position: Foucault is also convinced that the autonomous subject cannot be the source of meaning and coherence. This is already apparent in his examination of the "author function" (above, p. 126). The sentences which open and conclude his work *The Order of Things* and which describe (and apparently long for) the future disappearance of the human subject are even more famous (or, according to the reader's point of view, infamous): Foucault holds that "man is only a recent invention ..., a new wrinkle in our knowledge" [113.xxiii], and the last sentence of the book emphatically claims and wishes "that man would be erased, like a face drawn in sand at the edge of the sea" [113.387]. We will have to return to the controversy triggered by these and similar statements (below, pp. 147–149).

Accordingly, in his most important and influential works, Foucault was not concerned with the subject's freedom and individuality, but rather with the unconscious linguistic rules and mechanisms which restrict this freedom. Unlike de Saussure and the deconstructionists, however, Foucault is not interested in language as an abstract system of rules nor in an all-encompassing textuality, but in the social conditions of its use – if we want to use structuralist terminology, we may say that he is more interested in the *parole* than in the *langue*. To put it simply, we can say that Foucault explores the ways in which the use of language is a manifestation of power.

Perhaps the most accessible introduction to Foucault's methodology can be found in the inaugural lecture he held at the Collège de France in December, 1970 (English translation in [114.215–37]). In it, Foucault outlines a theoretical program for research projects which he wanted to undertake during the following years. As he explains at the beginning of his lecture [114.216], in human societies, discourse, the use of language, is not something free from all constraints, but instead is tightly controlled and organized. Certain areas are completely excluded from discourse: religious or moral taboos must not be addressed; the words of madmen are not considered serious discourse at all. A particularly clear example for these mechanisms of exclusion can be seen in the sciences: certain statements cannot be uttered within their boundaries. Within the discipline of physics, it is certainly possible to say that the universe will expand forever after the big bang, and it is equally admissible to say that this expansion will be reverted one day and the universe will end in a "big crunch," but if somebody were to say that this expansion is caused by the breathing of a god, he would position himself outside of the boundaries of the discursive field of physics. Hence, Foucault writes [114.223]: "Within its own limits, every discipline recognises true and false propositions, but it repulses a whole teratology of learning." (With the word "teratology," the study of monstrous creatures, Foucault here alludes to medieval maps which often depicted monsters and fabulous creatures at the confines of the known world.) Before an utterance can be judged to be true or false within a discipline, it has to be positioned and expressed within its limits; as Foucault writes vividly [114.224], it has to be "*dans le vrai*," "within the true." In the wake of ideas formulated by Nietzsche, Foucault claims that this "will to knowledge" is one of the strongest and most pervasive means of controlling human discourse.

All these mechanisms cause a "rarefaction" of discourse: not every individual is allowed to say everything in every situation, but certain rules control what we (can) say, and it is our task to analyze these rules. Foucault had already provided a methodology for such an analysis and raised some fundamental issues in his book *The Archaeology of Knowledge*, first published in 1969 [114]. In it, Foucault pleaded for a new historiographical project which would describe and analyze the various strata of discourse, very much like some sort of archeology. Foucault wants to explore the utterances (*énoncés*) in various disciplines. They all are subject to certain discursive rules which cause utterance "A" to be made in a given discipline at a certain point in time, rather than some other utterance. Hence, we must ask certain questions about these "discursive formations"; answering them will allow us to understand the system of their rules [114.50–5]:

ã» Who speaks? In which ways do discourses allow certain individuals to assume the role of the speaking subject while excluding others from this role, thus relegating them to the function of object of the discourse who are only spoken about? What status does the discourse confer upon the individuals who are allowed to assume this role? There are numerous constellations, as can be seen in a short remark which Foucault makes elsewhere [116.62]: in some situations such as the confession or the interrogation, it is not the position of the speaker which is powerful but that of the silent listener.

ã» Which institutional frameworks make discourse possible? How do they influence it by imposing certain formal conventions, preventing certain statements, sanctioning certain utterances as valuable and relevant while excluding others?

ã» What is the relation between the subject and the objects of discourse? How does she or he produce her utterances, take possession of these objects, subject them to her utterances? What is, on the other hand, the influence of the objects on the mode of discourse?

The totality of all rules which control the formation of an utterance and represent the "system of its enunciability" [114.129] is called an "archive" by Foucault. He writes: "the archive cannot be described in its totality" [114.130], but it is the framework within which every analysis of utterances and discursive formations has to take place.

In his book *The Archaeology of Power*, Foucault had already intimated that his methodology should explore the relation between discursive formations and non-discursive practices [114.162], and he had remarked that what is at stake in every discourse is power because discourse is a commodity which is in dispute in the political sphere [114.120]. However, he still declared that his main interest lay in analyzing the rules that were within the discourse or at the least "on its frontier" [114.74]. His subsequent course of research set out to fulfill the announcement he had made and take his analyses beyond the confines of discourse. This becomes clear, for example, in his 1975 book *Discipline and Punish* on the development and organization of the prison [115]. This work examines, on the one hand, the various social forms of discourse about crime and criminals and their reflections in social institutions such as forms of punishment; on the other hand, it analyzes the ways in which the inmates' bodies become a field upon which these various forms of discourse exert their power. In particular, Foucault's vigorous analysis of the modern prison system in which power has been transformed into anonymous "discipline" and hence become unassailable, outlines a new conception and definition of power: it no longer appears as sovereignty or coercion, but takes a variety of forms to hide its true character – as Foucault writes in another context [116.86]: "power is tolerable only on condition that it mask a substantial part of itself."

This methodology of exploring the relation between discourse and extralinguistic reality puts Foucault at odds with the positions of structuralism as well as with deconstruction, which is developing its concepts at the same time. Some of the most important differences between Foucault and the deconstructionists can be summarized thus:

- With his new approach, Foucault leaves the sphere of pure synchrony. This does not mean a return to conventional forms of historiography: his "archeology" does not attempt to discover "origins" and "developments," but emphasizes, in contrast to the overly smooth story lines of traditional historians, the discontinuity and disjointedness of human reality. Nevertheless, the sheer perception of and focus on a historical dimension is an important step beyond structuralist dogmas.

- For Foucault, language is no longer a system hermetically closed in itself; unlike structuralist *langue*, his "discourse" is closely connected with extralinguistic factors, especially questions of social and political power. This is a decisive difference to Derrida's position for whom there is "nothing outside of the text" (above, p. 123).

- In his earlier works, Foucault defined the task of scholarship as being exclusively focused on description and analysis. His later statements and especially his social commitment make it clear that political action can and must be one of the consequences of his insights – it is necessary to recognize and see through structures of dominance and control in order to fight against them. This is another fundamental difference to deconstruction and its political restraint (see above, p. 130, and cf. p. 29).

It has already been suggested that Foucault's influence was produced not so much because of the positive results of his work than because they offered numerous possibilities to ask novel questions and to pursue his ideas in different directions. Even when his writings make contributions to distinct disciplines, they appear to call for more thorough analyses rather than providing them. Undoubtedly, his conscious abstention from dogmatism and from totalizing theories and definitions have contributed to augmenting his influence, which has been decisive for a number of scholars (the entire movement of the New Historicism would not have been possible without Foucault's work; see below, p. 159). Hence, when we read his books such as *The Archaeology of Knowledge*, we receive negative definitions for a number of fundamental concepts such as "enunciation" (*énoncé*), "discursive practice" (*pratique discursive*), or "archive": Foucault explains carefully what these concepts are *not* [114.88–98]. But we do not get any clear and unambiguous definition. Even a concept as momentous and central to his theory as "power" is never clearly defined – power seems to be ubiquitous in all human relationships ("Power is everywhere," as he writes explicitly in [116.93]), but it eludes any attempts at unequivocal definition. On the other hand, this can be seen as a fundamental openness of his concepts, and it has encouraged many scholars to transfer Foucault's questions and terms to other disciplines. Scholars critical of his approach have described the situation in somewhat different terms: the vagueness of Foucault's terminology allowed other scholars to see in his concepts whatever they chose without taking the consequences of his theory into account; this is a criticism raised by Lentricchia in [235.86–102].

Objections to Foucault's Analysis of Discourse

Foucault's theories have not been undisputed, and we will now turn to this criticism. His opponents have rightly reproached him for being somewhat superficial in his use of historical evidence: his judgments about historical developments, they argue, are not always easy to accept; e.g., he postulates dramatic changes in the history of a certain discourse without substantiating such claims (see the examples given in articles by Page DuBois [88.102] or Paul Allen Miller [259.175]). Even admirers of his work have to admit that the factual informa-

tion they contain must sometimes be taken with a grain of salt (see Gary Gutting's remarks in [162]). This criticism is especially pertinent to his early work
when Foucault was primarily interested in discourse itself, not in its ramifica-
tions. Supporters of Foucault have been a bit too cavalier in their reply to this
objection: they claimed that the value of Foucault's research does not depend on
the historical accuracy of its details (see, e.g., the remarks of Roy Boyne [45.34
n. 8]). But Amy Richlin is right to emphasize [305.168]: "If you are going to
base major claims about the nature of historical change on historical research,
at least you should get it right." In addition to this factual inaccuracy, there are
a number of serious methodological problems:

- Foucault's methodology is good at explaining the ways in which a certain
  distribution of discursive power works in a certain historical situation; it
  is less good at analyzing the phenomenon of historical change: it is, in a
  strange manner, blind to the revolutions and revisions of such a distribution.
  Foucault himself was deeply aware that this was a central problem of his
  research: in *The Archaeology of Knowledge*, he returned to the phenomenon
  of historical change several times (such as [114.74–6 or 135–40]), but all
  his explanations remain vague and unsatisfactory. Though Foucault turned
  away from structuralism's pure synchrony, this difficulty can be explained as
  a legacy of the "blind spot" of any structuralist approach (see above, p. 29).

- As Said [314.222] remarked, the reason for this particular blindness can be
  found in Foucault's definition of power. It is certainly the case that power
  does occur in terms such as the ones analyzed by Foucault, as bureaucratic,
  discursive power without individual origin and without systematic oppression. But Said is right to emphasize that in history, we often find the phenomenon of personal power and active oppression, to which Foucault seems
  oblivious.

- A related issue is Foucault's perspective on the human individual. There can
  be no doubt that individual human beings have changed discursive structures through their actions and have influenced historical developments
  through their "will to power." In this regard, Foucault is an heir to the pre-
  conceptions of structuralism which also was more interested in depersonal-
  ized systems of rules than in individual words and actions.

- From the point of view of a professional historian, we may wonder to what
  extent Foucault's project of an archeology of discourse is capable of providing reliable information. Foucault himself is aware of these difficulties and
  admits that his research will never be able to view the totality of a given

cultural archive; for him, this is a necessary corollary of his methodology [114.157–60]. But we are entitled to ask how this conspicuous modesty in his methodological aspirations relates to the sweeping statements which we find in many passages of his books.

ঌ This question is intimately connected to another objection which Foucault himself had anticipated [114.205–6]: from where does his own discourse derive its authority? Can it be situated outside of the system of discursive fields; can it utter "truth(s)" without hiding its own will to power under such noble expressions? It is a testimonial to Foucault's intellectual sincerity that he is prepared to raise such questions about his own work, but he has not been willing or not been able to supply satisfactory answers, as his critics have rightly seen (see, e.g., Hubert L. Dreyfus and Paul Rabinow in [87.90–100], Habermas in [163.276–86], Hayden White in [377.106–14], Dosse in [86.1.337], and Wolfgang Detel in [81.53–7]).

We should, then, not regard Foucault's project of an archeology of discourse as replacing all other forms of historiography; instead, we should see it as a valuable addition which will allow us to come to grips with phenomena that would otherwise remain unseen. It should be evident that different historical perspectives will always be able to see different *partial* aspects of history, and Foucault's approach is no exception to this rule.

However, the aspect of Foucault's thought which turned out to be most difficult to accept was his emphasis on the thesis that the human subject is about to disappear. This has given him the reputation of being an "anti-humanist." Foucault's later work seems to imply, at least in part, a cautious retreat from his earlier positions. At the Collège de France, he taught several courses on the subject, and the last two volumes of his *History of Sexuality*, [118] and [117], study the emergence of the subject in antiquity (see below, p. 151). Moreover, in his later years, Foucault became involved in a number of political issues, especially the struggle of oppressed social groups whose human rights were being violated (such as prisoners, Vietnames refugees, or the Polish labor union Solidarność). This commitment can be understood as an acknowledgment that he was now prepared to pay more attention to individual actions and individual responsibility and, accordingly, to the existence of the human subject. Maybe we are entitled to replace his earlier, more provocative assertions (quoted above, p. 141) with the more cautious formulation which he used elsewhere [114.25–6] when he emphasized that his aim was not to abolish terms such as "author" or "book":

They must not be rejected definitively of course, but the tranquillity with which they are accepted must be disturbed; we must show that they do not come about of themselves, but are always the result of a construction the rules of which must be known, and the justification of which must be scrutinized: we must define in what conditions and in view of which analyses certain of them are legitimate; and we must indicate which of them can never be accepted in any circumstances.

However, Foucault has never explicitly retracted or withdrawn his earlier statements and has never been able (or willing) to obliterate the impression these words had made. If we consider the enormous implications they have, we will understand why they met with harsh, sometimes quite passionate criticism. Even if we disregard some of the more emotional contributions and just look at the most important arguments, it soon becomes clear why so many readers found Foucault's assertions hard to swallow. Foucault himself had, at the end of *The Archaeology of Knowledge*, predicted that there would be resistance to his theory [114.210–11]: over the course of the last decades, he writes, people were forced to accept that they, as human individuals (as "cogito"), had little or no control of a number of important areas of their existence, such as social institutions, language, or myths. Hence, Foucault says he understands that humans, after being robbed of the illusion of being in control of these aspects, feel unease about losing the liberty and control of their discourse. Even structuralist linguistics had conceded them as much: within the system of language, the *langue*, we are free to form every utterance (*parole*) we please. And aren't we all convinced that our thoughts are completely free and that nothing but outside forces can prevent us from expressing them? Foucault is convinced that we can no longer subscribe to these reassuring beliefs: discourse also obeys rules, and we can never control these rules and hardly perceive their existence.

It is certainly impossible to simply return to old-fashioned ideas about the autonomous subject, and we can agree with Foucault that our behavior, our language, and our mind are determined by rules beyond the individual's reach, and more so than we perceive. But does this mean that the human subject is disappearing or ought to disappear? Despite those radical announcements, it still hasn't seen fit to vanish. Again, the political consequences of this conviction are particularly striking and make Foucault's assumption appear more than dubious:

ชๅ Numerous groups fighting against political oppression at first welcomed

Foucault's analysis of discourse as a desirable tool for making the mechanisms and strategies of domination visible and thus helping their fight. Understandably, they pointed out that members of such groups first have to acquire a voice of their own, that their first aim is to obtain the status of a speaking subject. This criticism of Foucault's theories has, for example, been expressed by feminists who emphatically agreed with his analysis of sexuality as a sphere of the struggle for social power (see, e.g., the contribution by Nancy Hartsock [174]).

❧ Overall, we cannot avoid the question of how political action can still be said to be possible after the disappearance of the subject. Isn't this thesis just an attempt to escape the necessity of making social interaction possible through intersubjective communication and compromise? How can we establish categories such as responsibility or unfreedom (not to mention the highly problematic concept of human freedom) without recurring to the idea of the human subject?

These objections seem to be momentous enough to invalidate Foucault's thoughts about the human subject. But we are allowed to ask whether the questions Foucault raised, the methodology he suggested, and the inspirations he gave to research in the humanities can still be put to fruitful use if we do not share his opinions about the subject. I would argue that Foucault's own work is proof that this is indeed the case. In his later writings, he silently reintroduced the subject and examined the conditions and rules governing its emergence. It is a historical fact that there are a wide range of possibilities of becoming a subject – human beings have not regarded themselves a person or an individual in the same way in all societies and periods; the difference between freedom and constraint, "I" and society, doing and suffering has been defined in different ways in different cultures. This should give us pause: it seems more promising to examine these historically different ways of establishing the subject than to assume that there is one single, uniform way of defining its position. Foucault himself has led the way by looking at the subject in antiquity; we will examine these works in the next section.

Foucault and Antiquity

Foucault studied aspects of ancient society in the last two books he finished before his death. They are volumes 2 and 3 of his *History of Sexuality*, [117] and [118]. In order to understand his hypotheses and the intense discussion

about them, we must first have to take a brief look at the plan and the genesis of
the work as a whole. In 1976, Foucault published the first volume of what was
planned then as a series of six volumes on the history of sexuality in the Western
world; the French title was *La Volonté de savoir*, "The Will to Knowledge" [116].
In it, Foucault discusses the "repressive hypothesis" according to which sexuality and the discourse about it have been more and more censored and repressed
since the eighteenth and nineteenth centuries and have only been able to recover
from this repression in the most recent era. Foucault argues that this hypothesis is quite untrue; much rather, talking about sexuality has been multiplied
during this seemingly repressive period: disciplines such as medicine, psychology, psychoanalysis, and the legal system studied and discussed, described and
classified "abnormal" sexual behavior, thus establishing and making possible a
scientific discourse of and about sexuality. Other societies created an *ars erotica*,
an "art of loving" while this development led to a *scientia sexualis*, a "science of
sexuality."

Foucault suggests that this particular discourse should be an object of historical analysis [116.69]: "The history of sexuality ... must first be written from
the viewpoint of a history of discourses." Which constellations of power have
rendered this scientific discourse possible? Foucault argues that in this context,
power must not be seen as merely negative, refusing, and repressive, but we have
to understand that it is a productive feature. In such discourses, sexuality became one of the decisive factors of human personality (think of the importance
psychoanalysis attributes to aspects of sexuality). The "avowal" became the central form of speaking about sexuality, be it in the form of the confession, the
criminal interrogation, or the medical anamnesis. This production of sexuality as an area of knowledge coincided with the production of a certain truth
about sexuality: now, it became possible to speak of "natural" and "perverse"
forms; a "norm" and "departures" from this norm were established. Foucault
regarded this process as an important part of the emergence of what he called
"bio-power": in the eighteenth and nineteenth centuries, he claimed, we can
observe that power, in realms such as politics and economics, shifts from being
a merely punitive factor to being normative and regulative. Its main areas of
action now were the disciplining of the human body and control of the development of populations; both areas are intimately connected with the normal-
ization and control of sexuality.

This first volume of the planned work offered not so much a historical study
of sexuality as the theoretical blueprint for such an analysis which Foucault proposed to undertake in the following years. The program of this analysis appeared

to be based on the analysis of discourse such as Foucault had outlined and practiced it in his prior works. But no continuation appeared for the next eight years, and when, in 1984, two more volumes were published, they came as a major surprise. Foucault starts *The Use of Pleasure* [117] with an introduction which contains a lengthy criticism of his earlier work and proposes an entirely new methodology for the whole project of the *History of Sexuality*: his further research, he writes, has indicated that it was only possible to understand why sexuality could become a moral problem in the eighteenth and nineteenth centuries if one had previously analyzed the ways in which human beings came, in the course of history, to regard themselves as "subjects of desire." This process began in antiquity; hence, the two volumes published in 1984 studied the emergence of the individual person in antiquity. In *The Use of Pleasure* [117], Foucault studies Greek sexual norms in the fourth century BCE, paying particular attention to the differences between Greek and later Christian values. Greek morality did not consider sexual desire as being negative or harmful *per se*, but saw it as a very strong urge which was dangerous because of its excessive power and, unless used in the right way, threatened to overwhelm a human being and make it the slave of her or his own passions. Hence, the free Greek male (Greek morality is almost exclusively concerned with free males) needed to restrain himself and was not allowed to give way to this desire in its full extent. Unlike Christian morality, Greek rules about sexuality saw the danger not in some kind of pollution, but in human enslavement to emotions [117.79–80]; hence, they did not distinguish between what was allowed and what was forbidden, but between excess and moderation [117.114]. The proper use of our sexual desires belongs into the comprehensive field of a general conduct of life which is meant to help humans become subjects controlling and governing their bodies and minds. However, the general rules of this conduct made philosophers as well as physicians suggest that men should abstain from sexuality as much as they could. This laid the groundwork for the later (Christian) morality which esteemed virginity and sexual abstention. Foucault then analyzes the similarities, but also the differences between Greek and later Christian ideas about marriage, especially the rules regarding mutual fidelity in married couples.

But the main focus of Greek ethics was not so much on married life as on pederasty. Foucault first underlines the fundamental difference between the Greek concept and Christian beliefs: for the Greeks, it was completely obvious that adult men would feel sexually attracted to handsome young men as well as to beautiful women. However, the structure of this relationship posed problems: the socially accepted form of this relationship was an older man pursuing and getting involved with a decidedly younger boy. This boy, being significantly younger, was in a socially inferior position. On the one hand, his older companion tried to pressure him into giving in to his advances; on the other hand, he was supposed not to give in too soon and not to let himself be degraded into a pure object of sexual lust. The reason for these contradictory expectations was that as a grown-up, he was expected to become a mature male who could control himself and take political responsibility in his city. This was a dilemma for the boy, and Greek philosophers devoted lengthy explanations to its solution. According to Foucault, Plato suggested one possible answer: in his dialogues, especially the *Phaedrus* and the *Symposium*, he discussed the nature of pederasty. He considered Eros, sexual desire, as a longing for beauty and truth, and thus made it transcend the narrow frame of pederasty proper. In this definition, both the loving adult and the beloved youth can play an active part since both are striving for truth.

Foucault considered these ethical ideas an important step toward "a history of 'ethics,' understood as the elaboration of a form of relation to self that enables an individual to fashion himself into a subject of ethical conduct" [117.251]. In *The Care of the Self* [118], he examines the modifications this ethics underwent until the second century CE. The idea, already common in classical times, that a human being needs to perfect himself, is developed into a full-blown system of "care of the self" (ἐπιμέλεια ἑαυτοῦ, *cura sui*) during the Hellenistic period, the time after the death of Alexander the Great in 323 BCE; whoever aspires to a philosophical ideal of life has to fulfill the requirements of this ethical system. As Foucault emphasizes, this systems demands a more severe, "ascetic" self-discipline from every individual not because of stricter moral rules but because of a new way of defining individual perfection [118.67].

It is in the frame of this redefinition of an ethical system that the rules concerning sexuality changed, too. Medical writings of this time emphasize more and more the violent nature of the sexual act, which jeopardizes the body's balance; hence, they suggest as much abstention as possible. In the classical period, the purpose of marriage had been defined as the procreation of offspring in order to continue the family's bloodline. Now, marriage is more and more seen as the connection of two individuals for a common life; hence, new duties ensue for both partners. The ideal of unconditional mutual faithfulness, which had already been expressed in classical texts, is now a frequent and normal requirement that expresses these new ethical ideas. Pederasty does not disappear competely, but it has to defend itself against this new ideal of marital community; its definition has to be redefined in a modified form that takes this new marital ideal into account in order to retain its philosophical justification. In the conclusion of his book, Foucault makes it clear that this ethics often continues and draws upon classical ideas and concepts, yet makes them conform to this model of the "care of the self," thus subordinating them to new ideals and rearranging their value. These new ideas prepare the way for Christian morality, but we must not neglect to perceive the important differences.

The Debate about Foucault's Interpretation of Ancient Sexuality

If we consider the critical judgments about the two volumes studying ancient society, we perceive a curiously divided opinion: while laypersons were full of admiration (Hinrich Fink-Eitel calls them an "ingenious analysis" [105.75]), many classicists were less impressed with these books. The reproach of factual inaccuracy and lack of evidence, which had already been raised against earlier publications (above, p. 145), was targeted at these books as well (for Glenn W. Bowersock, they constitute "one of the most serious, if well-intentioned, misrepresentations of antiquity that the modern world has yet beheld" [42.86]). Indubitably, scholars were right to point out a number of gaps and misrepresentations in Foucault's analysis of sexuality in the ancient world:

- ❧ Feminist critics have reproached Foucault for being completely oblivious of women as subjects; this has been argued by Richlin in a passionate and fascinating article [305] (cf. the contributions by Jean Grimshaw [156] and DuBois [88]). These critics rightly point out that there is enough evidence from the ancient world to avoid this blind spot of Foucault's work. Given this important gap, one should see Foucault's books not as a history of sexuality, but just as one small part of such a history.
- ❧ Even the male perspective is taken into account only in a small part. Foucault's selection of texts he analyzes is almost completely restricted to philosophical and medical documents. If he had also taken into consideration texts such as lyrical poems or love novels, he would have revised a number of his findings. Critics have rightly complained that his selection of the evidence has already decided about the results of his works, as in an article by David H. J. Larmour, Paul Allen Miller, and Charles Platter [229.25]: "Foucault reads and presents a selection of ancient evidence in a way that ensures that he 'finds' what he is looking for."
- ❧ In addition to these misrepresentations which result from neglecting certain genres, there is also a chronological and cultural bias. Foucault's *The*

Use of Pleasure [117] studies almost exclusively texts from Athenian authors; nevertheless, Foucault makes sweeping generalizations about "the Greeks." Moreover, in *The Care of the Self* [118], he uses texts from Greek and Roman authors without paying attention to cultural differences. This way, there is a serious misrepresentation, especially of Roman attitudes.

ě♥ Foucault reads even the material he uses in a biased way which disregards its complexities. As Pierre Hadot has shown [164], in Stoic and Epicurean texts, the notion of "care of the self" is not as central as claimed by Foucault; David Cohen and Richard Saller have questioned his interpretation of ancient marriage [57]. The clear and coherent picure of ancient sexuality which Foucault depicts contains a number of (sometimes significant) distortions.

In addition to these factual problems, there were also a number of methodological questions. We have already seen that for all those who had read the *Introduction* [116] to Foucault's *History of Sexuality* and were waiting for a continuation of the project, the two volumes published in 1984 constituted a major surprise. Foucault had not only altered the entire plan of his work in significant ways; the style of his presentation was completely different. There is hardly a trace anymore of the grand theories and hypotheses of his earlier work; concepts such as "discourse" and "power" are hardly mentioned. Instead, we find a historiographical approach; Foucault reads, summarizes, and interprets the ancient testimonies and tries to tease out their cultural context. This change in methodology is, on the one hand, in need of explanation (and Foucault's readers have sought and found a number of explanations); on the other hand, it provokes our judgment. Especially readers who had admired Foucault's prior works and had derived inspiration from them could not but be disappointed by his new methodology (see, e.g., Grimshaw's contribution [156]). Apparently, Foucault had returned to purely traditional forms of historiography. What had become of the analysis of discourse and the principle (which Foucault had emphasized again and again; see [114.55, 63, 70, 121–2, 164–5]) that he wanted to analyze discourse as an event of its own right, not as a translation of desires, thoughts, and systems? Here, in interpreting a text by pseudo-Lucian, Foucault states explicitly that he will make abstraction of the rhetorical and ironical elements of this passage in order to dissect its "erotic argumentation" (*argumentaire érotique*); this is a clear example of taking the text for a transparent medium of thoughts, thus degrading the discourse and "translating" it.

The volumes published in 1984 marked a sharp break with Foucault's earlier theoretical positions in other regards, too. Previously, Foucault had always refused to search for historical continuities; instead, he had emphasized the great rifts in historical developments [114.8–9]. In these new volumes, we find attempts to distinguish common features and differences between the classical and Hellenistic periods – this puts at least as much emphasis on the continuities as on the breaks. Now it could be assumed that Foucault was merely returning to solid and reliable criteria of historiography. The problem, however, was that Foucault's way of choosing and examining the evidence is not appropriate for exploring such developments. Miller rightly criticizes [259.175]: "Foucault ultimately privileges a static vision of history that precedes from one steady-state model to the next without any substantial transitional stages. ... We are given detailed snapshots of fourth-century Greece and of the first two centuries of imperial Rome, with only the barest outline of what occurs in between." In retrospect, this puts the high pretensions even of Foucault's earlier work in doubt: is an analysis of a social "archive" really possible, and to what extent can such research claim to be reliable and relevant? How many "discursive events" have to be collected in order to deliver valid data? Are some texts "more representative" than others? How can we find out which ones they are? Aren't certain areas of discourse lost forever because they have never been transmitted to us?

Nevertheless, a number of classicists gave a more positive assessment of Foucault's work and took these two volumes as inspiration to examine ancient sexuality in novel ways. However, if we take a closer look at these new contributions, we will soon become aware that their authors pay enthusiastic homage to *The Use of Pleasure* [117] and *The Care of the Self* [118], yet look more to the first volume of the series [116] for theoretical and methodological inspiration. Many of them are not so much interested in topics that had motivated Foucault (such as the emergence of the moral subject in antiquity) as in exploring and analyzing the differences between ancient and modern sexuality. As David M. Halperin, John J. Winkler, and Froma I. Zeitlin write [168.7]: whoever examines the discourses and practices of ancient sexuality "will find herself confronted in the ancient record by radically unfamiliar values, forms of behavior, and social practices, by ways of organizing and articulating experience that challenge modern notions about what life is like and that call into question the supposed universality of 'human nature' as we currently understand it." Hence, these scholars underline one aspect that is more implied than clearly expressed in Foucault's own writings: our modern perception of sexuality is not "natural" and eternally unchanging, but historically contingent and thus culturally just one way out of a great many possibilities; hence, it can be changed. As readers of Foucault's books emphasize, he himself has always been cautious in expressing this thought (see, e.g., Rabinow [297.347] or Susan Bordo [40.180]). Antiquity and the particular details of sexuality, especially of pederasty, that we can study in it teach us that our categories of homosexuality and heterosexuality are not terms for unalterable dispositions that are unconditionally defined in human nature, but constructs which are determined by the culture we live in (hence, this view is called "social constructivism"). In particular, this aspect has been emphasized by classicists who were active in the fight for gay rights, such as Halperin [166.26].

At the end of this chapter, we will try to sum up the discussion about Foucault's study of ancient texts and his influence on classical studies. Overall, my impression of the two volumes published in 1984 is rather negative. Cohen and Saller were right to say [57.56–9] that after the *Introduction* to the *History of Sexuality*, the public was justified in expecting a different continuation of the project. The first volume surpassed the two subsequent ones by far; this becomes clear when we see that even scholars who hold a positive opinion about these later studies tend to rely, in their own work, almost exclusively on vol. 1 and try to minimize the radical differences between the various parts. Whatever may have been the scholarly or personal reasons which made Foucault change the direction of his work so fundamentally, we have to respect them and should not reproach Foucault for writing the books he wrote and not books we would have found more important and more interesting ourselves. Nevertheless, we are free to follow his inspiration in different ways than he has done himself.

This is exactly what the German philosopher Detel has done in a recent book [81], which is among the most fascinating and substantial contributions to the debate about Foucault's interpretation of ancient sexuality. Detel makes quite explicit what is the aim of his book [81.2]: "It is a bold attempt to say what Foucault's historical perspective and better historical knowledge should have led him to say about the texts he studied, but which he did not." In a number of penetrating analyses, Detel succeeds in demonstrating that Foucault's excessive focus on the single aspect of sexuality has prevented him from a real understanding of ethical phenomena, which are the subject of his studies [81.78]: "The ethical work of the ancient world is at the same time educational work in a much more comprehensive sense and complex sense than Foucault is prepared to admit." In particular, Detel argues convincingly that the connection between sexuality and questions of political power is much more intimate than Foucault had seen; as an example, he remarks that ancient marriage is situated [81.161] "at a juncture between political patriarchy, scientific economic knowledge, and ethical self-discipline."

Detel's book clearly demonstrates that Foucault has inspired new and fruit-ful ways of thinking about the ancient world, and the new interest in ancient sexuality which his example has stimulated is more than welcome in our disci-pline – the vivid discussion about his work has fostered fascinating research and produced a greater methodological awareness. (However, as Richlin [305.169] has reminded us, we may legitimately wonder whether Foucault's work was re-ally necessary for this to happen; as she understandably writes, "that's the kind of thing that feminist historians were doing all along.") On the other hand, one may regret that classical studies has concentrated almost exclusively on this sin-gle aspect of Foucault's work. His explorations of ancient sexuality are certainly important and fascinating; they certainly help us understand the relativity of our own categories in this field which we take for unalterable and "natural"; nev-ertheless, I would argue that other ideas which Foucault proposed merit more attention for our work on the ancient world. Personally, I find it quite sad that in classical studies, the earlier, more political work of Foucault has been almost dismissed and displaced by attention to the *History of Sexuality*. When we study ancient texts, it would certainly be worthwhile pursuing a number of questions which Foucault defined as foremost for analyzing discourse [119.1.787]: "Which special types of discursive practice can be found in a given period? Which rela-tions between these different practices can be established? Which relations be-tween different forms of practice can be established? What is the relation they have to non-discursive forms of practice such as political, social, or economic practices? Which changes can these forms of practice undergo?"

Such questions will hardly allow us to draw a complete and comprehensive picture of a certain period (we have seen that Foucault's "archeology" is more an addition to than a replacement for other, more conventional forms of histo-riography, above, p. 147). But to ask them with regard to individual problems, individual texts, and individual cultural phenomena, to use them in a local, not a global manner appears to be a valid and promising way of research for clas-sical studies. In the next chapter, we will see a theoretical approach which was inspired precisely by such questions and Foucault's methodology in answering them.

Further Reading

Reading Foucault demands concentration and mental discipline, yet his books are not as difficult and forbidding to read as the texts of the deconstruction-ists. Without a doubt, Foucault's own writings provide the best introduction to his work. In addition to his inaugural lecture at the Collège de France, which is an especially accessible summary of his major ideas ([114.215–37], mentioned above, p. 142), I would particularly recommend *The Archaeology of Knowledge* [114] for a first approach; it contains the most important concepts of his earlier work. Another way of accessing his theoretical position are the numerous smaller articles and published interviews. A complete collection of the original French texts can be found in [119]; the English translation [120] contains a selection of the material; in the English-speaking world, the collection *The Foucault Reader*, edited by Paul Rabinow [297], is very popular. The debate about ancient sexuality has produced numerous publications, some of which are excellent. In addition to Wolfgang Detel's book [81], mentioned above, a small selection would comprise *Before Sexuality*, a volume edited by David M. Halperin, John J. Winkler, and Froma I. Zeitlin [167]; Bruce Thornton's *Eros* [353], the collection *Rethinking Sexuality*, edited by David H. J. Larmour, Paul Allen Miller, and Charles Platter [228], and the highly entertaining *Courtesans and Fishcakes* by James Davidson [70] (the three books mentioned last are all, to varying degrees, critical of Foucault's ideas). Issue 2:1 (1990) of the journal *differences. A Journal of Feminist Cultural Studies* is entirely devoted to the topic "Sexuality in Greek and Roman Society."

Chapter 10
New Historicism

In the two preceding chapters, we saw the differences, but also the similarities between the approaches of deconstruction and of Foucault. It is important to keep these theoretical positions in mind if we want to understand what defines the so-called New Historicism (the term is problematical, and we will have to come back to it). In the USA, deconstruction was the predominant, if not undisputed strand of literary theory in the 1980s. But its tendency to postulate an insurmountable boundary between the text and the outside world carried the danger of becoming just another modish version of immanent close reading which placed the great canonical texts into the empty space of linguistic *différance*. It was not only the more traditional groups of literary criticism who were dissatisfied with this situation, but also a number of innovative scholars argued strongly in favor of putting literature back into its social and historical context. In particular, a group of younger critics who taught English Renaissance literature at the University of California at Berkeley argued in favor of such a new direction. This was certainly no coincidence: in the early 1980s, Foucault held several appointments as a visiting professor at Berkeley, and he exerted a thorough influence on these scholars. In 1982, Stephen Greenblatt (b. 1943), one of the leading thinkers of this group, wrote an introductory essay for a special issue of the journal *Genre* [147] in which he labeled the methodology he and his colleagues were using a "New Historicism." Henceforth, a new brand of criticism was available in the supermarket of literary theory, and the customers (who were a bit sick of deconstruction which had been around for several years now) eagerly accepted this "new and improved" product. However, Greenblatt soon had to admit that New Historicism was not quite what many readers wished to see in it. In the programmatical article "Towards a Poetics of Culture," he wrote [149.1]: it was "a practice rather than a doctrine, since as far as I can tell (and I should be the one to know) it's no doctrine at all." Nevertheless, neither literary critics working in academia nor the general public let themselves be discouraged: they all regarded New Historicism as the latest fashion you just had to follow. This became especially visible after the popular *New York Times Magazine* published an article about Greenblatt and his new methodology [33]: it was now indisputable that this was the successor to the superannuated deconstructionist model. Time and again, the scholars working in this field themselves emphasized that New Historicism was, as H. Aram Veeser writes [361.x], "a phrase without an adequate referent" or, as Louis A. Montrose says [266.392], just an invention of its commentators and detractors – in vain. It was perceived as the new theoretical paradigm. This in turn inspired its adherents to fulfill these general expectations and provide a theoretical foundation for the sort of research they had performed in a more implicit and intuitive manner. If we now turn to this relatively new movement, we must not forget that its adherents feel that it is common interests and questions which connects them rather than a full-blown theory.

New Historicism and Deconstruction

Undoubtedly, large parts of New Historicist thinking can be understood as a critical discussion of deconstructionist tenets. As we will see, New Historicists do not categorically reject the ideas of deconstruction, but their fundamental approach to texts is diametrically opposed to its principles. While deconstruction's main aim is to demonstrate that texts are "always already" severed from their original context (decontextualized) and that no historical context will ever be sufficient to guarantee the stability of their meaning, New Historicism goes in the opposite direction and emphasizes the contextualization of texts. New Historicists emphasize that texts do not originate in a historical vacuum; instead, they are produced in certain historical and social situations, and knowledge of these circumstances will at least not be detrimental to our interpretation of the text. However, it would be rash to assume that this is just a predictable swing of the critical pendulum in the opposite direction and that New Historicism is merely a rejection of the more outrageous deconstructionist paradoxes (as Lentricchia [236.86–7] seems to imply). New Historicism differs markedly from older, established attempts at historical contextualization in both theory and practice, as will be clear when we look at a number of significant details.

&ラ New Historicism considers literature as being just one among a multitude of social discourses that all participate in establishing and interpreting a common view of the world and of human society. They vehemently refuse to privilege literary texts in any way. Hence, they reject consciously (and sometimes provocatively) the conventional hierarchy (which seems so unalterable in older interpretations) of literary text, which must be interpreted, and historical "background," which has to act as a foil and to make the real object of our study appear in a better and clearer way. Greenblatt, for example, writes [148.95]: "history cannot simply be set against literary texts as either stable antithesis or stable background, and the protective isolation of those texts gives way to a sense of their interaction with other texts and hence of the permeability of their boundaries." There is hardly an aspect of New Historicism which has been more difficult to accept for conventional critics than this harsh juxtaposition of "high literature" and everyday texts such as diaries, legal acts, or political pamphlets; in this duet, the "obscure source is not at all meant to play the timid secondary part," as Andreas Höfele rightly says [183.113].

ᴁ If we look at the consequences of this refusal to make a sharp distinction between "high" literature and its historical "background," we see that New Historicism is prepared to read everyday texts in a close and careful way which had hitherto been reserved for literary works. If we want to understand the ways in which literature and other textual forms influence each other in a certain period, we must pay an equal amount of attention to both sorts of texts. Montrose [265.17], one of the main representatives of New Historicism, has vividly expressed this thus: New Historicism has developed a new form of intertextuality that does not put different authors and different texts in a diachronic dialogue, but instead establishes such a dialogue synchronically, within the same cultural system.

ᴁ Hence, the texts that interact and connect in such a system are no longer seen as masterworks that are produced for eternity and are stable and fixed for all time, but instead, New Historicism emphasizes the aspect of social action through texts. Like other forms of social discourse, literature wants to fulfill social functions. This explains the refusal to distinguish between a "background" and a "foreground": representatives of New Historicism do not consider symbolic actions (such as the theater or religious rituals) as a secondary phenomenon that merely interprets a reality which exists unproblematically and objectively. Instead, they emphasize that human beings always attribute meaning to social and historical circumstances right from the start. As Lee Patterson [285.60] writes, man "is a creature who is constituted by his own constitution of the symbolic activity that is culture."

ᴁ By expressing such views, New Historicism positions itself with regard to a question which has been discussed for a long time. One can say that there are two extreme positions concerning the relationship between literary texts (or other works of art) on the one hand and historical reality on the other. Humanistic theories of art often sought eternal values and truth in works of art which were supposed to be independent of the historical contingencies of their production. This view considers literature to be completely or almost completely autonomous. Political analyses such as Marxist readings, however, considered all artistic products to be part of an "ideological superstructure" which merely reflects the economic or social conditions of the society in which they were produced; hence, they see art as being completely determined. It is obvious that New Historicism rejects the first alternative; it refuses to see great art in some sort of intellectual vacuum. However, it replaces the Marxist distinction of basis and superstructure with the assumption of a mutual influence of material and cultural factors (see Montrose [265.23]). In this rejection of a crude cultural determinism, New Historicism is similar to "Cultural Materialism," a movement which has been influential especially in Great Britain. Its main representative, Raymond Williams (1921–88), also emphasized [378.99] that culture is not a mere reproduction of outside factors, but is as productive and active as economic or political actions.

All these points make it clear why New Historicism deserves to be called "new." It is certainly not a mere return to older attempts at historical contextualization or a reaction to the extreme positions of deconstruction. Much rather, its proponents take into account the arguments of deconstruction and other postmodern tendencies against the assumption that historical reality is unproblematic and can be understood and analyzed in simple, unambiguous ways. They share a general mistrust (frequent in the Western world since the 1970s) against the grand "master narratives" which purport to provide sweeping explanations of the course of world history. Marxism, for instance, claims that the entire history of humanity is marked by class struggle and will inevitably end with the victory of the proletariat. Montrose [266.411] expresses it thus: in New Historicism, like in other modern tendencies of historical narrative, we observe a "shift from History to histories."

This New Historicist rejection of all-embracing explanations entails a number of consequences. First, its adherents are modest enough to renounce any claim to an exhaustive interpretation of a text or a culture. Greenblatt, for example, writes that he consciously and voluntarily relinquishes [148.4] "the satisfying illusion of a 'whole reading,' the impression conveyed by powerful critics that had they but world enough and time, they could illuminate every corner of the text and knit together into a unified interpretive vision all of their discrete perceptions. My vision is necessarily more fragmentary." Moreover, the turn toward multiple "histories" explains one of the most striking aspects of New Historicist practice, its predilection for astonishing, often remote or apparently inconsequential anecdotes. It can almost be considered a trademark of New Historicism to begin one's studies with such a surprising story and lead one's readers into unfamiliar territory – Greenblatt, for example, starts a study of Shakespeare's tragedy *Henry V* [148.21] with an extract from a police report about Shakespeare's contemporary Christopher Marlowe (1564–93).

This New Historicist practice reveals the influence of an inspirational figure who is often quoted by its proponents (e.g., Montrose [266.399]), the American anthropologist Clifford Geertz (1926–2006). Geertz developed an anthropological methodology that he calls [132.24] the "semiotic approach to culture." According to him, cultural phenomena cannot be observed and described as "objective" behavioral patterns; instead, they must be understood as being embedded in a complex communicative system: by performing certain actions, the members of a culture want to make statements, they want to convey meaning. The anthropologist's task consists in understanding such statements; (s)he regards culture as a text which needs to be deciphered. As if they were learning a foreign language, anthropologists cannot take general rules as their point of departure, but must begin with individual phenomena and guess their significance. Anthropologists, then, try to explore which meaning a certain behavior has for those who are fluent in the language of a certain cultural system. At the same time, it is clear that every single action can only be understood by constantly referring to the entire cultural system. For this procedure, Geertz has coined the term "thick description," which has become a household word in cultural studies. Anthropological observation and description cannot just gather raw material and then, in a second step, go on to interpret it; much rather, every description of social facts will always and necessarily contain assumptions about their meaning. By such interpretative observation, anthropologists reach an understanding of the underlying cultural system [132, esp. 3–30].

Accordingly, Geertz's anthropological methodology consists in an interpretative ("thick") observation and description of local, often anecdotal phenomena [132.21]: "the anthropologist characteristically approaches such broader interpretations and more abstract analyses from the direction of exceedingly extended acquaintances with extremely small matters." Geertz himself is perfectly aware of the problems created by such an approach [132.21–3]: how can exact observation and thick description of such microphenomena ever lead to reliable generalizations? Geertz does not claim to have a theoretically unassailable answer to this question; instead, he laconically points to the role of the interpreter [132.23]: "Small facts speak to large issues, winks to epistemology, or sheep raids to revolution, because they are made to." This suggestion can be understood if we know that Geertz considers anthropology not a scientific discipline, but an art of interpretation; nevertheless, not everybody will find it quite satisfactory.

New Historicism adopts a number of strengths of Geertz's approach. When thick description is handled by a person who is knowledgeable about a culture and is talented as an interpreter of such communicative actions, it can really, in an unforgettable manner, open our eyes to overreaching relations by looking at small trivialities (and whoever has heard Greenblatt lecture knows that he is a true virtuoso in this regard). However, New Historicism also inherited Geertz's unwillingness for theoretical foundations of interpretation and thus a number of problems it shares with Geertz's anthropology, as we will see later.

What we have seen so far suggests that the relationship between New Historicism and deconstruction is much more complex than we first thought. It is certain that New Historicism is in many regards opposed to deconstruction, yet it is also apparent that it has learned a number of things from the deconstructionists and would not have been possible without their ideas. Geertz's position that cultural phenomena are texts which need to be read and interpreted can be compared (with a grain of salt, of course) with the deconstructionist claim that it is impossible to exit the world of texts (above, p. 123). New Historicism is also convinced that historical reality is not accessible in itself but has to adopt the form of a text – Montrose [265.20] here speaks of "the historicity of texts and the textuality of history."

Furthermore, New Historicists refuse to accept any clear-cut boundary between a work of art on the one hand and its historical background on the other; this immediately calls to mind the deconstructionist distrust of violent hierarchies (above, p. 132). If we examine these positions closely, we will get a clear idea of the difference between New Historicism and older historicizing approaches to literature: on the one hand, its adherents are not interested in finding out "how it really was," as the founder of the science of critical history, Leopold von Ranke (1795–1886), famously put it. Instead, they emphasize that "social actions are themselves always embedded in the systems of public signification, always grasped, even by their makers, in acts of interpretation" (Greenblatt [146.5]). Hence, they see the most important aim of their studies in recapturing these contemporary interpretations and are convinced that it is impossible to reach any historical reality beyond these interpretations. This also implies that New Historicists regard any "objectivity" of the historian herself or himself as a pure illusion. Modern observers are themselves part of cultural semiotic systems from which they cannot break away, and they will always see those past interpretations through the lenses of their own interpretive systems. Instead of lamenting this situation, New Historicists prefer to highlight the subjectivity of their studies by inserting autobiographical elements into their texts – the anecdote about a flight from Baltimore to Boston which closes Greenblatt's book *Renaissance Self-Fashioning* [146.255–7] has become famous in its own right.

Finally, the New Historicist fascination with things that at first sight appear to be marginal and unimportant can also be interpreted as a nod to deconstruction. When Greenblatt [148.4] writes that it was his aim "to look less at the presumed center of the literary domain than at its borders, to try to track what can only be glimpsed, as it were, at the margins of the text," this is comparable to strategies of reading which we have observed in Derrida's works and which consist in uncovering what texts try to exclude, hide, or repress (above, p. 114). However, despite all these points of contact, there can be no doubt that the influence of deconstruction on New Historicism is not as important as Michel Foucault's, and this is the topic to which we will now turn.

New Historicism and Michel Foucault

Michel Foucault's frequent visits to Berkeley had a massive influence on a number of New Historicists. What was especially important was his conception of power (above, p. 144). "According to Foucault, the most important mentor of New Historicism, power is ubiquitous not as a one-dimensional relationship between 'high' and 'low,' sovereign and subject, but as an unstable product of a multitude of social practices," as Höfele writes [183.108]. Power, understood in these terms, was at the center of Foucault's work; as he has himself written, we must "conceive of ... power without the king" [116.91]. New Historicism explores the multiplicity of cultural forms in which power manifests itself: theater and court ceremonies, exorcisms and trials. Again, we should be aware of the fact that New Historicism does not think of these cultural forms as mere reflections of or reactions to "real" power relations; instead, it emphasizes their social productivity (above, p. 160). When Montrose examines pastoral poetry and plays in Elizabethan England, he concludes that the theatrical performance of such plays was "more than an instrument of public relations ...; it was an extraordinarily elaborate and extended periodic ritual drama, in which the monarch physically and symbolically took possession of her domains" [264.101]. Monarchy itself is, to a large extent, theatricality; hence, the theater itself is a form of the struggle for power and of the application of political power.

Greenblatt coined another influential metaphor to capture this mechanism of power play: he studies power under the aspect of "social energy," which can adopt a number of forms and exert various effects in a society: "it is manifested in the capacity of certain verbal, aural, and visual traces to produce, shape, and organize collective physical and mental experiences. Hence it is associated with repeatable forms of pleasure and interest, with the capacity to arouse disquiet, pain, fear, the beating of the heart, pity, laughter, tension, relief, wonder" [148.6]. Such social energy cannot be appopriated and stored away for good; much rather, it circulates among the members of a society, is exchanged in a variety of forms, and is the object of negotiations and competition. In a now famous article, Greenblatt [148.94–128] analyzes the ways in which Shakespeare's theater appropriates the ritual of exorcism, which had been frowned upon and even outlawed by the official church and political authorities. In the absence of the ecclesiastical ritual, it was the theater which now fulfilled the desire to watch the mysterious and powerful fight between good and evil. On the other hand, the theater thus serves the aims of the official authorities by brandishing exorcism as a deceptive, "theatrical" spectacle. In such mechanisms, Greenblatt sees the "circulation of social energy" at work.

New Historicism is thus interested in such processes and in local, everyday manifestations of power (as opposed to the great political, diplomatical, or military actions described by conventional historiography); it shares this interest with a number of modern approaches in historiography. It is certainly possible to find a number of reasons for this change of perspective. For New Historicism, Catherine Gallagher [129.43] makes a convincing case by pointing out the political landscape in the USA during the 1980s: the great protest movements of the 1960s were over, and in the following decades even those who were not content with the current state of society and wished for a fundamental change had no hope of any global or general revolutionary upheaval. Hence, they turned to fostering small-scale change in their own surroundings. Such a form of activity could not but welcome Foucault's concept of power: only local resistance had any hope of succeeding in a fight against a ubiquitous, diffuse form of power, not an all-out fight.

Another aspect of New Historicism demonstrates that Gallagher's assumption about its origins is right, its genuine fascination with subversion, i.e., with all forces and elements which raise opposition against the dominant beliefs and institutions of a society (or, at least, try to do so). Greenblatt's work repeatedly emphasizes that works of art must not be understood as mere means used by the powers that be in order to secure their superiority. Shakespeare's theater, for example, has its own agenda and aims. It attempts, in its particular ways, to capture its share of social energy; this will bring it into a position of competition with or even opposition to official authorities. Hence, in the article just quoted, Greenblatt remarks that *King Lear* is by no means a simple repetition and inculcation of the official policy toward exorcism. Instead, its dramatic constellation puts this official position in doubt because it is the stage villains especially who share these official assumptions [148.120–7].

However, such forms of subversion cannot be said to be fundamental. In his book *Renaissance Self-Fashioning* [146], Greenblatt states that even people and literary characters who seek a position completely outside of the dominant ideology are bound to be deeply marked by this ideology. Subversion is only imaginable as a negation of social norms; hence, even the outsider will carry the marks of these norms (which (s)he rejects) in herself or himself: "the attempts to challenge this system ... are ... exposed as unwitting tributes to that social construction of identity against which they struggle" [146.209]. Such forms of subversion, then, will not only reinforce the dominant ideology; we can even say that authority produces such subversive and competing forces itself for it defines itself in opposition to such "aliens" which are depicted as being the absence of the "natural" order of things: "the alien is always constructed as a distorted image of the authority" [146.9]. Hence, power is in need of such counterimages in order to secure its own position [148.37]. New Historicism thus rejects the assumption that a dominant ideology is a completely monolithic and stable system; instead, it emphasizes the multitude of competing and conflicting elements it harbors. This view is again influenced by the positions of Williams ([378.112–13]; cf. Montrose's explanation [266.404–5]). Ultimately, all forces which seem to be opposing authority thus are incorporated into an overall scheme, a power structure which embraces and controls all subversion. We will have to return to this dialectical relation between "subversion" and "containment," as these polar oppositions have been labeled in a convenient shorthand.

Objections to New Historicism

As we have seen, quite a number of literary critics enthusiastically welcomed New Historicism as being the latest trend in the fashion of literary theory. Within a short period of time, this brought about a critical examination of its theoretical underpinnings. Greenblatt himself tried to explain that New Historicism was a form of practice, not of theory (above, p. 159). Yet this did not dissuade scholars from expecting a theoretical foundation for this practice from its adherents and from raising a number of objections against its premises. We will now examine some of the main points brought forward in this debate. Some of these points will sound familiar because, as we have seen, New Historicism derives some of its fundamental concepts from Foucault's theses, and also from deconstructionist positions.

One important objection was that the questions asked and the assumptions made by New Historicists fail to take individual human actors in history into account (see, e.g., Patterson [285.66–7]); similar arguments had already been made against Foucault's methodology (above, p. 146), and again, it is impossible to dismiss this argument. Greenblatt's metaphors of the circulation and mediation of social energy focuses on entire social groups (such as Protestants) or social institutions (such as the theater), and readers often get the impression that the individual author or the individual literary work are just arbitrary paradigms for an analysis of these anonymous forces which might as well be exchanged for other examples. On the other hand, we should again refrain from placing too much emphasis on this argument: every approach is capable of explaining and analyzing certain parts of literature and has a blind spot with regard to other parts. Since New Historicism is, from the outset, interested in the social effects of literary products, it follows logically that it will pay more attention to these collective phenomena than to individual texts. Nevertheless, we may certainly be permitted to ask whether a theory can really be satisfactory if it fails to perceive a distinction between, say, Shakespeare's plays and dozens of dramas written by his less impressive contemporaries.

This objection against New Historicism is especially justified because it is, in a paradoxical way, also guilty of a mistake which is the flip side of this coin. On the one hand, it refuses to privilege literary texts in any way and demonstrates, in its juxtapositions, that in Shakespeare's works, we find the same "negotiations" of social problems as in everyday texts. On the other hand, it always resorts to such works which conventional literary history had labeled "canonical" without being able to provide criteria for such value judgments itself (this point has been made by, e.g., Vincent P. Pecora [287.270–2]). But we may legitimately ask why such everyday texts should be compared to a tragedy or a poem, and not rather with other everyday documents. Greenblatt appears to try answering this question when he writes, "great art is an extraordinarily sensitive register of the complex struggles and harmonies of culture" [146.5]. But can this statement really explain what defines "great art"? To put it bluntly, is great art everything which is a sensitive means for registering social processes, and nothing else? It would appear that New Historicism here adopts traditional definitions of canonical or "great" literature uncritically and can thus be said to exploit them parasitically.

Another aspect of New Historicism which has been singled out for criticism is its method of analyzing literature by juxtaposing it with uncanonical, often anecdotal material. In a pointed formulation, Alan Liu writes [240.743]: "A New Historicist paradigm holds up to view a historical context on one side, a literary text on the other, and, in between, a connection of pure nothing." Liu makes an apt comparison when he refers to the method of double projection of slides which had been introduced into art history by the Swiss scholar Heinrich Wölfflin (1864–1945) and which invites the audience to compare two pictures [240.730–1]. Which criteria tell New Historicists which pictures should be compared and which aspects and qualities of the pictures should be focused on? Hitherto, New Historicism has failed to develop an adequate theoretical frame which could demonstrate that such comparisons display more than "facile associationism" (Dominick LaCapra [226.193]) or "arbitrary connectedness" (Montrose [266.400]). Again, the element of subjectivity plays an important role: as long as competent and creative critics undertake such juxtapositions, they will result in interesting and accurate observations. But this procedure is in danger of becoming ossified as a mere routine, and the surprise effect of such projections cannot be repeated indefinitely (see Höfele [183.122]). However, proponents of New Historicism might reply that it will be quite a while until it has applied its technique of juxtaposition to all possible periods and texts of literary history and that even a few innovative and surprising results certainly warrant longer experiments with this methodology.

In part, the theoretical problems we have just analyzed can be traced back to the work of the anthropologist Geertz: his method of "thick description" also presupposed that the observer and describer had at least an inkling of what he was looking for. Geertz himself was already acutely aware of this limitation [132.20]: "Cultural analysis is (or should be) guessing at meanings, assessing the guesses, and drawing explanatory conclusions from the better guesses, not discovering the Continent of Meaning and mapping out its bodiless landscape."

There is another issue with Geertz's "thick description" that remains problematical for New Historicism: which methodology warrants, on the basis of individual observations or of the analysis of anecdotes or a certain behavior, making inferences about the entirety of a cultural system (above, p. 163)? Despite all their shrewd and suggestive analyses of individual texts, New Historicists fail to come up with a convincing answer to the question of to what extent such phenomena can be considered symptomatic of an overarching system. Lentricchia [236.87–9] is certainly right to point out that such analyses take every element as a synecdoche, a miniature model of the entire structure, and that this presupposes a strongly deterministic view of history in which even the smallest actions and behaviors are controlled by immutable laws. Again, adherents of New Historicism have failed to provide a theoretical foundation for assuming such a strong determinism.

This leads us to the most intense debate which was occasioned by New Historicism, the problem of "subversion" and "containment" (for the terminology, see above, p. 167; cf. Montrose's explanation [266.402–3]): are all subversive impulses produced by the dominant ideology and, in the long run, controlled and even turned to its proper use by it, or is there such a thing as real subversion? This question is especially pertinent to literary works: are Shakespeare's plays just props of the English monarchy, or do they have a liberating and subversive effect? Questions like this have been discussed in classical studies for a long time: is Virgil's *Aeneid* merely a glorification of the Augustan order and its ideology, or can we hear in it voices which are critical of the established political system? Overall, the New Historicist answer to such questions is unequivocal: although it cautions that we should not imagine the dominant power as being completely homogeneous, in the end, it emphasizes that all dissident discourses are contained by this power, as Greenblatt writes [148.52]: "The subversive voices are produced by and within the affirmations of order; they are powerfully registered, but they do not undermine that order."

A number of arguments have been raised against this assumption. There can be no doubt that the view of historical developments which results from New Historicist interpretations is overly harmonizing: contradictions are neutralized in an all-encompassing order; there is a tendency to highlight the "both – and," as Patterson [285.62] rightly says. This desire for harmony can be seen in the favorite metaphors used by New Historicists: expressions such as "exchange," "negotiations," or "circulation" suggest a peaceful, commercial relationship. Yet such an impression of historical development is primarily produced by the particular perspective favored by New Historicists, who focus almost exclusively on "history as text." In "real" history, wars are fought, innocents are killed, and sometimes, bloody revolutions take place. As Patterson [285.62–3] and Pecora [287] rightly see, New Historicists, deeply involved in the world of their fascinating texts, are in danger of losing sight of such realities.

Finally, New Historicism has been attacked for being politically suspect or downright unacceptable, curiously enough both by conservative and liberal critics. Little needs to be said about the conservative attacks. Their representatives are deeply suspicious of the fact that New Historicism draws connections between lofty literary texts and social realities, and they claim this is nothing but a "gross misinterpretation of deathless prose," as Begley [33] writes (cf. Höfele [183.121]). Hence, they see in New Historicism yet another form of Marxist criticism which concentrates exclusively on power as the decisive element of human relationships and thus fails to do justice to other important aspects such as love and tolerance (Edward Pechter [286.292, 301]). Peacefully conversing in their cozy parlor, surrounded by the immortal classical works, conservative critics may think it is scandalous to look for traces of the struggle for social power in these texts; their driver and their maid may conceivably hold different opinions on this matter.

Critics on the political left, on the other hand, reproach New Historicism for propagating a depiction of society in which the dominant ideology manages to quell every opposition and which thus leads to absolute immobility. Patterson writes: [285.63]: "On the one hand Renaissance culture is an arena of social contradictions engaged in ceaseless strife, and yet on the other hand, nothing happens." This view, the critics hold, is basically nothing but an expression of political despair, not least explainable by the political situation in the USA during the presidency of Ronald Reagan (see Eagleton [90.198] and Patterson [285.69–71]). This is another problem which New Historicism inherited from its teachers, in this case from Foucault, against whom similar objections had been raised (above, p. 148): if power really is everywhere and none of our actions can escape it or effectively counteract it, is there any point in political commitment? Or are we really in a situation where all that counts is getting as big a share as possible of this power?

We certainly have to take these criticisms seriously, yet they do not add up to a complete condemnation of New Historicism. If somebody were to claim that its analyses of power structures capture the entirety of historical reality, (s)he would certainly be wrong. But this claim is not made by the proponents of New Historicism themselves; all it can do and wants to do is throw light on some aspects of culture and society, and I would argue that it succeeds in doing so in a fascinating and illuminating manner. Power certainly is not all there is, but we cannot deny that it leaves its mark on a major part of human behavior and is indeed intimately connected with numerous cultural and literary phenomena. The point is not whether every thesis proffered by New Historicists, every textual juxtaposition they suggest can be said to be valid. The most important achievement of New Historicism is that its methodology has opened our eyes to relations which neither conventional interpretations of texts, nor deconstruction with its eternally recurring *différance*, nor traditional historical analyses were able to perceive. Much remains to be done before the surprise effects of New Historicism will become a worn-out routine.

New Historicism and Antiquity

To a certain extent, New Historicism's methodology can be said to be familiar to classical studies: given the scarcity of the transmitted material, it has always been considered a matter of course to include texts which do not belong to "high" literature (such as grammatical or medical textbooks, documentary papyri or inscriptions, anthologies and anecdotes) in our analyses. Nevertheless, we have to admit that nothing which has been transmitted from antiquity can be compared to the multitude of personal and official documents of modern periods to which we still have access. Yet classics has hardly considered power, as defined in the terms outlined by Foucault, as an important category for analyzing texts.

Here, I will present Schmitz's recent study of the so-called Second Sophistic [319] as an example of an analysis inspired by the methodology of New Historicism. It is heavily influenced by the writings of the French sociologist Pierre Bourdieu (1930–2002), which is closely related to New Historicist positions (see especially his book *Distinction. A Social Critique of the Judgement of Taste* [41]).

The Second Sophistic was a highly visible rhetorical and cultural phenomenon in the Greek-speaking part of the Roman Empire, especially during the second and third centuries CE. Its representatives were famous for delivering declamations on mythical or historical topics, adopting the character and perspective of the actors involved in these situations: what would the father of a soldier who died at Marathon say to honor his son? What would Demosthenes say when he confronted King Philip II of Macedon? What were the arguments with which the Greeks tried to convince the angry Achilles to participate in the fight? In these declamations, the sophists did not use the Greek language which was usual in their own period, but closely imitated the classical Attic dialect of the fifth and fourth centuries BCE – a form of language which was removed from their own by half a millennium. They were expected to extemporize their speeches.

All of this sounds as if it was the weird hobbyhorse of some nerdy scholars in their ivory towers, but in fact, some of the most successful and celebrated sophists were powerful politicians. Herodes Atticus, the unofficial king of Sophistic, was perhaps the wealthiest man of his time and a close friend of the Emperor Hadrian; he even became consul in Rome. In inscriptions honoring local politicians throughout the Eastern Roman Empire, terms such as "sophist" (σοφιστής) and "orator" (ῥήτωρ) are often used as honorary titles. Classical studies has always been somewhat helpless when it came to explaining the blatant contradiction between this unworldly cultural movement on the one hand and the elevated political and social position of its representatives on the other.

Hence, this new analysis does not look at the Second Sophistic as a cultural phenomenon which can be examined in isolation, but puts its social effects in the center of the study: in a New Historicist manner, it considers culture neither an area completely isolated from social developments nor a mere reflection of its circumstances, but as actively involved in creating and establishing social structures and reproducing the power of the elite. This social functionality can be seen at work in a number of aspects of the Second Sophistic:

- The ideal to which education (παιδεία) aspired was clearly defined: only those who mastered the classicizing Attic language and could perform public declamations in it were considered to be well-educated. The sophist was a perfect embodiment of this ideal.
- According to the prevailing ideology of the period, only a well-educated man was capable of exercising political power. The sophists, in their dazzling performances, made a highly visible demonstration of superior education as a form of legitimation for political superiority; in so doing, they acted as representatives of the entire elite. On these public occasions, the lower classes made a symbolic rehearsal of their role in the political process: since they did not master the complex and difficult rules of Atticism, they were condemned to silence. They could thus comprehend and internalize their lack of political participation.
- Within the elite itself, we find a degree of competition and rivalry which is difficult to understand by modern measures: everyone wanted to be foremost and outrank his colleagues (formulae such as "the first in the city" or "the first in the province" were bestowed as official titles and proudly displayed in honorary inscriptions). One manifestation of this competitiveness which is still visible today are the numerous splendid buildings and monuments in Greece and Asia Minor. Wealthy and powerful citizens spent their money to erect them in order to heighten their reputation and outdo

their competitors. This phenomenon (and similarly, donating large sums of money to public causes, accepting costly offices, or traveling widely for the sake of one's city) is called "euergetism." The Second Sophistic should be seen in the same context: public oratory and education also offered opportunities to compete with other members of the elite and outdo them. At the same time, this manner of competition created a sense of togetherness between the competitors: they shared the same education, had read the same works of literature, and felt superior to the masses who lacked this refinement.

એ At the same time, the sophists' declamations also offered their hearers occasions for identifying with accepted values: the sophists often made appeal to their pride of being heirs to the great tradition of Greek culture, thus allowing them to feel included in the superiority that Greek education bestowed.

Hence, a phenomenon such as the splendid performance of a sophist, which at first sight appears to be so marginal and isolated, can be understood, in New Historicist terms, as a typical example of the symbolic appropriation of social energy. In his particular manner, the sophist, who is alone allowed to speak in front of a mass of people who have to remain silent, is participating in power; he acquires reputation and represents, in his particular role, his elevated social rank. This appropriation of social energy explains why some men were prepared to spend so much time and labor on mastering the complicated rules of sophistic oratory. In spite of its seemingly irrelevant and geeky topics, then, the second sophistic was not a phenomenon situated in an ivory tower, but played an important role in the social system and in the struggle for power.

Further Reading

As we have seen, New Historicism considers itself to be a practice rather than a theoretical position. Hence, the only way to become acquainted with it is to watch its proponents at work, as it were. One factor which makes this somewhat difficult is the fact that the majority of works which belong to this approach focus on one particular area of literary history, English Renaissance poetry. There are a number of volumes which collect particularly important or inspiring articles, such as *Practicing the New Historicism*, edited by Catherine Gallagher and Stephen Greenblatt [130], or the books edited by H. Aram Veeser ([360] and [362]); in both, you will find helpful and substantial introductions by the editor. Greenblatt's *Shakespearean Negotiations* [148] is a collection of previously published articles by the most prominent proponent of New Historicism which also offers a good introduction to this approach. A painstaking discussion of the tenets and foundations of New Historicism can be found in Brook Thomas's book [347].

Chapter 11
Feminist Approaches/Gender Studies

One point we have to emphasize at the beginning of this chapter even more strongly than for other theoretical positions we have seen is that feminist approaches in literary studies do not constitute a coherent theoretical position or a methodology. This is not due to some lack of logical rigor in its proponents, but rather a conscious rejection of the demand for a monolithic model of thought. Feminist criticism has made use of a number of the methodologies and approaches we have seen in the preceding chapters; in particular, it has utilized deconstruction and strategies of reading influenced by psychoanalysis. One strand of these various feminist approaches results in the subdiscipline of gender studies which has been particularly lively during the last decade. This genealogy is clearly visible, yet it should not mislead us into assuming that feminism is defunct in literary studies and that gender studies have taken its place. Much rather, both still coexist, and if we emphasize such genealogical links on the following pages, this should primarily be understood as a means for making intellectual connections comprehensible.

The Feminist Movement and Definitions of "Woman"

As its name suggests, feminist criticism is derived from the political movement of feminism, so we will look briefly at the history of feminism. Women's struggle for equal rights in the Western world began in the nineteenth century. However, it was not until the first half of the twentieth century that the main demands of women were fulfilled in most Western countries, such as the right to own property, access to schools and universities, and the right to vote. However, women soon found out that this formal equality had not led to a significant change in their actual social and economic circumstances. One of the key texts of feminism which supported this statement through painstaking historical analyses of the situation of women was Simone de Beauvoir's (1908–86) study *The Second Sex* [32], first published in 1949. As the title of this truly revolutionary and groundbreaking work implies, the French philosopher argues that women have always been considered and treated as the "second" sex. In Western history and thought, "human" has always been equated with "male" (as a term such as "mankind" suggests). Women were defined as "the other," in opposition and contrast to men, and this alterity was usually perceived as being deficient: women are not human beings in the full sense of the term. In philosophy, art, and literature, the woman usually is the object toward which the male subject directs his gaze and his desire.

Simone de Beauvoir's book was the inspiration for a number of political movements that, since the 1960s, began to fight for women's liberation, especially in the USA. These movements are often called the "second wave" of feminism (after the first wave, the struggle for formal equality in the nineteenth century). Again, women demanded legal and sexual equality, such as "equal wages for equal labor," or the right to decide themselves about their sexuality and especially about their pregnancy. But activists in this second phase of feminism were especially committed to uncovering and condemning ideas which degrade and belittle women in our society. For this overarching goal, feminism was and still is active in a number of political, economical, and cultural fields. It is not a monolithic movement or political party, but should be seen as a lively plurality of opinions and attitudes. There is, however, one fundamental distinction which we need to grasp if we want to understand this sometimes bewildering variety of standpoints and especially the different feminist approaches in criticism. All representatives of feminism fight for equal rights for women, but they base this demand on different assumptions:

ﻉ Since antiquity, philosophers have argued for a fundamental equality of man and woman. They claim that the only natural differences between the sexes are bodily; intellectual and psychical differences are only produced by education and socialization and can accordingly also be abolished. This had been argued by Plato in his *Republic* (451c – 452c) when he demanded that women should be allowed to become guardians too and should therefore have the same education as men. The pithiest formulation was provided by the French Jesuit François Poullain de la Barre (1647–1723) in his pamphlet *The Equality of the Two Sexes*, published in 1673: "L'esprit n'a point de sexe," "the mind has no sex" [293.89]. This standpoint is labeled "social constructivism" because it holds that the differences between the sexes are mainly produced by social mechanisms (see above, p. 156, for social constructivism in the study of sexuality).

ą❧ The opposing point of view is called essentialism. It argues that there are fundamental and irreducible differences between the sexes. Feminist representatives of this view often depict the feminine in positive terms such as wholeness, physicalness, solidarity, and empathy (as opposed to the alienated and aggressive world created by a society dominated by males). Emphasizing these female values is seen as a means for improving the entire human society; this can be understood as an attribute of social Utopianism.

Constructivism is undoubtedly the dominant position in modern feminism: only very few feminists would actually call themselves, in a positive sense, "essentialists." Nevertheless, the debate about the question of which human attributes are marked by our upbringing and which are caused genetically ("nature vs. nurture") is by no means closed, neither for our sexuality nor for any other area of our lives. Moreover, we need to remember that both positions entail consequences which can be problematic:

ą❧ If men and women really are fundamentally different, it is difficult to avoid a hierarchization into "better" and "less good" attributes. For centuries, men have been successful in using these differences to assign women an inferior position in society – why should this change if we believe these fundamental differences exist?

ą❧ If, on the other hand, femininity is just a social construction, the feminist movement will disintegrate into an infinite number of micro-movements since there are as many forms of femininity as there are cultures, nations, social classes, etc. Struggling for the equality of "women" would become difficult or even impossible since there is no such thing as a general notion of "woman." What is particularly relevant to our topic here: in this case, we would have to wonder whether ancient constructions of femininity are so radically different from our modern perceptions that analyzing ancient culture in these modern terms would become utterly impossible.

Feminism in Literary Criticism

After these general remarks, we can now explore the ways in which feminist ideas have exerted influenc on literary criticism. The need to introduce feminist approaches into literary studies was felt at an early stage: in her book, de Beauvoir had already analyzed texts by male authors to provide examples of the negative view of women and femininity. But the relationship between feminism in general and feminist approaches in literary criticism is not without its share of problems. Some of the questions with which feminist criticism was confronted are these:

- How should we define the hierarchy between feminism as a revolutionary political movement on the one hand and feminist literary criticism on the other? Are feminist studies in literary criticism merely a continuation of the political struggle by different means? Is it already a betrayal of the political aims of feminism (namely, to fundamentally change the patriarchal structures of society) if we allow it to become embedded in a culture of scholarship which purports to be interested in "objective" knowledge, without any political ax to grind?

- Similar questions arise in the microcosm of the academic world. Many feminists fear that male-dominated society will merely pretend to accept feminist approaches, but will always reject any real change of power structures and play down and minimize the importance and revolutionary potential of these approaches by embracing them. It was often asked whether we should not consider the entire structure and style of scholarship with its special language, its rituals, and hierarchies a field dominated by male values which aims to preserve these values. On the other hand, feminists have argued that such an integration into the academic world is the only way to enter the world of male power, engage it in a dialogue, and bring about fundamental changes.

- For the feminist critics themselves, the most imminent danger was that of becoming completely ghettoized. It was understandable that women in academia emphasized the need to look, for example, at women in history and art, and feminists saw it as their own duty to carry out such research themselves. But it was all too easy for the idea that "only women will be able to do feminist research" to become reversed into "women can only do feminist research." This is especially difficult for younger scholars at the beginning of their careers: understandably, they try to avoid becoming locked into such a niche of the academic system. However, this begets the danger that scholarship will return to "business as usual" and marginalize, neglect, or relegate all research about women and femininity to an irrelevant position.

We will meet these and similar questions again when we now turn to the individual manifestations of feminist criticism. Roughly speaking, we can distinguish between an Anglo-American and a French form of feminist criticism. These are of course oversimplifying labels, but they are useful if we remember that these geographical terms are just a convenient shorthand. French feminism originated in France, but it has been exported to and is now practiced in many other countries, not least in the USA. One can even say that many French feminists are more well-known and respected in American academia than in France itself.

French Feminism

The most prominent representatives of French feminism are probably Hélène Cixous (b. 1937), Luce Irigaray (b. 1934), and Julia Kristeva (b. 1941), none of whom, by the way, was born in France. Without losing sight of significant differences, we can say that the work of the former two follows similar premises. For both, the leading question is: How is it possible for women to express themselves in a language which is fundamentally alien to them because it is through and through dominated by a male perspective? Their assumption that the order of language is one aspect of the political order of the sexes follows the lead of the French psychoanalytical critic Jacques Lacan (see below, p. 203), who emphasized the pivotal function of the "name of the father" in the emergence of the human subject. Hence, language in itself is "phallocentric," i.e., marked by the phallus, the symbol of paternal power, and does not allow women to position themselves as subjects. If women want to take this position, they have to search for completely innovative forms of expression which will destroy this conventional linguistic structure. Irigaray and Cixous have coined several names for this new language, such as *écriture féminine*, "feminine writing," *parler femme*, "womanspeak," or *langue maternelle*, "mother tongue," but have described it in quite similar terms: this sort of language refuses to follow a strict (male) logic; instead of offering only one immutable sense, it offers a plurality; its effect is a liberation from the oppression caused by the "name of the father." As Cixous writes [54.358]: "Her language does not contain, it carries; it does not hold back, it makes possible." Both try to ground the qualities of this specifically female language in the characteristics of the female body: whereas man's sexuality is limited to his penis, woman is represented as possessing a plurality of sexual organs which allow a multiple "bliss" (*jouissance*; see above, p. 126). Women will feel this bliss when they produce and read texts in this female language. In their own works, Irigaray and Cixous themselves try to utilize this female language and refuse, for example, to follow the rules of logic and grammar which they feel to be restrictive. Readers have to decide for themselves whether they regard this as irritating or liberating. I must confess that for me, it is quite annoying, but this may be irrelevant: as a man, I am not the addressee of such texts and may be following the prejudices of phallocentrism of which I am deeply unaware.

While the works of Julia Kristeva are related to the positions just outlined in a number of ways, we can also observe momentous differences: for Hélène Cixous especially, "feminine writing" appeared to be a term for the potential of a language which is still waiting to be created rather than a means of expression and a literature already in existence (in this respect, it is comparable to Barthes's "writerly texts"; above, p. 53). Kristeva, on the other hand, suggests that such a liberation from the restrictive laws of phallocentric language exists already. In her book *Revolution in Poetic Language* [221.19–106], first published in 1974, she distinguishes, again taking her cues from Lacan, a "semiotic" and a "symbolic" phase in our use of language. The latter term denotes our entrance into the linguistic order dominated by the "name of the father," in which signifiers and signifieds are clearly differentiated. Yet before entering this phase, in a pre-Oedipal period which is a mere theoretical construct, human beings are imbued with desires that cannot be expressed or understood linguistically; in this phase, outside and inside, subject and object are not yet distinguished. This "semiotic phase" is superseded by our entrance into the world of language and logic, but this linguistic order will never succeed in completely restraining or oppressing the semiotic potential within us. Modern avant-garde literature such as the poems of Isidore Ducasse de Lautréamont (1846–70) or Stéphane Mallarmé (1842–98) have, according to Kristeva, succeeded in recovering, at least in part, this semiotic phase by destroying the conventional order of language and refusing to submit to the univocality of the symbolic phase [221.81]: "The theory of the unconscious seeks the very thing that poetic language practices within and against the social order: the ultimate means of its transformation or subversion, the precondition for its survival and revolution."

Kristeva calls such a subversive deformation of language "poetic" (*langage poétique*); she never says explicitly that this poetic language is identical with "feminine writing" – terms such as "male" or "female" make no sense when we speak about the semiotic phase, which is situated before any awareness of gender. In other contributions (such as [222]), Kristeva has also expressed strong doubts about some positions of French feminism; her hope is not to see a victory of these seemingly feminine values over the seemingly male ones, but to participate in a movement which will build a world without restrictive gender distinctions. Nevertheless, feminists were justified in quoting her as an author-

ity insofar as the liberation of humanity from the phallocentric rules of language
is part of her agenda, too. However, in Kristeva's approach, terms such as "feminine" and "male" become metaphors for certain linguistic and literary phenomena rather than concrete terms for the actual situation of women and men.

Pragmatic Feminism in Literary Criticism

I hope it has become clear that the French strand of feminism in literary studies is of a markedly theoretical nature, not targeted toward concrete political
aims. Hence, for those who expected and demanded immediate revolutionary
effects of feminist activism, writings such as those just described could not but
be disappointing. Especially in the USA, the reception of this French feminism
was quite ambivalent: while one group of feminists welcomed it wholeheart-
edly and considered its emphasis on a utopian feminine speech as a liberation
from the restrictions of male political structures, others remained more skeptical. To quote but one example, the American critic Ann Rosalind Jones, in her
essay "Writing the Body" first published in 1981 [207], critized these features of
French feminism:

> ❧ Our bodies are inscribed by a number of cultural and not least linguistic
> factors (as has been shown, e.g., by the writings of M. Foucault); hence, the
> female body cannot be considered a secure point of departure for feminine
> language. In particular, the female body is too much an object of male pro-
> jections, desires, and phantasms to serve as a source of an authentic female
> subjectivity.
> ❧ Not only is French feminism in danger of succumbing to a naive female es-
> sentialism, it also fails to pay sufficient attention to the differing cultural cir-
> cumstances of women: women in the Third World, for example, certainly
> have other, more pressing needs than liberating their language from pater-
> nal laws. It would be utterly pretentious to claim that because of apparent
> bodily similarities, one is capable of speaking for women of all periods, all
> social classes, and all geographical origins.
> ❧ Finally (and this is certainly the most important objection): the space which
> French feminism described as being specifically female is exactly the space to
> which men have always relegated women and femininity. When, for exam-
> ple, Cixous writes "More so than men who are coaxed toward social success,
> toward sublimation, women are body" [54.48], even the worst anti-femi-
> nists could subscribe to this sentence. Their version would read: "Women

ought to be happy about their bodies and their 'womanspeak' and leave areas such as power, politics, and serious matters to us men." Hidden behind the overwhelming, orgasmic, irrational bliss lies the well-known concept of female hysteria which has been used for centuries to marginalize and trivialize women. Far from being a liberating force, this strand of feminism actually is a prop of male dominance and really is detrimental to the political ambitions of feminism as a whole.

These arguments can be thought of as typical of the criticism raised against French feminism by numerous American feminists. We will have to come back to the question if and to what extent they are justified. But first, we will try to get to know Anglo-American feminist criticism. In many ways, it can be said to be more pragmatic, closer to actual texts, but also less philosophical in nature than its French counterpart. The following sections do not claim to give a comprehensive picture of this Anglo-American branch, but they present some of the most important areas where it has been active.

Women as authors

One of the demands of feminism was that the "female side of history," which had all too often been forgotten or repressed, be given its proper place (this has sometimes been called "herstory," in opposition to the dominant "history"). It is within this framework that feminist criticism began to search for neglected and marginalized female writers. This had two effects: on the one hand, authors who hitherto had not been published and read were presented to a wider readership; on the other hand, female authors who were already well known were read in novel ways. This movement was especially momentous in the USA, where the problem of evaluating literature is considered more important than in many other cultures. For a long time, there seemed to exist a silent agreement among all educated people on which literary works really were "great books." Feminists rightly were suspicious that this was a "gentleman's agreement" which excluded women from taking a place in the canon (as Lilian S. Robinson [309.116] wrote). This agreement has important effects not only for American academia, but also for society in general: since most American colleges offer "great books courses" of some sort as part of the core curriculum and since many Americans go to college and take one of these classes, the question of which authors should be included in these courses as representing "the best in Western civilization" is of enormous political importance. Hence, feminists were justifiably appalled that there were almost no women in this canon of great literature. A photograph taken at New York's Columbia University nicely epitomizes this debate. Columbia had not accepted women into its college until 1983. Its main library, Butler Library, has a list of male classical authors (such as Plato, Aristotle, Demosthenes, Cicero, and Virgil) carved into the architrave above the main entrance. In May, 1989, women covered this inscription with a banner that displayed a counter-canon of female authors such as Christine de Pizan, Juana Inés de la Cruz, the Brontë sisters, Emily Dickinson, and Virgina Woolf. This feminist demand for a revision of the canon was paralleled by efforts of a number of other groups who felt underrepresented in the conventional canon, such as ethnic or racial minorities, homosexuals, or socially disadvantaged classes.

But it soon became clear that this strategy in itself was not sufficient to overcome feminist grievances. Of course it is possible to add works to the traditional canon or to establish other traditions (such as a canon of literature written by women or by blacks). Nonetheless, a number of literary critics, even those who opposed the conventional canon, still had the impression that only the works included in the traditional canon had real literary value. And indeed, it is difficult to deny that many works written by women appear to be less accomplished than those written by men, when we judge them by our usual criteria. The reason for this is obvious: in the past, women were often denied access to schools and universities; they had either no opportunity at all for acquiring philosophical, scientific, or linguistic knowledge and especially familiarity with the great literary tradition, or they had to obtain this knowledge laboriously as autodidacts. Hence, women often wrote not in the genres that were considered especially important and lofty (such as Epic poetry, philosophical treatises, or sublime lyric such as the ode), but in genres that were marginal (such as the novel; see the book *Edging Women out* by Gaye Tuchman and Nina E. Fortin [358]), or the texts they wrote were not considered to be literature at all because they were diaries, letters, or similar personal documents. Hence, a revision of the canon could not mean merely to look for texts written by women which might fit into this traditional canon, it also had to entail a fundamental debate about the criteria for belonging to this canon.

From the perspective of classical studies, such discussions may appear to be rather immaterial: for ancient literature, this process of canonization was terminated many centuries ago. The vicissitudes of transmission have decided in our place what is worthy of reading and what is not. Literacy in general was far less widespread than it is today, and women were confined to the house even more than in the modern world. We have evidence for very few women who overcame these difficulties and wrote literary texts (such as the scanty remains of Sappho's lyrics in Greek and the elegies of Sulpicia in Latin), but it must be doubted whether many more than these few texts ever existed, and if they did, we are not in a position to discover them; they have been lost irremediably. But if we look closely, we see that this does not mean that the discussion of the canon is unnecessary for classicists. The only chance for our classical texts to be considered relevant for today's world is their claim to represent more than merely a fortuitous snapshot of a remote past. Demands for a revision of canons are an important criterion for this claim. If we maintain that classical literature represents a value that transcends cultural and historical boundaries, we do this because we believe there is some universal human element alive in it which is more than a mirror image of the dominant, old prejudices of an elite of predominantly white, wealthy, heterosexual, male readers. If we as classicists fail to convey the message that our literature speaks to more people than just this one restricted group, the situation of these texts in a world which becomes more multicultural and multifaceted every day is indeed desperate. Hence, demands such as those raised by feminist readers have to be taken seriously by classicists as well.

Women as readers

These remarks bring us to a second facet of feminist criticism. If ancient literature provides very few works written by women, we can at least explore the ways in which the transmitted literature can be read from a female perspective. This question entails a combination of reader-response approaches (above, chapter 6) with feminist criticism. As an example of such an approach, we can look at Judith Fetterley's (b. 1938) study *The Resisting Reader* ([104]; some key passages are reprinted in [369.564–73]). Fetterley analyzes what it means to read a number of great books of American authors *as a woman*. Washington Irving's (1783–1859) famous short story "Rip van Winkle," for example, invites its readers, by subtle textual strategies, to identify with the male protagonist, against his wife. Female readers do not find a place of their own in this text [104.11]: "The consequence for the female reader is a divided self. She is asked to identify with Rip and against herself ..., to laugh at Dame Van Winkle and accept that she represents 'woman', to be at once both repressor and repressed, and ultimately to realize that she is neither." Fetterley discovers similar strands of hatred against or fear of the female in other stories and novels. This makes reading such texts in an unproblematic, positive way impossible for women. Women, Fetterly argues, are excluded from large parts of American literature; if they want to read such works, they have to adopt a certain reading position [104.XXII]: "the first act of the feminist critic must be to become a resisting rather than an assenting reader and, by this refusal to assent, to begin the process of exorcizing the male mind that has been implanted in us."

Fetterley's study demonstrates a problem that we have seen in a similar fashion in the attempts to define a specifically female language: apparently, the biological sex alone is not sufficient to define a reader as "female"; instead, a woman reading these texts must resist the mechanisms they implement and actively withstand their suggestions. Not every woman reading texts, then, is a female reader – if she does not resist, she will be reading like and as a man. Some feminist critics have taken this argument one step further: according to them, some strategies of reading are always and unavoidably patriarchal. If you read a text under the assumption that it offers only one legitimate meaning and that all approaches which do not arrive at this meaning must necessarily be illegitimate, you are, these scholars hold, following strategies of reading which must be called patriarchal.

This invites us to look back upon the debate between French and Anglo-American feminism: adherents of French feminism argued that the followers of a more pragmatical approach were not radical enough in breaking with such practices and could hence never really escape the rules of patriarchy. According to them, only a departure for completely uncharted territories such as "feminine writing" can offer the revolutionary stimulus that will allow us to break up the ossified, oppressive structures which constrain women. Undoubtedly, both positions have powerful arguments, and the decision which of them we prefer is a fundamentally political choice which confronts every movement in search of social change: am I still faithful to my aim if I attempt to bring about this change in small steps and by accepting compromises with the established order, or will this make me a traitor to my movement or even a minion of this established order, and is it better to remain in a position of fundamental opposition, even at the risk of failing to achieve anything? There appears to be no completely satisfactory response to these questions – however, I would argue that the pragmatic approach has in its favor the fact that it has often been much more successful.

Images of women in literature

The question of how women (should) read is intimately connected to the third area in which feminist criticism has provided a number of new perspectives to literary studies. It is here presented as the last in the series; chronologically, it was actually the first to develop. Feminist readers, who had become sensitized to nuances of texts by their current struggle for equal rights, looked at literature with a different kind of attention and discovered that women are only rarely assigned an active and positive role in the works which are generally read and admired; instead, they are regularly depicted from the perspective of male prejudices – even if these works are written by women. De Beauvoir had already studied a couple of literary works in her study *The Second Sex*; in 1970, Kate Millett (b. 1934) published *Sexual Politics*, one of the earliest examples of feminist criticism, and analyzed the image of women in five modern authors. She concluded that this image was deeply marked by oppressive, patriarchal prejudices [260.237–61].

During the earliest phases of political feminism, such analyses often sounded quite accusatory, and feminists demanded that literature depict strong, independent women as role models. But this approach was soon considered to be somewhat naive: it reduces literary texts to the stories they narrate, without paying attention to their literary form, and it treats novels as historical documents. Hence, in a caustic remark, the Norwegian critic Toril Moi (b. 1953) called such an approach "a search reminiscent of The Soviet Writers Congress's demand for socialist realism in 1934. Instead of strong happy tractor drivers and factory workers, we are now, presumably, to demand strong, happy *women* tractor drivers" [262.8]. Moi is right to point out that this methodology is bound to fail when applied to postmodern, non-realistic texts.

From Images of Women to Gender Studies

Hence, in the following period, the emphasis of such analyses shifted from the "what" to the "how" of literary texts. Feminist criticism was no longer interested in accusing single authors of being hostile to women; instead, it now attempted to analyze the mechanisms that produce images of women which correspond to certain male desires, fears, or phantasms. It soon became apparent that the depiction of women can often be seen to fall into certain stereotypical, male-defined categories (the headings used here are merely intended as a set of instructive examples; they are taken from an article by Natascha Würzbach [387.141]):

- Madonna, mother, idealized lover: these can be read as male attempts at making women available to their desires;
- witch, harlot, *femme fatale*: these demonizations betray male fears of the menacing, alien nature of woman;

ह‍ comical crone, silly blonde, hysteric: these can be seen as male strategies
of belittling, marginalizing, and domesticating women to overcome their
deep-rooted anxiety of female uncanniness.

Such studies help us undestand how a certain branch of feminist criticism
could develop into gender studes. It was de Beauvoir especially who had emphasized that our ideas of feminineness are chiefly influenced by cultural factors.
The most famous and oft-quoted sentence of her study, at the beginning of volume 2, reads [32.267]: "One is not born, but rather becomes, a woman" ("On ne
naît pas femme : on le devient"). Our natural sex merely defines our body. Yet
all factors that we consider, consciously or unconsciously, as defining of "man-
liness" and "feminineness" are cultural, not natural, as becomes clear when we
remember that they are different in different human societies. However, our education and socialization familiarize us with such gender roles at such an early
stage of our lives that we hold them to be completely natural. We are so used
to believing that men are (and should be) active, rational, and strong; women,
on the other hand, passive, emotional, and tender, that we all find it difficult to
see such prejudices for what they really are. And even if we succeed in recognizing their social and cultural constructedness, this does not warrant that in
our everyday actions and thoughts we will be able to liberate ourselves from the
burden of such stereotypes.

This distinction between a natural "sex" (restricted to our bodies) and a cultural "gender" (defined by social factors) has been universally accepted. Gender studies sees as its aim to analyze the ways in which gender is culturally constructed and influences our lives. Of course, this approach is not restricted to
literature; instead, it treats all cultural phenomena that take part in this process
and help identify and fix gender roles – these can be academic disciplines such
as medicine or philosophy, and the arts, but also mass media like film and television, advertisements, or popular music, to name but a few examples. And of
course, gender studies are not restricted to analyzing the creation of feminineness; much rather, both genders are seen as being in a relational position: female
is constructed as a counterimage of male and vice versa. Gender studies analyze
the ways in which such constructions proceed and act, they look at the effects
they have on our society, and they ask which mechanisms make these constructions appear to be perfectly "natural" to all actors.

Gender studies, too, want to achieve a change in the relationship between
men and women, but they aim to do so in a less immediate way than most
strands of feminist criticism. Proponents of gender studies point out that it

is to the advantage of misogynous mechanisms if the differences between sex and gender appear to be minimal – if you accept that women are less rational and strong than men "by their nature," you will not doubt that the leading role in society should belong to men. Hence, uncovering such constructions as being constructions is already a liberating act. Nevertheless, not all feminists are happy about the development of gender studies in academia: they are concerned that it will fit into the academic environment too snugly and be just one discipline out of a great many (and one that will not be particularly respected). Such concerns are not easy to dismiss: for all those who disdain feminism, assigning feminist approaches a narrowly restricted place in the academic world, then marginalizing them, and finally declaring them irrelevant was certainly a much more efficient way of combating feminism than outright resistance. This is not to say that such developments are an inevitable consequence of a cynical plot of patriarchy, but it explains why some feminists saw gender studies not only as a chance, but also as a risk to feminism.

Queer Theory

Another approach which was much discussed during the 1990s can be seen as a way of coping with these difficulties of gender studies. "Queer theory" (the name is derived from a term for homosexuals which was first used as an insult but became adopted by the homosexual community itself) is even more radical in doubting the naturalness of categories of human sexuality than gender studies. Judith Butler (b. 1956), for example, in her book *Gender Trouble* [50] which was first published in 1990, wonders whether the distinction between "sex" and "gender" is really meaningful. She argues that we should abandon the belief that there is such a thing as a natural sex which will only subsequently be assigned the cultural value of a gender role. Instead, Butler holds, we always encounter sexuality in the form of such roles charged with cultural expectations and limitations [50.16]: " 'persons' only become intelligible through becoming gendered in conformity with recognizable standards of gender intelligibility." "Natural" sex is always already a construction of our mind, not some objectively existing substance; it is not a raw material which will only later be marked with a cultural stamp. Paradoxically, one could say that logically, gender precedes sex and sex is only produced by and through gender.

Queer theory claims that it is particularly the categories of sexual desire which define and create gender roles. Modern thinking (at least in the Western world) sees our sexuality in stable and fixed terms: there is heterosexuality and there is homosexuality (and because some individuals cannot be positioned on this terminological matrix, there also is bisexuality which, however, does not play an important role in our way of thinking about sexuality). Queer theory follows suggestions made by Foucault (above, p. 156) and puts this binary opposition in question. It has radical doubts about the "naturalness" of these categories and argues that even our sexual orientation and desire are culturally constructed.

Such a position is at first deeply unsettling: we have a feeling that nothing is as intimately connected with our inner self, is as immediately natural as our sexual desire. But classicists should be quick to recognize the value of this approach: the institution of pederasty (above, p. 151) which played such an important role in Athenian society presupposes that adult men feel attracted to and aroused by handsome youths, but will also marry and have children with their wives. Our modern matrix of "heterosexuality vs. homosexuality" does not seem to work in such cases.

Butler aims to analyze the mechanisms of socially santioned sexual desire which ensure that such seemingly stable and "naturally" based roles are produced. Since the beginnings of human society, we can observe a number of attempts to detect a natural, stable core of sexuality beyond all social constructs. There is, for example, the account of biblical creation which describes the origin of man and woman and their mutual attraction as ordained by God; there is the version of Plato who, in the *Symposium*, has Aristophanes tell a myth according to which every human being longs for the other half that will make her or him a complete being again, or there are psychological explanations which suggest that every human is orginally oriented toward bisexuality and has to learn by repression and social taboos, in the course of her or his development, to direct her or his desire towards a certain target. As in the case of gender roles, the analysis of sexual desire from a "queer" perspective often concludes that such seemingly "natural" foundations are always constructs which obey certain social and cultural rules. Butler holds that gender-roles are only defined by social constructions of desire. Hence, she calls gender "performative": it is not a core of our subjectivity that we could somehow possess in a definite manner, but must constantly be (re)produced by social interaction.

There are no clear-cut boundaries between feminist criticism, gender studies, and queer theory (see the overview by Eve Kosofsky Sedgwick [325.271]). If we want to define some criteria for distinguishing them, we could see their positions as an increasing fascination with the tenets of deconstruction: for feminist criticism in its first phase, the category "woman" was unproblematic and immediately available. Gender studies began to doubt whether this is really the case and turned to analyzing the ways in which gender roles are produced via arbitrary binary oppositions. Queer theory takes this position another step further and regards our entire sexuality as a product of social discourses and hence of mechanisms of power (this makes it clear that Foucault's thinking, especially his books about the history of sexuality, have exerted an important influence on queer theory). This entails as a consequence that queer theory explores a wide range of social practices, as J. Butler writes [50.3]: "gender intersects with racial, class, ethnic, sexual, and regional modalities of discursively constituted identities." Thus, queer theory transcends the boundaries of literary studies in the narrow sense of the word and becomes part of a more encompassing cultural studies approach.

Gender Studies and Attic Drama

Gender studies have been quite successful and influential in classics since the mid-1980s. Especially in the USA, there is a steady flow of studies examining the construction of femininity and masculinity in ancient literature, philosophy, mythology, religion, or art (or at least taking this aspect into account). A number of disciplines such as ancient history, archeology, epigraphy, papyrology, or the study of ancient law have pursued the question of what life in the ancient world really was like for women. The numerous studies of ancient sexuality (above, p. 158) also belong to this success story of gender studies in classics.

One area where gender studies have been particularly active and respected during the last years is classical Attic drama, i.e., tragedy and comedy of the fifth and fourth centuries BCE. It is fairly obvious that questions of gender roles and gender differences are at the core of this genre: on the Attic stage, all roles, even female ones, were exclusively played by men. At the same time, we see immediately that female characters on stage are granted an amount of liberty and initiative which Athenian men would not have tolerated in the everyday lives of their wives and daughters – a Medea, Clytemnestra, or even Lysistrata could only exist on the tragic or comic stage, not in reality. Finally, the field of theater studies also is a good example of the difficulties and problems we face when we try to study women in antiquity: even a problem which appears to be as simple as the question of whether women were at least allowed to participate in the dramatic performances as spectators has not found a definitive answer to this day.

Even if women were present, there can be no doubt that the dramatic discourse itself was addressed at the adult, free, male citizens of Athens. Why, then, did female characters have such important functions in this discourse? Scholars explain that for the male citizens, they were the counterimage, the "other" which, by its very alterity, helped define and focus their own identity (for this concept, see above, p. 167). The American scholar Froma I. Zeitlin, in an essay with the telling title "Playing the Other" first published in 1985, has analyzed this aspect of Attic drama (reprinted in [388.341–74], also in [381.63–96]). Zeitlin examines four aspects of this dialectical relation between the genders on the Attic stage:

- Attic tragedy emphasizes the suffering of the human body. Now the body, in Greek thought, is especially connected with femininity [388.352]: "in a system defined by gender the role of representing the corporeal side of life in its helplessness and submission to constraints is primarily assigned to women."

- Greek tragedies typically have their place at the entrance of a house, at the threshold of exterior (which has male connotations) and interior (with female connotations). Hence, it acts out male anxieties: men claim to control their entire families and thus also the interior of the house, only to discover in tragedy that this is not possible and that within the house, they will have to face a horrible fate: "they fail to lock up, to repress those powerful forces hidden in the recesses of the house" [388.355].

- Cunning and intrigue are especially important parts of tragic actions; they also carry female connotations. Hence, what we often see on stage is that male plots fail or are successful only when men succeed in securing the support of a woman.

- Being an actor, assuming a role without actually being the impersonated individual is also connected to femininity; hence, the entire sphere of theatricality has female connotations. As Zeitlin writes [388.363]: "theater uses the feminine for the purposes of imagining a fuller model for the masculine self, and 'playing the other' opens the self to those often banned emotions of fear and pity."

Tragedy, then, demonstrates to its male spectators that their lives would be incomplete without these female aspects; at the same time, the tragic play takes possession of this feminine side [388.364]: "tragedy arrives at closures that generally reassert male, often paternal (or civic), structures of authority, but before that the work of the drama is to open up the masculine view of the universe."

Another study which analyzes effects of gender on the Attic stage is Laura McClure's *Spoken Like a Woman*, published in 1999 [250]. McClure examines the differences between male and female discourse in Attic drama. Women typically speak within the house, to other women or to servants; discourse in public is an almost exclusively male domain. The differences between these forms of discourse become especially visible when writers explore their limits. A particularly clear example analyzed by McClure is the comedy *Thesmophoriazusae* ("Women Celebrating the Thesmophoria") which Aristophanes staged in 411 BCE. In it, a man is disguised as a woman to participate in this exclusively female ritual, but he is discovered after a short while. One of the factors undoing him is that Aristophanes has him use language which female characters do not normally use on stage: he constantly utters rude obscenities and scatological expressions which are usually reserved for men, thus betraying that he cannot be a woman.

There has been an intense debate about the political and social functions of Greek drama. Given that the dramatic performances in Athens were part of public religious rituals sponsored and organized by the city and attended by a large number of citizens, it seems plausible to assume that they played an important role in the public life and civic identity of Athenians. Gender studies has shown convincingly that categories of masculinity assumed important functions in this civic identity and that representations of women on stage were momentous for the definition of masculinity. This is an important aspect of Attic drama which had not been seen by classical studies until the advent of gender studies in the mid-1980s.

Further Reading

Since feminist criticism as well as gender studies are vast fields and since both are not clear-cut theoretical positions as much as a certain practice of looking at texts and cultural phenomena, it seems best to gain a first impression of this area by watching feminist critics working. There are two edited volumes which I would especially recommend: Elaine Showalter edited the volume *The New Feminist Criticism* [329] which contains a number of important and interesting contributions; the article "Feminist Criticism in the Wilderness" by Showalter herself [329.243–70] is especially clear and informative and could be an excellent point of departure for further forays into this field. For those who are not afraid of big books (1,200 pages!), the anthology *Feminisms*, edited by Robyn R. Warhol and Diane Price Herndl [369], offers a wealth of information: it contains numerous important essays in a convenient format. French feminism sometimes is challenging to read, but Hélène Cixous's often quoted article "The

Laugh of the Medusa" [54] is a good starting point. For a first introduction to the larger context and the theoretical issues, I would recommend Toril Moi's slim volume, *Sexual/Textual Politics* by [262].

If you want to see the ways in which feminist and gender approaches have been brought to ancient texts, you can begin with some special issues of academic journals which are dedicated to this topic: volume 6 (1973) of *Arethusa*, entitled "Women in Antiquity," contains the useful "Selected Bibliography on Women in Antiquity" by Sarah B. Pomeroy [291]; *Helios* 16 (1989) contains "Studies on Roman Women"; *Helios* 17:2 (1990) is a collection of feminist analyses of Ovid's works. Some of the contributions to the volume *Feminist Theory and the Classics*, edited by Nancy Sorkin Rabinowitz and Amy Richlin [298], are somewhat problematic, so this volume may not be the best starting point for readers who are unfamiliar with the topic. Gillian Clark's slim volume *Women in the Ancient World* [55] provides a clear and very helpful overview of modern scholarship; however, its primary focus is not on literature.

Chapter 12
Psychoanalytic Approaches

No other chapter in this book is as much in need of the caution mentioned in the introduction (above, p. 12): you should be aware that everything here is said from my subjective perspective. Hence, it is necessary to declare my point of view and my mental reservations right at the outset. The history of modern psychoanalysis begins with the work of Sigmund Freud (1856–1939), and Freud is also the starting point of the application of the psychoanalytical methodology to literary texts. Freud's concepts have, in a more or less trivialized form, become part of general knowledge; hence, this is not the place (nor is my knowledge sufficient) to give an outline of psychoanalysis in general. I will merely present, in a very brief manner, those parts of the psychoanalytical theory which can be of interest for scholars working in the field of literary criticism. Notwithstanding the fact that Freud himself was no literary critic, he has often adduced and made use of literary works in his writings. He derived what is probably his most well-known hypothesis from the interpretation of an ancient text – I mean, of course, his theory of the Oedipus complex.

We have to understand that this is not a mere detail of Freud's theories, but a central part of it. According to Freud, humans begin their lives without any idea of their subjectivity; for an infant, there are no clear boundaries between "I" and "not-I." In particular, it lives in a symbiotic relationship with its mother at this early stage of its life. As soon as it becomes aware that it and the mother are two different persons, it directs its desire toward her. But the place of the mother's lover is already taken, by its father, who threatens the child with (imaginary) castration. Hence, the child must abandon its erotic desire for its mother and repress this drive. We have to emphasize the importance of this step: the father establishes order by preventing the child from fulfilling its desire. It is this repression of Oedipal feelings (erotic longing for the mother, rivalry and hatred of the father) which turns the child that follows only the "pleasure principle" into a human being that enters the "reality principle." It is through this first act of repression that an unconscious, inaccessible for our usual mental activities, is established. The father and the "castration anxiety" which he inspires introduce the child into the world of rules, prohibitions, and authorities.

It is only one (if particularly embarrassing) out of several objections against this Freudian analysis of the Oedipus complex that this castration anxiety cannot be immediately applied to girls and that the "emergence of the human being" depicted in this theory really is an "emergence of the male." Another objection is the observation that Freud's theories of how our subjectivity is shaped in early infancy are only meaningful in societies where the nuclear family consisting of mother, father, and children is the predominant mode of environment for children; however, when we look at evidence across a wide historical and geographical range, we see that this is more the exception than the rule. Freud's assertions met vigorous objections from the very start, and as far as I can judge as a layman in psychoanalysis, these attacks were fully justified. The fact that an ever growing number of quarrels broke out between Freud and his various pupils and that the number of schools who compete and argue with each other are almost innumerable may not be sufficient to disprove psychoanalysis scientifically, but it leaves a devastating impression of its value and its contribution to sober analysis. Moreover, Freud's adherents display an unsavory habit of polemicizing against opponents by ascribing them psychic problems (there is a vivid example of this attitude in Françoise Meltzer's essay [254.5–6]), which is not apt to foster a dispassionate and levelheaded mode of argumentation.

The last years have produced a new wave of attacks on Freud's theories. One of the factors which triggered this intense debate was a phenomenon that irritated the general public especially in the USA, a number of lawsuits about supposed sexual abuse of children and alleged repressed memories. Psychoanalysts claimed that the traumatic experience of such an abuse is so unbearable for humans that it is regularly repressed into the unconscious and can only be recovered through the medium of psychoanalysis; they claimed that we have to acknowledge that a shocking proportion of the population experienced such abuse when they were children. Their opponents pointed out that this hypothesis quickly became a system of self-fulfilling prophecies: if the analyst succeeds in recovering such memories, he has proven the abuse; if the memories cannot be recovered, the mechanisms of repression are just too strong, which again proves that an immense and intolerable form of abuse has occurred. Discussion of these cases gained national attention when the American critic Frederick C. Crews published a skeptical article in the *New York Review of Books* of November 18, 1993 which triggered a long and intense debate (which was subsequently published as a book [65]; a defense of Freud's theories can be found in John Forrester's book *Dispatches from the Freud Wars* [111]).

This debate alerted the general public to the fact that fundamental doubts about the clinical and philosophical bases of psychoanalysis had been voiced for quite some time (an especially vigorous formulation can be found in the works of Adolf Grünbaum, see [158] and [159]). It should be clear why this discussion is of great importance for whoever attempts to apply the psychoanalytical model in other fields, such as literary criticism. If Freud's theories really lack a scientific basis, any interpretation of literary texts or cultural phenomena inspired by these theories cannot claim any form of authority; concepts derived from psychoanalysis such as "Oedipal" or "phallic" would be mere metaphors without any validity. This, however, is what is at stake here: as Peter Brooks has rightly said, any psychoanalytic interpretation cannot just be one out of many interpretations, but it has to lay particular claim to its validity [49.147]: "any 'psychoanalytic explanation' in another discipline always runs the risk of appearing to claim the last word, the final hermeneutical power." It will depend on our appraisal of Freud's theories whether we want to accept this claim for "the last word." If we like it or not, we are forced to take sides in these debates although we are not experts in the disciplines which they discuss.

When I tried to follow these discussions, my impression was that Freud's opponents are essentially right – his methodology is fundamentally flawed and cannot claim any measure of scientific reliability. What I found especially revealing was the fact that all the methodological and clinical mistakes Freud committed (such as the unbelievable blunders he made in the famous case of the "wolfman"; see the account by Patrick J. Mahony [245]) are defended in the vaguest possible terms by Freud's adherents: they seem to lack the courage to face the fact that their master committed such mistakes and that it needs arguing if we want to continue using his theories, in spite of such mistakes. Hence, I have serious and irreducible doubts about the value and validity of psychoanalytic interpretations in literary studies. I must ask readers to remember this prejudice when reading the following pages so they can form their own judgment about these matters.

Interpreting Dreams, Interpreting Literature

The Interpretation of Dreams [125], first published in 1900, is probably the work in which Freud made his most important contribution to literary studies. In it, he claims that "*the interpretation of dreams is the* via regia *to a knowledge of the unconsicous element in our psychic life*" ([125.441]; emphasis in the original text). Human beings have drives and impulses which influence our unconscious but cannot be expressed in our conscious lives and must thus be repressed. These drives find a means of expression in dreams. They are often of a sexual nature (such as sexual desire for the mother), and they are typically grounded in emotions, desires, or anxieties which we experience in early childhood. Yet even in dream, there is no undisguised fulfillment of such desires; they have to be encrypted by what Freud termed "dreamwork" in order to find an acceptable expression. The most important tools for such an encryption are condensation (several persons or events are combined), displacement (desires are directed onto trivial targets instead of forbidden ones), and an expression in pictures and symbols which can be represented in a dream "narrative" (considerations of representability, *Rücksicht auf Darstellbarkeit*). The task of the analyst consists in recovering the deeper dimensions of dreams which are hidden behind these surface phenomena, and thus in detecting the repressed desires.

Freud himself said repeatedly that literary texts are analogous to dreams. Thus, a psychoanalytic interpretation of a text takes as its starting point that a deeper, unconscious, and "true" meaning lies hidden beneath the text's visible surface and that interpretation consists in uncovering this deeper meaning. Freud argued that readers enjoy literature because in it, as in dreams, they find encrypted fulfillments of forbidden desires (without being conscious of this source of their pleasure). These basic tenets appear plausible at first sight. Whenever we read a literary text, we all have an impression that there is more to it than the objects, characters, and actions which it narrates on its surface. Hence, it seems reasonable to suggest that the task of literary criticism consists in detecting this unspecified "more." Nevertheless, such an approach raises a number of questions and problems which have not yet found an adequate solution. To better understand these problems, we must first take a brief look at the practice of psychoanalytical interpretation. Early attempts to make use of its methodology can be grouped into two categories:

    ⇢ Attempts to analyze the literary characters themselves according to Freud's principles. This is an approach that Freud himself employed when he examined, for example, the eponymous character Hamlet from Shakespeare's play and claimed that he had an Oedipus complex. However, there is a great danger of going beyond the information provided by the text and arriving at unfounded speculation. Literary characters are not living human beings, after all; they do not have an unconscious of their own.

৯ Hence, the logical consequence was not to analyze the characters, but their authors, for it is the authors who produce every part of a literary work. Psychoanalytic interpretations thus attempt to observe and analyze the psychic attitudes and complexes of the authors in their texts. Maybe the most famous (and at the same time infamous) example of such an approach is the study which the French psychoanalyst Marie Bonaparte (1882–1962) dedicated to the American writer Edgar Allan Poe (1809–49) in 1933 [38]; in it, she reads his literary work as an expression of psychic problems.

Very soon, scholars critical of such attempts raised the objection that these interpretations failed to see more in literary works than the biographies of their authors, or, to put it more precisely, than their authors' unconscious sexual desires. It is indeed difficult not to think of several jokes about psychoanalysis when one reads such reductive analyses. Obviously, these interpretations assume that in literature, we find the same mechanisms at work as in other manifestations of psychic problems; authors write to overcome the traumas they experienced in early childhood. On the one hand, this leads to a reductive form of "biographism" which sees the literary text as little more than a document of its author's life. On the other hand (and more importantly), this begs a number of difficult questions with regard to the status of the text and its interpretation: is literature really an expression of one (and just one) underlying meaning which an analyst can uncover if (s)he uses the correct methodology? Will the meaning thus uncovered supplant the original text, i.e., will the text itself be superfluous once we have found out what its hidden meaning is? Literary critics have argued against this assumption and pointed out that literature appears to have a wealth of meaning. A method of interpretation which claims that the "real" meaning of the famous simile of the cave in Plato's *Republic* (514a–517a) is just an expression of early infantine dreams of the uterus has lost all claims to being taken seriously. More recent contributions frequently claim that psychoanalytical approaches have now moved beyond the facile reductionism of these early attempts, but however hard I look, I find it impossible, even in newer interpretations of this sort, to see anything other than an attempt, albeit in more fashionable terms, to detect a mass of phallic symbols and Oedipal desires in every single text. If you find such "discoveries" exciting, psychoanalytical interpretations may be for you; personally, I have the impression that in this perspective, literature becomes a boring repetition of ever identical symbols.

Three Attempts at Psychoanalytic Interpretation

Until now, we have looked at Freud's psychoanalysis and its applications in literary criticism. There are, however, a number of approaches which are inspired by Freud's position, but follow him only in some areas while modifying others. Here, we will present three of these attempts briefly.

Carl Gustav Jung (1875–1961) had originally been a student and close collaborator of Freud's, but in 1913, a scholarly quarrel brought about a split between them. Jung called his own methodology "analytical psychology." Jung distinguishes between a "personal" and a "collective" unconscious. Jung held that while Freud's description of the former was adequate, the latter represented a psychic level which was even deeper. This element is present in all human beings from birth; it contains immemorial images, which Jung called "archetypes." They condense human experience in a number of powerful symbols such as mother earth, the divine infant, or monsters such as the centaurs, who are half human and half animal. The clearest occurences of these archetypes can be seen in the myths of various cultures, but they can also be found in literary works, albeit in a form which can be difficult to recognize because of the manifold transformations they have undergone. Jung's theories inspired several literary critics. Probably the most important of them is Northrop Frye (1912–91), whose book *Anatomy of Criticism* [126], first published in 1957, attempted to analyze literature as a systematic body of texts shaped by Jungian archetypes. Frye holds that there are fundamental genres (comedy, romance, tragedy, and satire) that are marked by archetypal myths which in turn represent the four seasons spring, summer, fall, and winter; his approach is often labeled "archetypal criticism." Another critic who could be named here is the philosopher Gaston Bachelard (1884–1962), who was quite influential in France for a while. He tries to understand poetry by deriving its qualities from primeval images related to the four elements water, air, earth, and fire; these images are related to, but not identical with Jung's archetypes.

Jung and the interpreters influenced by his theories avoid the biographical reductionism of Freudian analysis because what they see at work in myths or in literary texts is not the psyche of the individual author, but the collective symbolism of humanity. As far as I can see, hardly anyone still subscribes unconditionally to Jung's theory according to which archetypes are, as it were, part of our genetic disposition. Nevertheless, research done by Jungians (such as Karl Kerényi (1897–1973) for the area of classical myth; see his book *Introduction to a Science of Mythology* [212], written in collaboration with Jung) has brought to light a number of astonishing parallels and similarities between myths of different cultures and ages that can hardly be mere coincidences. Nevertheless, such interpretations face problems similar to the ones we observed in the structural analysis of narrative inaugurated by Propp (above, p. 46): are we really learning anything interesting and useful about literature when we hear that on a fundamental level, all comedies can be understood as being expressions of the same archetype?

The American critic Norman N. Holland (b. 1927) accepts some of Freud's fundamental concepts: literary texts are subject to unconscious mental phenomena. What makes his approach different is his attempt to combine elements of psychoanalytical criticism with reader-response criticism. His fundamental question is: Why do we derive pleasure from reading literary texts even though some of the events depicted in these texts would strike us as painful or embarrassing in our daily lives? It could be argued that this is, in fact, one of the oldest questions of literary criticism. Aristotle, in his *Poetics*, had already asked why we enjoy watching tragedies, and his reply was of a psychological nature: when we watch the action on stage, we are affected by emotions such as fear and pity and thus receive a "purification" ($\kappa\acute{\alpha}\theta\alpha\rho\sigma\iota\varsigma$). In an early phase of his work, Holland answered this question in an orthodox Freudian perspective [184.30]: "Literature transforms our primitive wishes and fears into significance and coherence, and this transformation gives us pleasure." According to the type of phantasms transformed by literature, Holland distinguished between oral, anal, urethral, phallic, Oedipal, latent, and genital texts and writers. Later, he became increasingly dissatisfied with this Freudian approach and emphasized the psychological involvement of the reader. In his book *5 Readers Reading*, first published in 1975, he examined the completely differing reactions of five students to the same literary text. His conclusion was [185.209]: "A reader responds to a literary work by assimilating it to his own psychological processes, that is, to his search for successful solutions within his identity theme to the multiple demands, both inner and outer, on his ego." Critics, however, have rightly pointed out the difficulty in detecting this "identity theme": isn't it again a kind of "text" which has to be read and interpreted?

Finally, we can turn to the American critic Harold Bloom (b. 1930). He considers Freud's theory of the Oedipus complex to be one of the most fundamental features of literary history. Bloom holds that all poets are in an Oedipal relationship of influence and competition with their predecessors whom they have to dislodge and supplant to make room for themselves. Bloom emphasizes that every poet cannot but misunderstand his "fathers" [36.30]: "Poetic influence –

when it involves two strong, authentic poets, – always proceeds by a misreading of the prior poet, an act of creative correction that is actually and necessarily a misinterpretation." This emphatic statement can be seen as related to the deconstructionist position that every reading is always a misreading (above, p. 122), and Bloom was indeed a colleague of de Man's at Yale for many years. However, Bloom himself obviously is not a deconstructionist: his view implies that such "misreadings" must be clearly identifiable as misrepresentations, so there must also be correct readings of texts.

Bloom's view of literary history as an Oedipal struggle of great poets certainly has the advantage of seeing in literary history more than a haphazard series of authors and works. But it is also obvious that this view can hardly be generalized: Bloom himself has to concede that for English literature, his pattern of Oedipal struggle cannot be applied to Shakespeare [36.11], and we may wonder whether the model of an "anxiety of influence" such as it has been described by Bloom is only applicable to periods of literary history that are dominated by Romantic ideas about creativity and the original genius. Furthermore, critics object to Bloom that his view of literature only looks at immanent criteria (are not factors such as political, social, and economic changes as important for the relationship between a poet and his predecessors?). In this one-sidedness, Bloom clearly is an heir to New Criticism which had been so dominant in the post-war USA (see above, p. 91).

Language and the Unconscious: Jacques Lacan

The strand of psychoanalytic criticism which has been most influential in modern literary theory is certainly the approach shaped by the French analyst Jacques Lacan (1901–81). We can best understand his position if we think of it as a synthesis of three different strands of thought:

ᴓ Freudian psychoanalysis;
ᴓ structural linguistics developed by Saussure (and Jakobson);
ᴓ and finally deconstruction, on which Lacan himself exerted a considerable influence.

While Lacan is thus quite remote from orthodox Freudianism (and was therefore excluded from or resigned from a number of psychoanalytic societies), he himself repeatedly claimed that his theories represented a return to what Freud really said (see, e.g., [224.179–80]); he held that Freud himself would have reached the same conclusions as he if he had had the concepts and methodology of Saussure's structuralism at his disposal.

Lacan likes to utilize an obscure style full of allusions, he quotes classical authors in their original language (the Greek passages adorned with numerous wrong accents), or he expresses his thought in mathematical formulae (which, at a closer look, are completely meaningless). There is no systematical account in his own writings; instead, it was only later readers of his contributions who formed a coherent system out of his oracular, fragmentary, often contradictory ideas. Hardly anyone will not have fundamental doubts reading Lacan's books: am I too stupid, or does he refuse to be understood? I freely admit that in Lacan's case, I followed the advice given in the introduction to this book (above, p. 3) and, after several attempts to make sense of his writings, gave up trying to understand him – after all, time is just to valuable to waste it on watching a self-appointed prophet playing his cryptic language games. Hence, the following brief outline is based on secondary accounts of Lacan's theory of which I found the explanations in Malcolm Bowie's book [43] and Meredith Skura's introductory article [330] particularly clear and helpful.

Like Freud, Lacan assumes that an imaginary confrontation with the father is especially important for the development of a child. For him, however, what is decisive is language with its mechanisms of absence and its relations (above, p. 118); hence, Lacan's most famous and quoted sentence reads [225.20]: "the unconscious is structured like a language." Lacan refers to Saussure when he reminds us of the fundamental differences between signifier and signified and claims that there is an impenetrable boundary between both, "a barrier resisting signification" [224.165]. However, Lacan goes beyond what Saussure wrote when he radically separates the signifier from the mental concept and emphasizes that in language (and thus in the unconscious), signifiers always refer to each other exclusively (for this separation and the deconstructionist idea of a "pure signifier," see above, p. 123). This is the basis of Lacan's famous notion of "an incessant sliding of the signified under the signifier" [224.170]: our longing is for the objects referred to by language, but we will never be able to fulfill this desire since it always eludes us because of the nature of language.

It is the father, or more precisely: the "name/no of the father" (in Lacan's playful expression *"le nom du père,"* both ideas are present and indistinguishable in the French pronunciation) that introduces the child into this world of empty references, into the "symbolic order" which Lacan also calls "the law." The child learns that our desires and needs are not always fulfilled right away, that "desire" can be for infinitely removed objects. Like Freud's theory, Lacan holds that this painful process cannot be avoided: only the introduction into this symbolic order allows us to find our position in family and society and thus to become a functional human being.

Again like Freud, Lacan applied his theories to literary texts, and emphasized the importance of this application by placing it at a very prominent position: he begins the collections of his writings, first published in 1966 [223], with a transcript of a seminar which he taught on Poe's short story "The Purloined Letter" (a story which had played a pivotal role in Bonaparte's psychoanalytic study of Poe's works). In it, we read about a letter which is extremely embarrassing and even dangerous for one of the characters but whose exact content is never revealed to the readers; it is stolen twice. Nobody can really possess this fateful letter; it always eludes attempts to grasp it and can best be hidden from view by being displayed openly. Lacan interprets this unseizable letter as a representation of the "pure signifier" [270.32]. Like a signifier, the letter always promises to reveal its secret; yet at the same time, it is clear that it will never fulfill this promise. Poe's story as read by Lacan demonstrates, in a symbolic way, what is the result of combining Freud's theories about the unconscious with the assumptions of structuralist linguistics. Lacan himself formulates the conclusions of his interpretation thus [223.1.71]: "Its essence is that the letter could transfer its effects to the inside: to the characters of the story, including the narrator, as well as to the outside: on us, readers, without anybody ever caring what it really meant. Which is the usual fate of everything that is written."

Further Reading

Since my personal reservations, prejudices, and gaps concerning the field of psychoanalytic criticism are especially marked, I would like to encourage and urge the reader to consult accounts which are more competent and more positive about psychoanalysis than the preceding chapter. Elizabeth Wright's edited volume *Psychoanalytic Criticism* [386] is particularly clear, and it contains a very helpful bibliography. A critical, but also very helpful account can be found in Terry Eagleton's book on literary theory [90.131–68] and Meredith Skura's article [330]. The volume *Literature and Psychoanalysis*, edited by Shoshana Felman [102], contains a number of contributions which exemplify the ways in which Lacan's ideas have been used for analyses of literary texts, a field which I could hardly touch upon here. Malcolm Bowie's book *Lacan* [43] is a good introduction to the works of this difficult thinker.

Conclusions?

As I said at the beginning of this book (above, p. 2), literary theory is concerned with questions of a sort that cannot be answered definitively – exactly as literature itself, which offers us inspirations and experiences that we will never consider as definitively settled. Hence, this book cannot offer final conclusions, but must have an open end.

If you have read your way through this introduction and followed any of the suggestions for further reading, you will also understand that this last chapter has to be merely preliminary in another sense as well: much that would be in need of careful explanation could only be mentioned in passing or had to be passed over. So this may be the right place to point out that some interesting and important positions could not be mentioned at all in this introduction (but they will be mentioned now, as a supplement):

&> Approaches that make use of the methodology of cultural anthropology for studying literary texts have been very prominent in classics since the 1970s. Scholars taking this direction are interested in exploring the relations between literature and social and religious rituals. They are not content with merely remarking that, for example, Attic tragedy is part of a religious ritual in honor of the god Dionysus, but they hold that this ritual aspect is mirrored in the texts themselves and was immediately visible to all contemporary hearers. A group of scholars working in Paris has been particularly important for the development of this approach; this group includes, among others, Jean-Pierre Vernant (1914–2007) and Pierre Vidal-Naquet (1930–2006); their contributions to the study of Greek tragedy have been collected in the volume *Myth and Tragedy in Ancient Greece* [366]. Another important influence has been the work of the German scholar Walter Burkert (b. 1931). One phenomenon which has been studied with particular attention are the "rites of passage," a concept which was first developed by the French anthropologist Arnold van Gennep (1873–1957) in a book published in 1909 [359]: many important stages in our social existence (such as coming of age, marrying, or taking important offices) are accompanied by elaborate rituals. Approaches influenced by cultural anthropology assume that reflections of such rituals can be found in numerous literary texts. Such interpretations argue that Greek culture is in many respects similar to primitive societies studied by anthropologists. This approach is often connected with the hypothesis (mentioned above, p. 111) that Greece was a preliterary society dominated by orality. An excellent introduction to this field (in German) is provided by Renate Schlesier [316].

❧ If I mention all forms of political criticism as a second theoretical approach which could not be treated in this volume, many readers will not consider this an important loss when they think of all the nonsense produced under that label in the totalitarian systems of the last century. But we have to be careful: political criticism is much more refined, various, and fascinating than the ossified Leninism of the Eastern bloc during the Cold War suggests. Scholars such as Louis Althusser (1918–90) in France, Theodor W. Adorno (1900–69) in Germany, Fredric Jameson (b. 1934) in the USA, or Terry Eagleton (b. 1943) in Great Britain have proposed a number of sophisticated and complex forms of Marxist criticism. As we have seen in the chapters on New Historicism (10) and on gender studies (11), newer theoretical positions do not consider literature and culture in general as a superstructure which merely reflects the political and economical circumstances, but emphasize the productivity and activity of cultural phenomena. Such political readings of literary texts pay particular attention to concepts such as ideology, subject, or interest (for a first approach, see Althusser's *For Marx* [4], Jameson's *The Political Unconscious* [199], Eagleton's *Ideology* [89], and Adorno's *Esthetic Theory* [2]).

❧ While conventional political criticism has been somewhat inactive since the 1990s (see the contributions collected in the volume *What's Left of Theory?* [51]), another strand has seen an enormous development. After the end of World War II, the former European colonies slowly gained their independence. The new field of postcolonial studies examines the ways in which this long political and economical dependency, the encounters of "primitive" and "developed" societies, and the liberation from colonial rule have manifested themselves in cultural productions (the classical contribution to this area is Edward W. Said's *Orientalism* [313], first published in 1978; a number of important contributions is collected in the volume *The Empire Writes Back* [7]). This approach has recently been adopted and applied in classical studies as well: the encounter of Rome, with its military and political superiority, and Greece, with its more developed culture, can be seen not only as a story of "cultural influence" and "reception," but also as a struggle for identity and cultural hegemony which can be analyzed in the categories provided by postcolonial studies (for examples of this new approach, see the overview in an article by Martin Hose [192] or the contributions in the volume *Being Greek under Rome*, edited by Simon Goldhill [141]).

ૐ I can only give a very brief nod to a theoretical approach which has been applied, especially in German scholarship, to the interpretation of cultural phenomena. The German sociologist Niklas Luhmann (1927–98) developed a theoretical position which he called "system theory" and which he applied to cultural production. In particular, he suggested exploring the ways in which culture can be understood as an "autopoietic system" which can no longer be understood and judged according to outside criteria but is a closed entity constantly reproducing itself. As a sociologist, Luhmann explored the ways in which this closed subsystem is connected to society as a whole. A number of literary critics, especially in Germany, have tried to follow his suggestions for their own work (see, e.g., Siegfried J. Schmidt's book [318]); I do not know of any attempts to make use of these suggestions in classical studies.

Whither Now?

This brings us to the end (if not to the conclusion) of this introductory book. You have read about important positions in literary theory, at least in outline. You will have become – or so I hope – more conscious, when interpreting texts, of the presuppositions you bring to literature, and you will now be able to recognize more easily the sometimes hidden premises that other interpretations follow. You will have found some of the approaches presented here more plausible and more interesting than others, and you will have taken the opportunity to look at some of the contributions listed in the "Further Reading" sections to familiarize yourself further with the methodologies and problems of these positions. Most important of all, you have learnt, while reading this book, to be critical of it and not to accept its assessments and explanations at face value. And now? Whither should you turn now?

Greek mythology tells us about the giant Antaeus. He was a son of Mother Earth. He forced all strangers to wrestle against him, and he was invincible at this sport because whenever he touched the earth, he would gain new strength. It was only Hercules who could finally beat and kill him by holding him in midair and crushing him there. This myth of Antaeus can be transferred to literary studies. Literary theory is a fascinating occupation which will enhance our attention to the manifold aspects, facets, problems, and devices of literary texts – but we always have to return to the texts in order to gain new strength. This does not mean that I subscribe to the criticism raised against "theory for theory's sake" mentioned above (p. 6). But it is obvious that nobody will be able to produce competent and meaningful studies of literary theory unless (s)he enjoys reading literary texts and has a vast and intense knowledge of literatures from as many periods and cultures as possible.

On the other hand, those readers who will have the most rewarding and inspiring encounters with literary texts are those who are able to view them from as many different perspectives as possible, who can think of as many questions to ask as possible. One of the reasons why we choose to spend our time reading literature (and literature from a remote past written in difficult languages) instead of pursuing more lucrative occupations (which may be quite as honorable) is our pleasure in discovering the strangeness of these texts: they allow us to transcend the boundaries of our own limited existence for some time and to see the world from a strange perspective. Literary theory is a means of helping us perceive this strangeness; it keeps us from lapsing into boredom and routine while we read, from perceiving these texts as mere confirmations of what we have always thought we knew instead of seeing them for what they really are: food for thought and provocations.

The way out of this book should be a way back to the texts. Readers should now adopt the cheerful pluralism which was mentioned several times in this introduction (see above, p. 4); they should now consider all the theories they have encountered their own possession and have the courage to think for themselves: maybe they can take a concept from here and a question from there to make a poem speak to them in a novel way and detect aspects they had not perceived before. Or reading such tragedy or such novel will open our eyes for new viewpoints or even lacunae of a certain theoretical approach which had not appeared to be very interesting before. Only competent readers will be capable of doing theory in a competent ways; only readers who are prepared to heighten their theoretical awareness will be able to encounter texts with the openness and attention appropriate to literature. The choice is not whether we want to do theory or not, the choice is whether we want to do good or bad theory. I finish this introduction by wishing that its readers may find it a pointer to good theory.

Additional Notes

9   Awareness of the fact that an "unprejudiced" approach to texts is but a mere illusion has become commonplace in works of literary theory, and Eagleton's formulation is often quoted or referred to; see Atkins [8.14], Barry [22.34–5], Selden, Widdowson, and Brooker [327.9], and Harrison [173.5]; in the introductory book by Nünning, Buchholz, and Jahn [280], it serves as an epigraph to the entire book.

10   For Compagnon [58], the fight against the prejudices of "common sense" is one of the decisive characteristics of literary theory.

11   A vivid and wonderful demonstration of the absurdity of the suggestion to explain different theoretical approaches by applying them to one individual text can be found in Crews [63], which collects a series of interpretations of A. A. Milne's (1882–1956) *Winnie-the-Pooh* (1926). Every interpretation is a spoof on a theoretical position in literary criticism, including a Marxist analysis, an exploration of the "sacramental meaning," and a psychoanalytic interpretation by "Karl Anschauung, M.D.," one of the last surviving students of Sigmund Freud's, entitled "A. A. Milne's Honey-Balloon-Pit-Gun-Tail-Bathtubcomplex," in an exhilarating German–English style.

26   For the often contradictory relationship between structuralism and the student revolts of May 1968, see Dosse [86.2.122–53].

35   A critical assessment of Lévi-Strauss's analysis of the Oedipus myth can be found in Scholes [321.68–74]; some general comments on his theory of myth appear in Kirk [216.42–83] and Lentricchia [235.124–9].

49   In his later essay "Actants, Actors, and Figures" [154.106–20], Greimas gives a lengthy explanation of his deductive methodology.

49   For arguments against Greimas's approach, see Scholes [321.102–7] and Culler [67.75–95, 232–5].

52   For the violent debate between Barthes and the Sorbonne professor Raymond Picard, see Dosse [86.1.223–8].

53   For Barthes as an undisputable authority in postmodern discourse, see the stimulating words of Detering [83.882–4].

54   Barthes has attempted a similar definition and classification of codes in his shorter essay "Textual Analysis of a Tale by Edgar Allan Poe" [27.261–93]. Readers who think *S/Z* is too complex and confusing may find this a convenent introduction to his narratological methodology.

66   For the decisive role of context in linguistic utterances, there is an instructive example in one of the contributions published under the name of Voloshinov, quoted in

Holquist [186.62–3].

67   For Bakhtin's criticism of the structuralist model of communication, see the illuminating explanations in Todorov [355.54–6].

68   Recent scholarship in the field of Slavic literature does not appear to accept Bakhtin's interpretation of Dostoevsky's novels; see the account in Möllendorff [263.56].

79   For Kristeva's important role in this decisive turning point of Barthes's work, see the account in Dosse [86.2.54–61].

79   The most thorough explanation of Riffaterre's methodology can be found in his *Semiotics of Poetry* [307]; there is a more succinct explanation in his "Compulsory Reader Response" [308]. Riffaterre's style is often quite dense and difficult (for this, he has been criticized as being elitist), so another way of approaching his theories would be to look at the critical discussion of his theses in Culler [68.80–99].

81   Genette has devoted an entire book to the phenomenon of the "paratext" [137] and another one to the "architext" [135].

85   Further important discussions of the use and abuse of the concept of intertextuality in the study of Latin literature can be found in the contributions of Conte and Barchiesi [62], Lyne [244], Thomas [349.1–11], and Fowler [121.115–37].

87   Examples of pragmatic and sociologist analyses of readers' attitudes can be found in Engelsing [95] or Wittmann [383]; an explanation of the methodology of this approach is Grimm [155].

88   Barner [21] shows some ways in which classical studies can compensate for the lack of ancient testimonies about actual readers.

89   Critics such as Holub [187.100] or Samuel Weber [372] have criticized Iser's most important book *The Act of Reading* [196] for its unnecessarily highfalutin style and zapping through a multitude of theoretical concepts without a clear reason; hence, his Constance lecture is probably an easier way to approach his methodology.

90   In developing the concept of *Leerstelle*, Iser is inspired by suggestions made by the Polish philosopher Roman Ingarden (1893–1970), whose book *The Literary Work of Art* [194] was published in 1931. It is still fascinating and engrossing to read; a number of arguments of contemporary reader-response criticism can already be found in Ingarden's book.

90   A critical debate of the arguments against Iser's theory, especially those proposed by Fish and Eagleton, can be found in Thomas [375.142–57].

102   Scholars such as Street [339] or Levine [237] have argued forcefully against the interpretations of Goody and Watt.

103   Thomas [350] is an excellent example of a very careful discussion of orality and literacy.

104   Finnegan [106] offers a very good introduction to this field.

106   There is an English translation of Wolf's *Prolegomena* (whose Latin style is rather difficult to understand) with an introduction and a commentary in [384].

109   In his posthumous book *The Singer Resumes the Tale* [242], Lord has given a vivid explanation of the oral poetry hypothesis and proposed arguments against some of the criticisms raised against it. In most of continental Europe, the Parry–Lord theses were not generally known before the 1970s; in 1979, Latacz edited a volume with a number of key contributions to this debate [230].

110   There is a wealth of scholarly literature on the adoption and dissemination of alphabetic writing in Greece; Heubeck [178.75–87] and Powell [294] provide a first introduction. For critical discussions of the Parry–Lord theses, see Austin [13.11–80] and Shive [328], as well as Erbse [96].

111   Examples of an "oral" interpretation of archaic and classical Greek culture can be found in Havelock [175], Gentili [138], and Rösler [311]; arguments against this view can be found in Latacz [231.357–95].

113   Public opinion about deconstruction was heavily influenced by an article in *Newsweek* (June 22, 1981); a particularly telling example of such an influential piece in the mass media (in this case, the *Washington Post*) is analyzed by Esch [98.379–83].

117   For the concept of "hearing oneself speak" which was first developed by Husserl, see the explanations in Habermas [163.169–72].

119   The clearest account of the important concept of *différance* can be found in an interview with Derrida [77.8–10].

120   De Man has been described as "capo di tutti capi" by, e.g., Lentricchia [235.283–4] and Merquior [255.249]. Such metaphors gain a significance which their authors had not intended when seen against the backdrop of the "de Man affair," described above, pp. 133–135.

122   For the deconstructionist theory of misreading, see the account in Culler [69.175–9].

123   A number of adherents of deconstruction take Merquior's point that an institutional-ized, automated form of deconstruction can turn into dreadful routine; see, e.g., Johnson [206.14–6] or Miller [258.131].

126   Two American critics, Steven Knapp and Walter Benn Michaels, have convincingly demonstrated that Hirsch's position is an empty one from a theoretical perspective; their contribution and the debate following it are collected in the volume *Against Theory*, edited by Mitchell [261].

128   The argument that deconstruction either does not take its own argument of the funda-mental unreadability of texts seriously or claims that its own texts somehow escape this condition is the objection mentioned most frequently; see, e.g., Abrams [1.25–6], Ellis [94.12–4], Harris [171.88], or Detering [83.883]. It is interesting to note that similar arguments against "nihilistic" positions have already been made in antiquity: Aristotle uses it when he argues against those who do not want to accept the universal valid-ity of the "law of contradiction" (nothing can be the case and not be the case at the same time) in his *Metaphysics* (K 6; 1062 b7–9: "If there are no true affirmations, the sentence 'there are no true affirmations' should also be false.").

131   For the philosophical implications of the debate between Derrida and Searle, see the account in Habermas [163.194–9]. A more positive assessment of Derrida's attitude in this discussion can be found in Scholes [322] and Rabinowitz [299.369–74].

133   There is a remarkably sober, factual, and helpful account of the de Man affair in Spitzer [336.61–96].

134   The assumption that de Man's entire intellectual work was nothing but a cover-up of his past mistakes is clearly absurd; there can be no doubt about that. Nonetheless, it is difficult not to feel uneasy when we read passages like this: "Not the fiction itself is to blame for the consequences but its falsely referential reading" [72.293], or "there can

never be enough guilt around to match the text-machine's infinite power to excuse"
[72.299].

135   Scholars such as Eagleton [90.124–7] or Lilla [239] have convincingly demonstrated
that in its consequences, deconstruction leads to political quietism and is thus, all outward appearances notwithstanding, a deeply conservative position.

136   For Gorgias as the first deconstructionist, see Felperin [103.104].

137   I do not accept Hose's claim [191] that decontextualization was the predominant mode
of interpretation in early Greek culture.

141   For Foucault's cautious, hesitant writing style which proceeds by provisional assumptions and frequent corrections, see the account in Holub [188.56–8]. The polemical
debate between Derrida and Foucault, which was quite vehement at times, is not only
mildly interesting as academic gossip, but teaches us a lot about the differing presuppositions and aims of deconstruction and discourse analysis; see Dosse [86.2.23–5],
Said [314.178–225, esp. 212–15], Boyne [45.53–87], and Larmour, Miller, and Platter
[229.6–9].

144   The relationship between discursive and non-discursive practices in Foucault's early
work is somewhat fuzzy; see the account in Dreyfus and Rabinow [87.84–6].

145   Dreyfus and Rabinow [87.79–85] explain the reasons why some of Foucault's key concepts remained so vague throughout his work; Detel [81.23] whimsically mentions the
"notorious énoncés."

146   Foucault's diffuse concept of power which does not allow resistance or escape is discussed by Habermas [163.266–93]; Detel [81.11–22] gives a good clarification of power
in Foucault's thinking.

147   Gutting [161.14] argues convincingly that Foucault's concept of "archeology" should
be seen as supplementing, not replacing other forms of historiography.

147   Foucault's political commitment is described by Dosse [86.2.248, 336–7]; he summarizes the topic of *The Care of the Self* [118] thus [86.2.349]: "The subject was back." For
Foucault's "return to the subject," also see Fink-Eitel [105.67–73].

153   A number of scholars have adduced texts from other genres than those analyzed by
Foucault and thus demonstrated the one-sidedness of his choice; see Miller on Catullus
[259] and Goldhill on the Greek novel [139]; for his neglect of Roman material, see
contributions by Richlin, [302] and [305.139].

154   For scholars who have tried to explain the change in direction of Foucault's work, see
Dosse [86.2.343–4], Fink-Eitel [105.67–76], Black [35], or Vizier [367]. Some readers have, according to their own ideological position, reproached or praised him for
returning to more traditional forms of historiography; see, e.g., Vegetti [364.925] or
Thornton [352.92].

154   Foucault's statement about the "*argumentaire érotique*" can be found on p. 281 of the
original French edition of *Le Souci de soi*. Unfortunately, the English edition [118.212]
misunderstands and mistranslates Foucault's text.

156   Not all activists for gay rights welcome extreme forms of social constructivism; see Larmour, Miller, and Platter [229.27–9].

156   Thornton [352.92] is probably right in criticizing scholars such as Winkler or Halperin
for downplaying the important differences between volume 1 and the later volumes of

Foucault's *History of Sexuality*.

162 For the similarities and differences between New Historicism and Cultural Materialism, see Höfele [183].

164 For the relationship between deconstruction and New Historicism, see the accounts in Thomas [347.24–50] and Patterson [285.57–63]. Liu [240.746–51] is rightly critical of the sometimes excessive obsession of New Historicists with autobiographical anecdotes. This aspect of New Historicism could be one of the reasons for the development of a recent fashion during the last years, especially in the USA. This approach emphasizes the "personal voice" in literary criticism; see the contributions in the volume *Compromising Traditions*, edited by Hallett and van Nortwick [165]. I find this approach so strange that I refrain from giving any assessment.

178 Feminist criticism of a constructivist interpretation of sex and gender can be found in, e.g., Soper [335].

179 For powerful arguments against the menace of isolation and ghettoization of feminist criticism, see Jehlen [205].

181 Kristeva [221.68] emphasizes that the "symbolic" and the "semiotic" are not chronologically subsequent phases in the development of humans, but rather theoretical constructs.

182 In addition to the pragmatic objections mentioned here, we also find penetrating criticisms of the philosophical foundations of French feminism; cf. the objections that Butler [50.79–93] raised against Kristeva's assumption of a semiotic phase.

184 For an overview of women as authors in the ancient world and their works, see Snyder [332]. Culler [69.43–64] provides a brief account of scholarship on the subject "women as readers."

185 For an example of the problems which female readers can have with texts from the ancient world, see Richlin [304].

188 For contributions which analyze different media and genres with regard to the production of gender roles, see the articles in volume 19 of the journal *Helios* which treat ancient texts from such diverse areas as medicine, the interpretation of dreams, and magic.

191 Clark's slim volume [55] provides a very useful overview of scholarship on women's lives in the ancient world. Pomeroy [292] was a groundbreaking work which still remains valuable and very readable; Fant and Lefkowitz (eds) [99] is a helpful collection of the ancient source material, edited by. For the question of whether women were allowed to watch theatrical performances, see the opposing views of Henderson [177] and Goldhill [140], as well as the collection of ancient testimonies by Podlecki [290].

199 The danger of reductionism has been seen by some psychoanalysts themselves; cf. this passage in Jung [211.65–83]:

> If we were to interpret Plato's metaphor in Freudian terms we would naturally arrive at the uterus, and would have proved that even a mind like Plato's was still struck on a primitive level of infantile sexuality. But we would have completely overlooked what Plato actually created out of the primitive determinants of his philosophical ideas; we would have missed the essential point and

merely discovered that he had infantile sexual fantasies like any other mortal. Such a discovery could be of value only for a man who regarded Plato as superhuman, and who can now state with satisfaction that Plato too was an ordinary human being. But who would want to regard Plato as a god? Surely only one who is dominated by infantile fantasies and therefore possesses a neurotic mentality. For him the reduction to common human truths is salutary on medical grounds, but this would have nothing whatever to do with the meaning of Plato's parable.

201   Justified criticisms of Holland's methodology can be found in Wright [386.57–8] or Culler [68.52–3]. Brooks [48] offers an interesting combination of Freudian psychoanalysis and reader-response criticism.

203   Because of his obscure writing and his often nonsensical use of mathematical formulae and scientific concepts, Lacan has been one of the main targets of the attacks by Sokal and Bricmont [333], who accuse a number of poststructuralist critics of "intellectual imposture."

204   In its function of an allegory of the signifier, the letter has a similar role in Lacan's interpretation of Poe's story as the phallus in some of his other writings: the phallus also is "empty," it "is the signifier intended to designate as a whole the effects of the signified, in that the signifier conditions them by its presence as a signifier" [224.316].

References and Bibliography

[1] Abrams, Meyer Howard: *Doing Things with Texts. Essays in Criticism and Critical Theory*, New York: W. W. Norton, 1989.

[2] Adorno, Theodor W.: *Esthetic Theory*, London: Routledge, 1984 [original German edn Frankfurt am Main 1970].

[3] Allen, Graham: *Intertextuality*, London: Routledge, 2000.

[4] Althusser, Louis: *For Marx*, New York: Random House, 1969 [original French edn Paris 1966].

[5] Andersen, Øivind: "Mündlichkeit und Schriftlichkeit im frühen Griechentum," *Antike und Abendland* 33 (1987) 29–44.

[6] Arnold, Heinz Ludwig, and Detering, Heinrich, eds: *Grundzüge der Literaturwissenschaft* (dtv 4704), Munich: dtv, 1996.

[7] Ashcroft, Bill, Griffiths, Gareth, and Tiffin, Helen, eds: *The Empire Writes Back. Theory and Practice in Post-Colonial Literatures*, 2nd edn. London: Routledge, 1989.

[8] Atkins, G. Douglas: "Introduction: Literary Theory, Critical Practice, and the Classroom," in [9], 1–23.

[9] Atkins, G. Douglas, and Morrow, Laura, eds: *Contemporary Literary Theory*, Amherst: University of Massachusetts Press, 1989.

[10] *Atti del convegno internazionale "Letterature classiche e narratologia"* (Materiali e contributi per la storia della narrativa greco-latina 3), Naples: Liguori, 1981.

[11] Attridge, Derek: "The Linguistic Model and Its Applications," in [326], 58–84.

[12] Austin, John Langshaw: *How To Do Things with Words*, 2nd edn. Cambridge, MA: Harvard University Press, 1975.

[13] Austin, Norman: *Archery at the Dark Side of the Moon. Poetic Problems in Homer's Odyssey*, Berkeley: University of California Press, 1975.

[14] Baasner, Rainer, and Zens, Maria: *Methoden und Modelle der Literaturwissenschaft. Eine Einführung*, Berlin: Erich Schmidt Verlag, 1996.

[15] Bakhtin, Mikhail M.: *Die Ästhetik des Wortes* (Edition Suhrkamp 967), Frankfurt am Main: Suhrkamp, 1979.

[16] Bakhtin, Mikhail M.: *The Dialogic Imagination. Four Essays*, Austin: University of Texas Press, 1981.

[17] Bakhtin, Mikhail M.: *Problems of Dostoevsky's Poetics*, Minneapolis: University of Minnesota Press, 1984 [original Russian edn 1929, 2nd edn 1963].

[18] Bakhtin, Mikhail M.: *Rabelais and His World*, Bloomington: Indiana University Press, 1984 [original Russian edn 1965].

[19] Bakhtin, Mikhail M.: "Das Problem des Textes in der Linguistik, Philologie und in anderen Humanwissenschaften. Versuch einer philosophischen Analyse," *Poetica* 22 (1990) 436–87 [original Russian edn 1976].

[20] Bal, Mieke: *Narratology. Introduction to the Theory of Narrative*, 2nd edn. Toronto: University of Toronto Press, 1997.

[21] Barner, Wilfried: "Neuphilologische Rezeptionsforschung und die Möglichkeiten der Klassischen Philologie," *Poetica* 9 (1977) 499–521.

[22] Barry, Peter: *Beginning Theory. An Introduction to Literary and Cultural Theory*, Manchester: Manchester University Press, 1995.

[23] Barthes, Roland: *S/Z*, New York: Hill & Wang, 1974 [original French edn Paris 1970].

[24] Barthes, Roland: *The Pleasure of the Text*, New York: Hill & Wang, 1975 [original French edn Paris 1974].

[25] Barthes, Roland: *Image, Music, Text*, New York: Hill & Wang, 1977.

[26] Barthes, Roland: *The Rustle of Language*, Berkeley, CA: University of California Press, 1989 [original French edn Paris 1984].

[27] Barthes, Roland: *The Semiotic Challenge*, New York: Hill & Wang, 1988 [original French edn Paris 1985].

[28] Barthes, Roland: *Œuvres complètes 1: 1942–1965*, Paris: Éditions du Seuil, 1993.

[29] Barthes, Roland: *Œuvres complètes 2: 1966–1973*, Paris: Éditions du Seuil, 1994.

[30] Barthes, Roland: *Œuvres complètes 3: 1974–1980*, Paris: Éditions du Seuil, 1995.

[31] Baur, Detlev: "Welchen Weingott nehmen wir zum Wild? Mehr als Geist der Gegenwart: Bernhard Zimmermanns gelehrte Tragödienrezeption bleibt einseitig," *Frankfurter Allgemeine Zeitung* 42 (1998) 44.

[32] Beauvoir, Simone de: *The Second Sex*, New York: Knopf, 1953 [reprint 1989; original French edn Paris 1949].

[33] Begley, Adam: "The Tempest around Stephen Greenblatt," *New York Times Magazine* (1993) 32–8.

[34] Benjamin, Andrew, ed.: *Post-Structuralist Classics*, London: Routledge, 1988.

[35] Black, Joel: "Taking the Sex out of Sexuality: Foucault's Failed History," in [228], 42–60.

[36] Bloom, Harold: *The Anxiety of Influence. A Theory of Poetry*, Oxford: Oxford University Press, 1973.

[37] Bogdal, Klaus-Michael, ed.: *Neue Literaturtheorien. Eine Einführung* (WV Studium 156), Opladen: Westdeutscher Verlag, 1990.

[38] Bonaparte, Marie: *The Life and Works of Edgar Allan Poe. A Psycho-analytic Interpretation*, London: Imago, 1949 [original French edn Paris 1933].

[39] Booth, Wayne C.: *The Rhetoric of Fiction*, 2nd edn. Chicago: University of Chicago Press, 1983.

[40] Bordo, Susan: "Feminism, Foucault and the Politics of the Body," in [300], 179–202.

[41] Bourdieu, Pierre: *Distinction. A Social Critique of the Judgement of Taste*, London: Routledge, 1986 [original French edn Paris 1979].

[42] Bowersock, Glen Warren: *Fiction as History. Nero to Julian* (Sather Classical Lectures 58), Berkeley: University of California Press, 1994.

[43] Bowie, Malcolm: *Lacan*, Cambridge, MA: Harvard University Press, 1991.

[44] Bowra, Cecil M.: *Heroic Poetry*, London: Macmillan, 1952.

[45] Boyne, Roy: *Foucault and Derrida. The Other Side of Reason*, London: Routledge, 1990.

[46] Brackert, Helmut, and Stückrath, Jörn, eds: *Literaturwissenschaft. Ein Grundkurs*, 6th edn. Reinbek bei Hamburg: Rowohlt, 2000.

[47] Brooks, Cleanth: *The Well Wrought Urn. Studies in the Structure of Poetry*, New York: Harcourt Brace, 1947 [reprint San Diego 1975].

[48] Brooks, Peter: *Reading for the Plot. Design and Intention in Narrative*, New York: Knopf, 1984 [reprint Cambridge, MA 1996].

[49] Brooks, Peter: "The Idea of a Psychoanalytic Literary Criticism," in [253], 145–59.

[50] Butler, Judith: *Gender Trouble. Feminism and the Subversion of Identity*, New York: Routledge, 1990.

[51] Butler, Judith, Guillory, John, and Thomas, Kendall, eds: *What's Left of Theory? New Work on the Politics of Literary Theory*, New York: Routledge, 2000.

[52] Cavallo, Guglielmo, Fedeli, Paolo, and Giardina, Andrea, eds: *Lo Spazio letterario di Roma antica* (5 vols), Rome: Salerno, 1989–91.

[53] Chomsky, Noam: *Aspects of the Theory of Syntax*, Cambridge, MA: MIT Press, 1965.

[54] Cixous, Hélène: "The Laugh of the Medusa," in [369], 347–62 [original French edn in *L'Arc* 61 (1975) 39–54].

[55] Clark, Gillian: *Women in the Ancient World* (New Surveys in the Classics 21), 2nd edn. Oxford: Oxford University Press, 1993.

[56] Clark, Katerina, and Holquist, Michael: *Mikhail Bakhtin*, Cambridge, MA: Harvard University Press, 1984.

[57] Cohen, David, and Saller, Richard: "Foucault on Sexuality in Greco-Roman Antiquity," in [142], 35–59.

[58] Compagnon, Antoine: *Literature, Theory, and Common Sense*, Princeton University Press, 2004 [original French edn Paris 1998].

[59] Conte, Gian Biagio: *The Rhetoric of Imitation. Genre and Poetic Memory in Virgil and Other Latin Poets*, Ithaca, NY: Cornell University Press, 1986.

[60] Conte, Gian Biagio: "Empirical and Theoretical Approaches to Literary Genre," in [127], 104–23.

[61] Conte, Gian Biagio: *Genres and Readers. Lucretius, Love Elegy, Pliny's Encyclopedia*, Baltimore, MD: Johns Hopkins University Press, 1994.

[62] Conte, Gian Biagio, and Barchiesi, Alessandro: "Imitazione e arte allusiva: modi e funzioni dell'intertestualità," in [52], 1.81–114.

[63] Crews, Frederick C.: *The Pooh Perplex. A Freshman Casebook*, New York: Dutton, 1963 [reprint Chicago 2003].

[64] Crews, Frederick C., ed.: *Unauthorized Freud. Doubters Confront a Legend*, New York: Penguin, 1998.

[65] Crews, Frederick C., et al.: *The Memory Wars. Freud's Legacy in Dispute*, New York: New York Review of Books, 1995.

[66] Crosman, Robert: "Do Readers Make Meaning?," in [344], 149–64.

[67] Culler, Jonathan: *Structuralist Poetics. Structuralism, Linguistics, and the Study of Literature*, Ithaca, NY: Cornell University Press, 1975.

[68] Culler, Jonathan: *The Pursuit of Signs. Semiotics, Literature, Deconstruction*, Ithaca, NY: Cornell University Press, 1981.

[69] Culler, Jonathan: *On Deconstruction. Theory and Criticism after Structuralism*, Ithaca, NY: Cornell University Press, 1982.

[70] Davidson, James: *Courtesans and Fishcakes. The Consuming Passions of Classical Athens*, London: HarperCollins, 1997.

[71] Delcroix, Maurice, and Hallyn, Fernand, eds: *Méthodes du texte. Introduction aux études littéraires*, Paris: Duculot, 1987.

[72] de Man, Paul: *Allegories of Reading. Figural Language in Rousseau, Nietzsche, Rilke, and Proust*, New Haven, CT: Yale University Press, 1979.

[73] de Man, Paul: *Blindness and Insight. Essays in the Rhetoric of Contemporary Criticism*, 2nd edn. Minneapolis: University of Minnesota Press, 1983.

[74] de Man, Paul: *The Resistance to Theory*, Minneapolis: University of Minnesota Press, 1986.

[75] Derrida, Jacques: *Of Grammatology*, Baltimore, MD: Johns Hopkins University Press, 1976 [original French edn Paris 1967].

[76] Derrida, Jacques: *Writing and Difference*, Chicago: University of Chicago Press, 1978 [reprint London 2001; original French edn Paris 1967].

[77] Derrida, Jacques: *Positions*, Chicago: University of Chicago Press, 1981 [original French edn Paris 1972].

[78] Derrida, Jacques: *Margins of Philosophy*, Chicago: University of Chicago Press, 1982 [original French edn Paris 1972].

[79] Derrida, Jacques: *Limited Inc.*, Evanston, IL: Northwestern University Press, 1988.

[80] Derrida, Jacques: "Like the Sound of the Sea Deep Within a Shell: Paul de Man's War," in [169], 127–64 [original edn in *Critical Inquiry* 14 (1988) 590–652].

[81] Detel, Wolfgang: *Foucault and Classical Antiquity. Power, Ethics and Knowledge*, Cambridge: Cambridge University Press, 2005 [original German edn Frankfurt am Main 1998].

[82] Detering, Heinrich: "'Grundzüge der Literaturwissenschaft.' Eine Einleitung," in [6], 9–23.

[83] Detering, Heinrich: "Die Tode Nietzsches. Zur antitheologischen Theologie der Postmoderne," *Merkur* 52 (1998) 876–89.

[84] Diels, Hermann, and Kranz, Walther, eds: *Die Fragmente der Vorsokratiker* (3 vols), 6th edn. Berlin: Weidmann, 1951–52 [reprint 1996].

[85] Döpp, Siegmar, ed.: *Karnevaleske Phänomene in antiken und nachantiken Kulturen und Literaturen. Stätten und Formen der Kommunikation im Altertum 1* (Bochumer Altertumswissenschaftliches Colloquium 13), Trier: Wissenschaftlicher Verlag Trier, 1993.

[86] Dosse, François: *History of Structuralism* (2 vols), Minneapolis: University of Minnesota Press, 1997 [original French edn Paris 1992].

[87] Dreyfus, Hubert L., and Rabinow, Paul: *Michel Foucault: Beyond Structuralism and Hermeneutics. Second Edition with an Afterword by and an Interview with Michel Foucault*, Chicago: University of Chicago Press, 1983.

[88] DuBois, Page: "The Subject in Antiquity after Foucault," in [228], 85–103.

[89] Eagleton, Terry: *Ideology. An Introduction*, London: Verso, 1991.

[90] Eagleton, Terry: *Literary Theory. An Introduction*, 2nd edn. Oxford: Blackwell, 1996.

[91] Easterling, Patricia E., ed.: *The Cambridge Companion to Greek Tragedy*, Cambridge: Cambridge University Press, 1997.

[92] Edmunds, Lowell: *From a Sabine Jar. Reading Horace, Odes 1, 9*, Chapel Hill: University of North Carolina Press, 1992.

[93] Ehrmann, Jacques, ed.: *Structuralism*, Garden City, NY: Anchor Books, 1966.

[94] Ellis, John M.: *Against Deconstruction*, Princeton: Princeton University Press, 1989.

[95] Engelsing, Rolf: *Der Bürger als Leser. Lesergeschichte in Deutschland 1500–1800*, Stuttgart: Metzler, 1974.

[96] Erbse, Hartmut: "Milman Parry und Homer," *Hermes* 122 (1994) 257–74.

[97] Erlich, Victor: *Russian Formalism. History–Doctrine* (Slavistic Printings and Reprintings 4), 3rd edn. New Haven: Yale University Press, 1981.

[98] Esch, Deborah: "Deconstruction," in [151], 374–91.

[99] Fant, Maureen, and Lefkowitz, Mary: *Women's Life in Greece and Rome*, 2nd edn. Baltimore, MD: Johns Hopkins University Press, 1992.

[100] Farrell, Joseph: *Vergil's Georgics and the Traditions of Ancient Epic. The Art of Allusion in Literary History*, New York: Oxford University Press, 1991.

[101] Farrell, Joseph: "The Virgilian Intertext," in [247], 222–38.

[102] Felman, Shoshana, ed.: *Literature and Psychoanalysis. The Question of Reading: Otherwise* (Yale French Studies 55/56), New Haven, CT: Yale University Press, 1977 [reprint Baltimore 1982].

[103] Felperin, Howard: *Beyond Deconstruction. The Uses and Abuses of Literary Theory*, Oxford: Oxford University Press, 1985.

[104] Fetterley, Judith: *The Resisting Reader. A Feminist Approach to American Fiction*, Bloomington: Indiana University Press, 1978.

[105] Fink-Eitel, Hinrich: *Foucault. An Introduction*, Philadelphia: Pennbridge Books, 1997 [original German edn Hamburg 1988].

[106] Finnegan, Ruth: *Oral Poetry. Its Nature, Significance and Social Context*, 2nd edn. Bloomington: Indiana University Press, 1992.

[107] Fish, Stanley: *Is There a Text in This Class? The Authority of Interpretive Communities*, Cambridge, MA: Harvard University Press, 1980.

[108] Fish, Stanley: *Doing What Comes Naturally. Change, Rhetoric and the Practice of Theory in Literary and Legal Studies*, Durham, NC: Duke University Press, 1989.

[109] Flesch, William: "Ancestral Voices: De Man and His Defenders," in [169], 173–84.

[110] Foley, Helene P., ed.: *Reflections of Women in Antiquity*, Philadelphia, PA: Gordon & Breach Science Publishers, 1981.

[111] Forrester, John: *Dispatches from the Freud Wars. Psychoanalysis and Its Passions*, Cambridge, MA: Harvard University Press, 1997.

[112]   Foucault, Michel: *Madness and Civilization. A History of Insanity in the Age of Reason*, New York: Pantheon Books, 1965 [original French edn Paris 1961].

[113]   Foucault, Michel: *The Order of Things: An Archaeology of the Human Sciences*, New York: Pantheon Books, 1970 [original French edn Paris 1966].

[114]   Foucault, Michel: *The Archaeology of Knowledge, and the Discourse on Language*, New York: Pantheon Books, 1972 [original French edn *L'Archéologie du savoir*, Paris 1969, and *L'Ordre du discours. Leçon inaugurale au Collège de France prononcée le 2 décembre 1970*, Paris 1971].

[115]   Foucault, Michel: *Discipline and Punish: the Birth of the Prison*, New York: Pantheon Books, 1977 [original French edn Paris 1975].

[116]   Foucault, Michel: *An Introduction* (The History of Sexuality vol. 1), New York: Pantheon Books, 1978 [original French edn Paris 1976].

[117]   Foucault, Michel: *The Use of Pleasure* (The History of Sexuality vol. 2), New York: Pantheon Books, 1985 [original French edn Paris 1984].

[118]   Foucault, Michel: *The Care of the Self* (The History of Sexuality vol. 3), New York: Pantheon Books, 1986 [original French edn Paris 1984].

[119]   Foucault, Michel: *Dits et écrits 1954–1988* (4 vols), Paris: Gallimard, 1994.

[120]   Foucault, Michel: *The Essential Works of Foucault, 1954–1988* (3 vols), New York: New Press, 1997–2000 [selection from original French edn [119]].

[121]   Fowler, Don: *Roman Constructions. Readings in Postmodern Latin*, Oxford: Oxford University Press, 2000.

[122]   Fowler, Don P., and Fowler, Peta G.: "Literary Theory and Classical Studies," in [190], 871–5 [rd].

[123]   Foxhall, Lin: "Pandora Unbound: A Feminist Critique of Foucault's History of Sexuality," in [228], 122–37.

[124]   Frank, Manfred: *What Is Neostructuralism?*, Minneapolis: University of Minnesota Press, 1989 [original German edn Frankfurt am Main 1984].

[125]   Freud, Sigmund: *The Interpretation of Dreams*, Ware: Macmillan, 1997 [original German edn Vienna 1900].

[126]   Frye, Northrop: *Anatomy of Criticism*, Princeton, NJ: Princeton University Press, 1957.

[127]   Galinsky, Karl, ed.: *The Interpretation of Roman Poetry: Empiricism or Hermeneutics?* (Studien zur Klassischen Philologie 67), Frankfurt am Main: Peter Lang, 1992.

[128]   Galinsky, Karl: "Introduction: The Current State of the Interpretation of Roman Poetry and the Contemporary Critical Scene," in [127], 1–40.

[129]   Gallagher, Catherine: "Marxism and the New Historicism," in [360], 37–48.

[130]   Gallagher, Catherine, and Greenblatt, Stephen, eds: *Practicing New Historicism*, Chicago: University of Chicago Press, 2000.

[131]   Gallop, Jane: *Reading Lacan*, Ithaca, NY: Cornell University Press, 1985.

[132]   Geertz, Clifford: *The Interpretation of Cultures. Selected Essays*, New York: Basic Books, 1973 [reprint London 1993].

[133]   Genette, Gérard: *Narrative Discourse. An Essay in Method*, Ithaca, NY: Cornell University Press, 1980 [original French edn Paris 1972].

[134] Genette, Gérard: *Narrative Discourse Revisited*, Ithaca, NY: Cornell University Press, 1988 [original French edn Paris 1983].

[135] Genette, Gérard: *The Architext. An Introduction*, Berkeley: University of California Press, 1992 [original French edn Paris 1979].

[136] Genette, Gérard: *Palimpsests. Literature in the Second Degree*, Lincoln: University of Nebraska Press, 1997 [original French edn Paris 1982].

[137] Genette, Gérard: *Thresholds. Paratexts of Interpretation*, Cambridge: Cambridge University Press, 1997 [original French edn Paris 1987].

[138] Gentili, Bruno: *Poetry and Its Public in Ancient Greece. From Homer to the Fifth Century*, Baltimore, MD: Johns Hopkins University Press, 1988 [original Italian edn Rome 1985].

[139] Goldhill, Simon: *Foucault's Virginity. Ancient Erotic Fiction and the History of Sexuality*, Cambridge: Cambridge University Press, 1995.

[140] Goldhill, Simon: "The Audience of Athenian Tragedy," in [91], 54–68.

[141] Goldhill, Simon, ed.: *Being Greek under Rome. Cultural Identity, the Second Sophistic and the Development of Empire*, Cambridge: Cambridge University Press, 2001.

[142] Goldstein, Jan, ed.: *Foucault and the Writing of History*, Oxford: Blackwell, 1994.

[143] Goody, Jack, ed.: *Literacy in Traditional Societies*, Cambridge: Cambridge University Press, 1968.

[144] Goody, Jack, and Watt, Ian: "The Consequences of Literacy," in [143], 27–68.

[145] Graff, Gerald: "Deconstruction as Dogma, or, 'Come Back to the Raft Ag'in, Strether Honey!'," *Georgia Review* 34 (1980) 404–21.

[146] Greenblatt, Stephen J.: *Renaissance Self-Fashioning. From More to Shakespeare*, Chicago: University of Chicago Press, 1980.

[147] Greenblatt, Stephen J.: "Introduction," *Genre* 15 (1982) 3–6.

[148] Greenblatt, Stephen J.: *Shakespearean Negotiations. The Circulation of Social Energy in Renaissance England*, Berkeley: University of California Press, 1988 [reprint Oxford 1997].

[149] Greenblatt, Stephen J.: "Towards a Poetics of Culture," in [360], 1–14.

[150] Greenblatt, Stephen J.: *Hamlet in Purgatory*, Princeton, NJ: Princeton University Press, 2001.

[151] Greenblatt, Stephen J., and Gunn, Giles, eds: *Redrawing the Boundaries. The Transformation of English and American Literary Studies*, New York: Modern Language Association of America, 1992 [reprint 1996].

[152] Greimas, Algirdas Julien: *Structural Semantics. An Attempt at a Method*, Lincoln: University of Nebraska Press, 1983 [original French edn Paris 1966].

[153] Greimas, Algirdas Julien: *Du sens. Essais sémiotiques*, Paris: Seuil, 1970.

[154] Greimas, Algirdas Julien: *On Meaning. Selected Writings in Semiotic Theory*, London: F. Pinter, 1987 [original French edn Paris 1970].

[155] Grimm, Gunther: *Rezeptionsgeschichte. Grundlegung einer Theorie* (UTB 691), Munich: W. Fink, 1977.

[156] Grimshaw, Jean: "Practices of Freedom," in [300], 51–72.

[157] Groden, Michael, Kreiswirth, Martin, and Szeman, Imre, eds: *The Johns Hopkins Guide to Literary Theory & Criticism*, 2nd edn. Baltimore, MD: Johns Hopkins University Press, 2005.

[158] Grünbaum, Adolf: *The Foundations of Psychoanalysis. A Philosophical Critique*, Berkeley: University of California Press, 1984.

[159] Grünbaum, Adolf: *Psychoanalyse in wissenschaftstheoretischer Sicht. Zum Werk Sigmund Freuds und seiner Rezeption* (Konstanzer Bibliothek 5), Konstanz: Universitätsverlag Konstanz, 1987.

[160] Gutting, Gary, ed.: *The Cambridge Companion to Foucault*, Cambridge: Cambridge University Press, 1994.

[161] Gutting, Gary: "Introduction. Michel Foucault: A User's Manual," in [160], 1–27.

[162] Gutting, Gary: "Foucault and the History of Madness," in [160], 47–70.

[163] Habermas, Jürgen: *The Philosophical Discourse of Modernity. Twelve Lectures*, Cambridge, MA: MIT Press, 1987 [original German edn Frankfurt am Main 1985].

[164] Hadot, Pierre: "Réflexion sur la notion de « culture de soi »," in [256], 261–8.

[165] Hallett, Judith P., and Nortwick, Thomas van, eds: *Compromising Traditions. The Personal Voice in Classical Scholarship*, London: Routledge, 1996.

[166] Halperin, David M.: "Historicizing the Subject of Desire: Sexual Preferences and Erotic Identities in the Pseudo-Lucianic Erôtes," in [142], 19–34.

[167] Halperin, David M., Winkler, John J., and Zeitlin, Froma I., eds: *Before Sexuality. The Construction of Erotic Experience in the Ancient Greek World*, Princeton, NJ: Princeton University Press, 1990.

[168] Halperin, David M., Winkler, John J., and Zeitlin, Froma I.: "Introduction," in [167], 3–20.

[169] Hamacher, Werner, Hertz, Neil, and Kennan, Thomas, eds: *Responses. On Paul de Man's Wartime Journalism*, Lincoln: University of Nebraska Press, 1989.

[170] Hamburger, Käte: *The Logic of Literature*, 2nd edn. Bloomington: Indiana University Press, 1973 [original German edn Stuttgart 1968].

[171] Harris, Wendell V.: *Literary Meaning. Reclaiming the Study of Literature*, New York: New York University Press, 1996.

[172] Harrison, Stephen J., ed.: *Texts, Ideas, and the Classics. Scholarship, Theory, and Classical Literature*, Oxford: Oxford University Press, 2001.

[173] Harrison, Stephen J.: "General Introduction: Working Together," in [172], 1–18.

[174] Hartsock, Nancy: "Foucault on Power: A Useful Theory for Women?," in [276], 157–75.

[175] Havelock, Eric A.: *Preface to Plato*, Cambridge, MA: Harvard University Press, 1963.

[176] Heidegger, Martin: *Pathmarks*, Cambridge: Cambridge University Press, 1998 [original German edn Frankfurt am Main 1976].

[177] Henderson, Jeffrey: "Women and the Athenian Dramatic Festivals," *Transactions of the American Philological Association* 121 (1991) 133–47.

[178] Heubeck, Alfred: *Schrift* (Archaeologia Homerica III, X), Göttingen: Vandenhoeck & Ruprecht, 1979.

[179] Hexter, Ralph, and Selden, Daniel, eds: *Innovations of Antiquity*, New York: Routledge, 1992.

[180] Hierdeis, Irmgard: *'Die Gleichheit der Geschlechter' und 'Die Erziehung der Frauen'* *bei Poullain de la Barre (1647–1723). Zur Modernität eines Vergessenen,* Frankfurt am Main: P. Lang, 1993.

[181] Hinds, Stephen: *Allusion and Intertext. Dynamics of Appropriation in Roman Poetry,* Cambridge: Cambridge University Press, 1998.

[182] Hirsch, Eric Donald, Jr: *Validity in Interpretation,* New Haven, CT: Yale University Press, 1967.

[183] Höfele, Andreas: "New Historicism/Cultural Materialism," *Deutsche Shakespeare Gesellschaft West. Jahrbuch* (1992) 107–23.

[184] Holland, Norman N.: *The Dynamics of Literary Response,* New York: Oxford University Press, 1968.

[185] Holland, Norman N.: *5 Readers Reading,* New Haven, CT: Yale University Press, 1975.

[186] Holquist, Michael: *Dialogism. Bakhtin and his World,* London: Routledge, 1990.

[187] Holub, Robert C.: *Reception Theory. A Critical Introduction,* London: Methuen, 1984.

[188] Holub, Robert C.: *Crossing Borders. Reception Theory, Poststructuralism, Deconstruction,* Madison: University of Wisconsin Press, 1992.

[189] Holzhausen, Jens, ed.: Ψυχή – *Seele – anima. Festschrift für Karin Alt zum 7. Mai 1998* (Beiträge zur Altertumskunde 109), Leipzig: Teubner, 1998.

[190] Hornblower, Simon, and Spawforth, Antony: *The Oxford Classical Dictionary,* 3rd edn. Oxford: Oxford University Press, 1996.

[191] Hose, Martin: "Fragment und Kontext. Zwei Methoden der Interpretation in der griechischen Literatur," in [189], 89–112.

[192] Hose, Martin: "Post-colonial Theory and Greek Literature in Rome," *Greek, Roman, and Byzantine Studies* 40 (1999) 303–26.

[193] Ihwe, Jens, ed.: *Literaturwissenschaft und Linguistik. Ergebnisse und Perspektiven.* Vol. 3: *Zur linguistischen Basis der Literaturwissenschaft 2* (Ars poetica 8), Frankfurt am Main: Athenäum, 1972.

[194] Ingarden, Roman: *The Literary Work of Art; an Investigation on the Borderlines of Ontology, Logic, and Theory of Literature. With an Appendix on the Functions of Language in the Theater,* Evanston, IL: Northwestern University Press, 1973 [original German edn Tübingen 1972].

[195] Iser, Wolfgang: *The Implied Reader. Patterns of Communication in Prose Fiction from Bunyan to Beckett,* Baltimore, MD: Johns Hopkins University Press, 1974 [original German edn Munich 1979].

[196] Iser, Wolfgang: *The Act of Reading. A Theory of Aesthetic Response,* Baltimore, MD: Johns Hopkins University Press, 1978 [original German edn Munich 1976].

[197] Jakobson, Roman: *Language in Literature,* Cambridge, MA: Harvard University Press, 1987.

[198] Jakobson, Roman, and Lévi-Strauss, Claude: "« Les Chats » de Charles Baudelaire," *L'Homme* 2 (1962) 5–21.

[199] Jameson, Fredric: *The Political Unconscious. Narrative As a Socially Symbolic Act,* Ithaca, NY: Cornell University Press, 1981.

[200] Jannidis, Fotis, Lauer, Gerhard, Martinez, Matias, and Winko, Simone, eds: *Texte zur Theorie der Autorschaft* (Reclam 18058), Stuttgart: Reclam, 2000.

[201] Jauss, Hans Robert: *Literaturgeschichte als Provokation* (Edition Suhrkamp 418), Frankfurt am Main: Suhrkamp, 1970.

[202] Jauss, Hans Robert: "Der Leser als Instanz einer neuen Geschichte der Literatur," *Poetica* 7 (1975) 325–44.

[203] Jauss, Hans Robert: *Toward an Aesthetic of Reception*, Minneapolis: University of Minnesota Press, 1982 [original German edn Frankfurt am Main 1970].

[204] Jefferson, Ann, and Robey, David, eds: *Modern Literary Theory. A Comparative Introduction*, 2nd edn. London: Batsford, 1986.

[205] Jehlen, Myra: "Archimedes and the Paradox of Feminist Criticism," in [369], 191–212 [first published in *Signs. Journal of Women in Culture and Society* 6 (1981) 575–602].

[206] Johnson, Barbara: *A World of Difference*, Baltimore, MD: Johns Hopkins University Press, 1987.

[207] Jones, Ann Rosalind: "Writing the Body. Toward an Understanding of L'Écriture féminine," in [369], 370–83 [first published in *Feminist Studies* 7 (1981) 247–63].

[208] Jong, Irene J. F. de: *A Narratological Commentary on the Odyssey*, Cambridge: Cambridge University Press, 2001.

[209] Jong, Irene J. F. de: *Narrators and Focalizers. The Presentation of the Story in the Iliad*, 2nd edn. London: Bristol Classical Press, 2004.

[210] Jong, Irene J. F. de, and Sullivan, John Patrick, eds: *Modern Critical Theory and Classical Literature* (Mnemosyne Suppl. 130), Leiden: Brill, 1994.

[211] Jung, Carl Gustav: *The Spirit in Man, Art, and Literature*, Princeton, NJ: Princeton University Press, 1971.

[212] Jung, Carl Gustav, and Kerényi, Karl: *Introduction to a Science of Mythology. The Myth of the Divine Child and the Mysteries of Eleusis*, London: Routledge, 1951 [original German edn Amsterdam 1941].

[213] Kaufmann, Walter, ed.: *The Portable Nietzsche*, New York: Penguin, 1954.

[214] Kennedy, George A.: "Ancient Antecedents of Modern Literary Theory," *American Journal of Philology* 110 (1989) 492–8.

[215] Kinser, Samuel: *Rabelais's Carnival. Text, Context, Metatext*, Berkeley: University of California Press, 1990.

[216] Kirk, Geoffrey S.: *Myth. Its Meaning and Function in Ancient and Other Societies* (Sather Classical Lectures 40), Berkeley: University of California Press, 1970.

[217] Knapp, Steven, and Michaels, Walter Benn: "Against Theory," in [261], 11–30 [first published in *Critical Inquiry* 8 (1982) 723–42].

[218] Kresic, Stephen, ed.: *Contemporary Literary Hermeneutics and Interpretation of Classical Texts. Herméneutique littéraire et interprétation des textes classiques*, Ottawa: University of Ottawa Press, 1981 [= *Revue de l'Université d'Ottawa/University of Ottawa Quarterly* 50 (1980) 325–642].

[219] Kristeva, Julia: Σημειωτική. *Recherches pour une sémanalyse*, Paris: Seuil, 1969 [quoted after the abridged edn Paris 1978].

[220] Kristeva, Julia: *Desire in Language. A Semiotic Approach to Literature and Art*, New York: Columbia University Press, 1980.

[221] Kristeva, Julia: *Revolution in Poetic Language*, New York: Columbia University Press, 1984 [original French edn Paris 1974].

[222] Kristeva, Julia: "Women's Time," in [369], 860–79 [original French edn in *Cahiers de recherche des sciences des textes et documents* 5 (1979) 5–19].

[223] Lacan, Jacques: *Écrits*, Paris: Seuil, 1966 [2 vols].

[224] Lacan, Jacques: *Écrits. A Selection*, New York: Norton, 1977 [original French edn [223]].

[225] Lacan, Jacques: *The Four Fundamental Concepts of Psycho-Analysis*, New York: W. W. Norton, 1977 [original French edn Paris 1973].

[226] LaCapra, Dominick: *Soundings in Critical Theory*, Ithaca, NY: Cornell University Press, 1989.

[227] Lämmert, Eberhard: *Bauformen des Erzählens*, Stuttgart: Metzler, 1955.

[228] Larmour, David H. J., Miller, Paul Allen, and Platter, Charles, eds: *Rethinking Sexuality. Foucault and Classical Antiquity*, Princeton, NJ: Princeton University Press, 1998.

[229] Larmour, David H. J., Miller, Paul Allen, and Platter, Charles: "Introduction. Situating The History of Sexuality," in [228], 3–41.

[230] Latacz, Joachim, ed.: *Homer. Tradition und Neuerung* (Wege der Forschung 463), Darmstadt: Wissenschaftliche Buchgesellschaft, 1979.

[231] Latacz, Joachim: *Erschlieung der Antike. Kleine Schriften zur Literatur der Griechen und Römer*, Stuttgart: Teubner, 1994.

[232] Latacz, Joachim: "Die Gräzistik der Gegenwart. Versuch einer Standortbestimmung," in [323], 41–89.

[233] Leitch, Vincent B.: *Deconstructive Criticism. An Advanced Introduction*, New York: Columbia University Press, 1983.

[234] Lemon, Lee T., and Reis, Marion J., eds: *Russian Formalist Criticism: Four Essays*, Lincoln: University of Nebraska Press, 1965.

[235] Lentricchia, Frank: *After the New Criticism*, Chicago: University of Chicago Press, 1980.

[236] Lentricchia, Frank: *Ariel and the Police. Michel Foucault, William James, Wallace Stevens*, Madison: University of Wisconsin Press, 1988.

[237] Levine, Kenneth: *The Social Context of Literacy*, London: Routledge, 1986.

[238] Lévi-Strauss, Claude: *Structural Anthropology*, New York: Basic Books, 1963 [original French edn Paris 1958].

[239] Lilla, Mark: "The Politics of Jacques Derrida," *The New York Review of Books* 45 (June 25, 1998) 36–41.

[240] Liu, Alan: "The Power of Formalism. The New Historicism," *English Literary History* 56 (1989) 721–71.

[241] Lord, Albert Bates: *The Singer of Tales* (Harvard Studies in Comparative Literature 24), Cambridge, MA: Harvard University Press, 1960.

[242] Lord, Albert Bates: *The Singer Resumes the Tale*, Ithaca, NY: Cornell University Press, 1995.

[243] Lyne, R. O. A. M: *Further Voices in Vergil's Aeneid*, Oxford: Oxford University Press, 1987 [reprint 1992].

[244] Lyne, R. O. A. M: "Vergil's Aeneid: Subversion by Intertextuality. Catullus 66.39–40 and Other Examples," *Greece & Rome* 41 (1994) 187–204.

[245] Mahony, Patrick J.: *Cries of the Wolf Man*, New York: International Universities Press, 1984.

[246] Makaryk, Irena R., ed.: *Encyclopedia of Contemporary Literary Theory. Approaches, Scholars, Terms*, Toronto: University of Toronto Press, 1993.

[247] Martindale, Charles, ed.: *The Cambridge Companion to Virgil*, Cambridge: Cambridge University Press, 1997.

[248] Matejka, Ladislav, and Pomorska, Krystyna, eds: *Readings in Russian Poetics. Formalist and Structuralist Views*, Cambridge, MA: MIT Press, 1971.

[249] Maurach, Gregor: *Methoden der Latinistik. Ein Lehrbuch zum Selbstunterricht*, Darmstadt: Wissenschaftliche Buchgesellschaft, 1998.

[250] McClure, Laura: *Spoken Like a Woman. Speech and Gender in Athenian Drama*, Princeton, NJ: Princeton University Press, 1999.

[251] McLuhan, Marshall: *The Gutenberg Galaxy. The Making of Typographic Man*, Toronto: University of Toronto Press, 1962.

[252] Medvedev, Pavel N.: *The Formal Method in Literary Scholarship. A Critical Introduction to Sociological Poetics*, Baltimore, MD: Johns Hopkins University Press, 1978.

[253] Meltzer, Françoise, ed.: *The Trials of Psychoanalysis*, Chicago: University of Chicago Press, 1988.

[254] Meltzer, Françoise: "Introduction: Partitive Plays, Pipe Dreams," in [253], 1–7.

[255] Merquior, José G.: *From Prague to Paris. A Critique of Structuralist and Post-Structuralist Thought*, London: Verso, 1986.

[256] *Michel Foucault philosophe. Rencontre internationale Paris, 9, 10, 11 janvier 1988*, Paris: Seuil, 1989.

[257] Miller, J. Hillis, ed.: *Aspects of Narrative. Selected Papers from the English Institute*, New York: Columbia University Press, 1971.

[258] Miller, J. Hillis: *Theory Now and Then*, Durham, NC: Duke University Press, 1991.

[259] Miller, Paul Allen: "Catullan Consciousness, the 'Care of the Self,' and the Force of the Negative in History," in [228], 171–203.

[260] Millett, Kate: *Sexual Politics*, Garden City: Doubleday, 1970 [reprint New York 1990].

[261] Mitchell, W. J. Thomas, ed.: *Against Theory. Literary Studies and the New Pragmatism*, Chicago: University of Chicago Press, 1985.

[262] Moi, Toril: *Sexual/Textual Politics. Feminist Literary Theory*, London: Routledge, 1985.

[263] Möllendorff, Peter von: *Grundlagen einer Ästhetik der Alten Komödie. Untersuchungen zu Aristophanes und Michail Bachtin*, Munich: Narr, 1995.

[264] Montrose, Louis A.: "'Eliza, Queene of Shepheardes,' and the Pastoral of Power," in [362], 88–115 [first published in *English Literary Renaissance* 10 (1980) 153–82].

[265] Montrose, Louis A.: "Professing the Renaissance: The Poetics and Politics of Culture," in [360], 15–36.

[266] Montrose, Louis A.: "New Historicisms," in [151], 392–418.

[267] Morris, Ian, and Powell, Barry, eds: *A New Companion to Homer* (Mnemosyne Supplement 163), Leiden: Brill, 1996.

[268] Morrison, James V.: *Homeric Misdirection. False Prediction in the Iliad*, Ann Arbor: University of Michigan Press, 1992.

[269] Most, Glenn W.: "Simonides' Ode to Scopas in Context," in [210], 127–52.

[270] Muller, John P., and Richardson, William J., eds: *The Purloined Poe. Lacan, Derrida, and Psychoanalytic Reading*, Baltimore, MD: Johns Hopkins University Press, 1988.

[271] Mund-Dopchie, Monique: *La Survie d'Eschyle à la Renaissance : éditions, traductions, commentaires et imitations*, Leuven: Peeters, 1984.

[272] Munk-Olsen, Birger: *L'Étude des auteurs classiques latins aux XIe et XIIe siècles* (2 vols), Paris: Éditions du CNRS, 1982–5.

[273] Nauta, Ruurd R.: "Historicizing Reading: The Aesthetics of Reception and Horace's 'Soracte Ode'," in [210], 207–30.

[274] Neukam, Peter, ed.: *Antike Literatur – Mensch, Sprache, Welt*, Munich: Bayerischer Schulbuch Verlag, 2000.

[275] Newton, Judith Lowder: "History as Usual? Feminism and the 'New Historicism'," in [360], 152–67.

[276] Nicholson, Linda J., ed.: *Feminism/Postmodernism*, New York: Routledge, 1990.

[277] Nietzsche, Friedrich: *Early Greek Philosophy & other Essays*, New York: Russell & Russell, 1964.

[278] Norris, Christopher: *Deconstruction. Theory and Practice*, 2nd edn. London: Routledge, 1991.

[279] Nünning, Ansgar: "Vom Nutzen und Nachteil literaturwissenschaftlicher Theorien, Modelle und Methoden für das Studium: eine Einführung in eine studentInnenorientierte Einführung," in [280], 1–12.

[280] Nünning, Ansgar, Buchholz, Sabine, and Jahn, Manfred, eds: *Literaturwissenschaftliche Theorien, Modelle und Methoden. Eine Einführung* (WTV-Handbücher zum literaturwissenschaftlichen Studium 1), Trier: Wissenschaftlicher Verlag Trier, 1995.

[281] Olsen, Stein Haugom: *The End of Literary Theory*, Cambridge: Cambridge University Press, 1987.

[282] Ong, Walter J: *Orality and Literacy. The Technologizing of the Word*, London: Routledge, 1982.

[283] Parry, Milman: *The Making of Homeric Verse. The Collected Papers*, Oxford: Oxford University Press, 1971 [reprint New York 1987].

[284] Pasquali, Giorgio: *Pagine stravaganti di un filologo*. Vol. 2: *Terze pagine stravaganti. Stravaganze quarte e supreme*, Florence: Le Lettere, 1994.

[285] Patterson, Lee: *Negotiating the Past. The Historical Understanding of Medieval Literature*, Madison: University of Wisconsin Press, 1987.

[286] Pechter, Edward: "The New Historicism and Its Discontents: Politicizing Renaissance Drama," *PMLA* 102 (1987) 292–303.

[287] Pecora, Vincent P.: "The Limits of Local Knowledge," in [360], 243–76.

[288] Picard, Raymond: *New Criticism or New Fraud?*, Pullman: Washington State University Press, 1969 [original French edn Paris 1965].

[289] Platter, Charles: "The Uninvited Guest: Aristophanes in Bakhtin's 'History of Laughter'," *Arethusa* 26 (1993) 201–16.

[290] Podlecki, Anthony J.: "Could Women Attend the Theater in Ancient Athens? A Collection of Testimonia," *Ancient World* 21 (1990) 27–43.

[291] Pomeroy, Sarah B.: "Selected Bibliography on Women in Antiquity," *Arethusa* 6 (1973) 127–57.

[292] Pomeroy, Sarah B.: *Goddesses, Whores, Wives, and Slaves. Women in Classical Antiquity*, New York: Schocken Books, 1975.

[293] Poullain de La Barre, François: *The Equality of the Two Sexes*, Lewiston, NY: Edward Mellen Press, 1989.

[294] Powell, Barry B.: "Homer and Writing," in [267], 3–32.

[295] Prince, Gerald: *A Dictionary of Narratology*, Lincoln: University of Nebraska Press, 1987.

[296] Propp, Vladimir: *Morphology of the Folktale*, 2nd edn. Austin: University of Texas Press, 1968 [original Russian edn Leningrad 1928].

[297] Rabinow, Paul, ed.: *The Foucault Reader*, New York: Pantheon Books, 1984.

[298] Rabinowitz, Nancy Sorkin, and Richlin, Amy: *Feminist Theory and the Classics*, New York: Routledge, 1993.

[299] Rabinowitz, Peter J.: "Speech Act Theory and Literary Studies," in [326], 347–74.

[300] Ramazanoğlu, Caroline: *Up against Foucault. Explorations of Some Tensions between Foucault and Feminism*, London: Routledge, 1993.

[301] Renner, Rolf Günter, and Habekost, Engelbert, eds: *Lexikon literaturtheoretischer Werke* (Kröners Taschenausgabe 425), Stuttgart: Kröner, 1995.

[302] Richlin, Amy: "Zeus and Metis: Foucault, Feminism, Classics," *Helios* 18 (1991) 160–80.

[303] Richlin, Amy, ed.: *Pornography and Representation in Greece and Rome*, New York: Oxford University Press, 1992.

[304] Richlin, Amy: "Reading Ovid's Rapes," in [303], 158–79.

[305] Richlin, Amy: "Foucault's *History of Sexuality*: A Useful Theory for Women?," in [228], 138–70.

[306] Riffaterre, Michael: "Describing Poetic Structures: Two Approaches to Baudelaire's les Chats," in [93], 188–230 [first published in *Yale French Studies* 36/37 (1966) 200–242].

[307] Riffaterre, Michael: *Semiotics of Poetry*, Bloomington: Indiana University Press, 1978.

[308] Riffaterre, Michael: "Compulsory Reader Response: the Intertextual Drive," in [385], 56–78.

[309] Robinson, Lilian S.: "Treason Our Text. Feminist Challenges to the Literary Canon," in [369], 115–29 [first published in *Tulsa Studies in Women's Literature* 2 (1983) 83–98].

[310] Rosenmeyer, Thomas G.: *Deina ta polla. A Classicist's Checklist of Twenty Literary-Critical Positions* (Arethusa Monographs 12), Buffalo: Department of Classics, State University of New York at Buffalo, 1988.

[311] Rösler, Wolfgang: *Dichter und Gruppe. Eine Untersuchung zu den Bedingungen und zur historischen Funktion früher griechischer Lyrik am Beispiel Alkaios*, Munich: W. Fink, 1980.

[312] Rösler, Wolfgang: "Michail Bachtin und die Karnevalskultur im antiken Griechenland," *Quaderni Urbinati di Cultura Classica* 52 (1986) 25–44.

[313] Said, Edward W.: *Orientalism. Western Concepts of the Orient*, New York: Pantheon Books, 1978.

[314] Said, Edward W.: *The World, the Text, and the Critic*, Cambridge, MA: Harvard University Press, 1983.

[315] Saussure, Ferdinand de: *Course in General Linguistics*, New York: McGraw-Hill, 1959 [original French edn Paris 1915].

[316] Schlesier, Renate: *Kulte, Mythen und Gelehrte. Anthropologie der Antike seit 1800*, Frankfurt am Main: Fischer, 1994.

[317] Schmid, Wolf, and Stempel, Wolf-Dieter, eds: *Dialog der Texte. Hamburger Kolloquium zur Intertextualität* (Wiener Slawistischer Almanach Sonderband 11), Vienna: Gesellschaft zur Förderung slawistischer Studien, 1983.

[318] Schmidt, Siegfried J.: *Die Selbstorganisation des Sozialsystems Literatur im 18. Jahrhundert*, Frankfurt am Main: Suhrkamp, 1989.

[319] Schmitz, Thomas A.: *Bildung und Macht. Zur sozialen und politischen Funktion der zweiten Sophistik in der griechischen Welt der Kaiserzeit* (Zetemata 97), Munich: C. H. Beck, 1997.

[320] Schmitz, Thomas A.: "'I Hate All Common Things': The Reader's Role in Callimachus' *Aetia* Prologue," *Harvard Studies in Classical Philology* 99 (1999) 151–78.

[321] Scholes, Robert: *Structuralism in Literature. An Introduction*, New Haven, CT: Yale University Press, 1974.

[322] Scholes, Robert: "Deconstruction and Communication," *Critical Inquiry* 14 (1988) 278–95.

[323] Schwinge, Ernst-Richard, ed.: *Die Wissenschaften vom Altertum am Ende des 2. Jahrtausends n. Chr.*, Stuttgart: Teubner, 1995.

[324] Searle, John: "Reiterating the Difference. A Reply to Derrida," *Glyph* 1 (1977) 198–208.

[325] Sedgwick, Eve Kosofsky: "Gender Criticism," in [151], 271–302.

[326] Selden, Raman, ed.: *The Cambridge History of Literary Criticism 8: From Formalism to Poststructuralism*, Cambridge: Cambridge University Press, 1995.

[327] Selden, Raman, Widdowson, Peter, and Brooker, Peter: *A Reader's Guide to Contemporary Literary Theory*, 4th edn. London: Prentice Hall, 1997.

[328] Shive, David: *Naming Achilles*, New York: Oxford University Press, 1987.

[329] Showalter, Elaine, ed.: *The New Feminist Criticism. Essays on Women, Literature, and Theory*, New York: Virago Press, 1985.

[330] Skura, Meredith: "Psychoanalytic Criticism," in [151], 349–73.

[331] Slater, Niall W.: *Reading Petronius*, Baltimore, MD: Johns Hopkins University Press, 1990.

[332] Snyder, Jane McIntosh: *The Woman and the Lyre. Women Writers in Classical Greece and Rome*, Carbondale: Southern Illinois University Press, 1989.

[333] Sokal, Alan D., and Bricmont, Jean: *Intellectual Impostures. Postmodern Philosophers' Abuse of Science*, London: Profile Books, 1998 [original French edn Paris 1997].

[334] Sontag, Susan: *Against Interpretation*, New York: Farrar, Straus & Giroux, 1966 [reprint 1990].

[335] Soper, Kate: "Productive Contradictions," in [300], 29–50.

[336] Spitzer, Alan Barrie: *Historical Truth and Lies about the Past. Reflections on Dewey, Dreyfus, de Man, and Reagan*, Chapel Hill: University of North Carolina Press, 1996.

[337] Stanzel, Franz K.: *A Theory of Narrative*, Cambridge: Cambridge University Press, 1984 [original German edn Göttingen 1979].

[338] Stierle, Karlheinz: "Werk und Intertextualität," in [317], 7–26.

[339] Street, Brian V.: *Literacy in Theory and Practice*, Cambridge: Cambridge University Press, 1984.

[340] Striedter, Jurij: "The Russian Formalist Theory of Prose," *PTL: A Journal of Descriptive Poetics and Theory of Literature* 2 (1977) 429–70.

[341] Striedter, Jurij: "The Russian Formalist Theory of Literary Evolution," *PTL: A Journal of Descriptive Poetics and Theory of Literature* 3 (1978) 1–24.

[342] Striedter, Jurij, ed.: *Russischer Formalismus. Texte zur allgemeinen Literaturtheorie und zur Theorie der Prosa* (UTB 40), 3rd edn. Munich: W. Fink, 1981.

[343] Suleiman, Susan R.: "Introduction: Varieties of Audience-Oriented Criticism," in [344], 3–45.

[344] Suleiman, Susan R., and Crosman, Inge, eds: *The Reader in the Text. Essays on Audience and Interpretation*, Princeton, NJ: Princeton University Press, 1980.

[345] Tadié, Jean-Yves: *La Critique littéraire au XXe siècle*, Paris: Pierre Belfond, 1987.

[346] Teuber, Bernhard: "Zur Schreibkunst eines Zirkusreiters: Karnevaleskes Erzählen im 'Goldenen Esel' und die Sorge um sich in der antiken Ethik," in [85], 179–238.

[347] Thomas, Brook: *The New Historicism and Other Old-Fashioned Topics*, Princeton, NJ: Princeton University Press, 1991.

[348] Thomas, Brook: "Restaging the Reception of Iser's Early Work or Sides Not Taken in Discussions of the Aesthetic," *New Literary History* 31 (2000) 13–43.

[349] Thomas, Richard F.: *Reading Virgil and His Texts. Studies in Intertextuality*, Ann Arbor: University of Michigan Press, 1999.

[350] Thomas, Rosalind: *Literacy and Orality in Ancient Greece*, Cambridge: Cambridge University Press, 1992.

[351] Thornton, Bruce: "Constructionism and Ancient Greek Texts," *Helios* 18 (1991) 181–93.

[352] Thornton, Bruce: "Idolon Theatri: Foucault and the Classicists," *Classical and Modern Literature* 12 (1991) 81–100.

[353] Thornton, Bruce: *Eros. The Myth of Ancient Greek Sexuality*, Boulder, CO: Westview Press, 1997.

[354] Todorov, Tzvetan: *The Fantastic. A Structural Approach to a Literary Genre*, Ithaca, NY: Cornell University Press, 1975 [original French edn Paris 1970].

[355] Todorov, Tzvetan: *Mikhail Bakhtin. The Dialogical Principle*, Minneapolis: University of Minnesota Press, 1984 [original French edn Paris 1981].

[356] Todorov, Tzvetan: *Literature and Its Theorists. A Personal View of Twentieth-Century Criticism*, Ithaca, NY: Cornell University Press, 1987 [original French edn Paris 1984].

[357] Tompkins, Jane P., ed.: *Reader-Response Criticism. From Formalism to Post-Structuralism*, Baltimore, MD: Johns Hopkins University Press, 1980.

[358] Tuchman, Gaye, and Fortin, Nina E.: *Edging Women Out. Victorian Novelists, Publishers, and Social Change*, New Haven, CT: Yale University Press, 1989.

[359] Gennep, Arnold van: *The Rites of Passage*, London: Routledge, 1960 [original French edn Paris 1909].

[360] Veeser, H. Aram, ed.: *The New Historicism*, New York: Routledge, 1989.

[361] Veeser, H. Aram: "Introduction," in [360], ix–xvi.

[362] Veeser, H. Aram, ed.: *The New Historicism Reader*, New York: Routledge, 1994.

[363] Veeser, H. Aram: "The New Historicism," in [362], 1–32.

[364] Vegetti, Mario: "Foucault et les Anciens," *Critique* 42 (1986) 925–32.

[365] Ventris, Michael, and Chadwick, John: "Evidence for Greek Dialect in the Mycenaean Archives," *Journal for Hellenic Studies* 73 (1953) 84–103.

[366] Vernant, Jean-Pierre, and Vidal-Naquet, Pierre: *Myth and Tragedy in Ancient Greece*, New York: Zone Books, 1988 [original French edn in 2 vols, 1972 and 1986].

[367] Vizier, Alain: "Incipit Philosophia," in [228], 61–84.

[368] Voloshinov, Valentin N.: *Marxism and the Philosophy of Language*, New York: Seminar Press, 1973 [original Russian edn Leningrad 1930].

[369] Warhol, Robyn R., and Herndl, Diane Price, eds: *Feminisms. An Anthology of Literary Theory and Criticism*, 2nd edn. New Brunswick, NJ: Rutgers University Press, 1997.

[370] Warning, Rainer, ed.: *Rezeptionsästhetik. Theorie und Praxis* (UTB 303), 2nd edn. Munich: W. Fink, 1979.

[371] Weber, Samuel, ed.: *Demarcating the Disciplines. Philosophy, Literature, Art* (Glyph Textual Studies 1), Minneapolis: University of Minnesota Press, 1986.

[372] Weber, Samuel: "Caught in the Act of Reading," in [371], 181–214.

[373] Weinrich, Harald: *Literatur für Leser. Essays und Aufsätze zur Literaturwissenschaft*, Stuttgart: W. Kohlhammer, 1971 [reprint Munich 1986].

[374] Wellek, René: *The Attack on Literature and Other Essays*, Chapel Hill: University of North Carolina Press, 1982.

[375] Wellek, René, and Warren, Austin: *Theory of Literature*, 3rd edn. New York: Harcourt Brace, 1956 [reprint San Diego 1977].

[376] Wheeler, Stephen M.: *A Discourse of Wonders. Audience and Performance in Ovid's Metamorphoses*, Philadelphia: University of Pennsylvania Press, 1999.

[377] White, Hayden: *The Content of The Form. Narrative Discourse and Historical Representation*, Baltimore, MD: Johns Hopkins University Press, 1987.

[378] Williams, Raymond: *Marxism and Literature*, Oxford: Oxford University Press, 1977.

[379] Wimsatt, William Kurtz: *The Verbal Icon. Studies in the Meaning of Poetry*, Lexington: University of Kentucky Press, 1954.

[380]   Winkler, John J: *Auctor & Actor. A Narratological Reading of Apuleius's The Golden Ass*, Berkeley: University of California Press, 1985.

[381]   Winkler, John J., and Zeitlin, Froma I., eds: *Nothing to Do with Dionysos? Athenian Drama in Its Social Context*, Princeton, NJ: Princeton Univerity Press, 1990.

[382]   Winko, Simone: "Literarische Wertung und Kanonbildung," in [6], 585–600.

[383]   Wittmann, Reinhard: *Buchmarkt und Lektüre im 18. und 19. Jahrhundert. Beiträge zum literarischen Leben 1750–1880*, Tübingen: Niemeyer, 1982.

[384]   Wolf, Friedrich August: *Prolegomena to Homer 1795. Translated with Introduction and Notes*, 2nd edn. Princeton, NJ: Princeton University Press, 1988.

[385]   Worton, Michael, and Still, Judith, eds: *Intertextuality: Theories and Practices*, Manchester: Manchester University Press, 1990.

[386]   Wright, Elizabeth, ed.: *Psychoanalytic Criticism. A Reappraisal*, 2nd edn. Cambridge: Polity Press, 1998.

[387]   Würzbach, Natascha: "Einführung in die Theorie und Praxis der feministisch orientierten Literaturwissenschaft," in [280], 137–52.

[388]   Zeitlin, Froma I.: *Playing the Other. Gender and Society in Classical Greek Literature*, Chicago: University of Chicago Press, 1996.

Index

Numbers in *bold* refer to main entries.